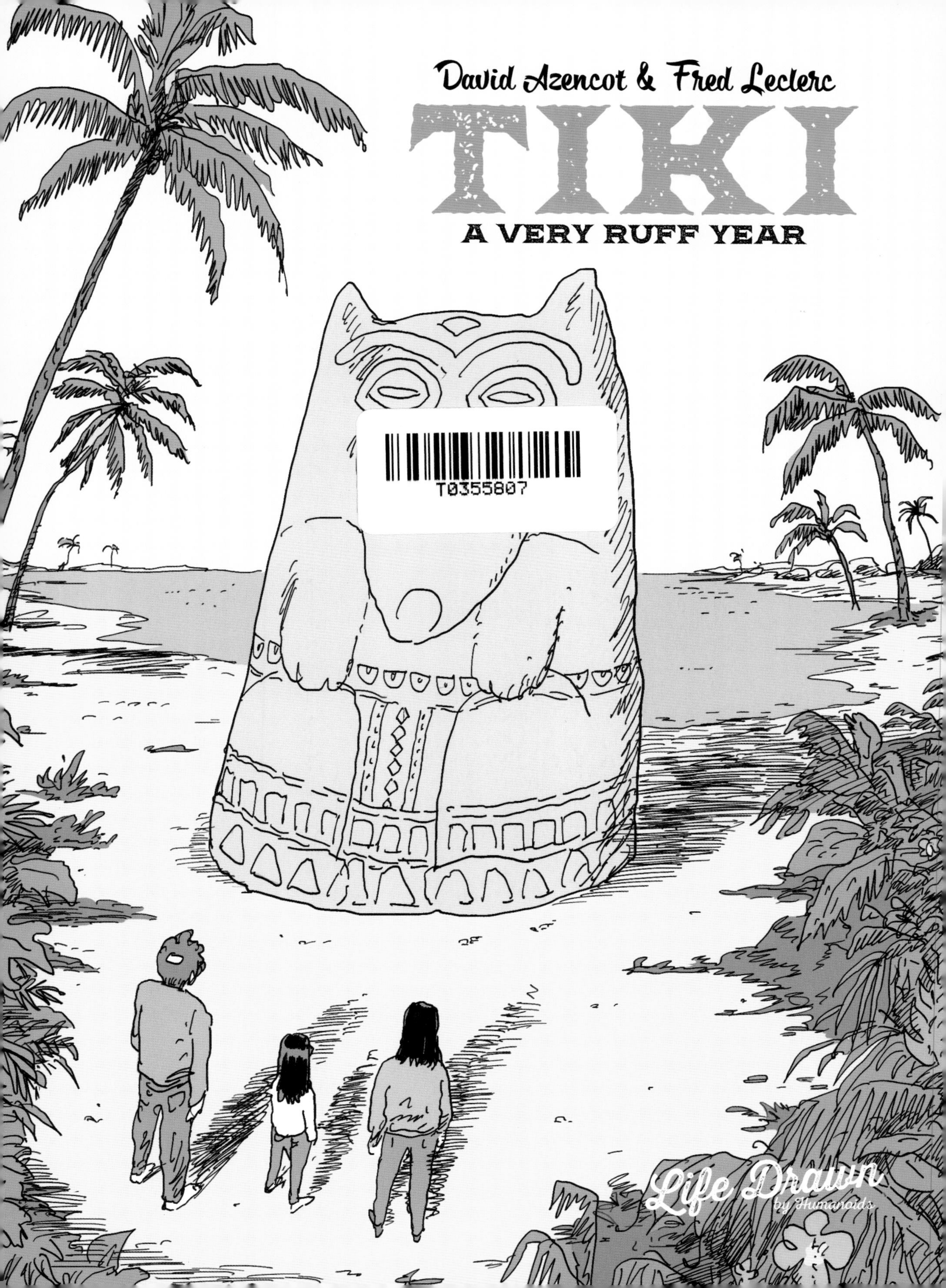
David Azencot & Fred Leclerc
TIKI
A VERY RUFF YEAR
Life Drawn
by Humanoids

David Azencot & Fred Leclerc
Writers

Fred Leclerc
Artist

Lucie Firoud
Color Artist

Nanette McGuinness
Translator

Jonathan Stevenson
Letterer &
English-Language Edition Editor

Alex Lecocq
Original Edition Editor

Vincent Henry
Original Edition Publisher

Sandy Tanaka
Designer

Jerry Frissen
Senior Art Director

Mark Waid
Publisher

Rights and Licensing - licensing@humanoids.com
Press and Social Media - pr@humanoids.com

TIKI: A VERY RUFF YEAR. First Printing. This book is a publication of Humanoids, Inc. 8033 Sunset Blvd. #628, Los Angeles, CA 90046. Copyright Humanoids, Inc., Los Angeles (USA). All rights reserved. Humanoids® and the Humanoids logo are registered trademarks of Humanoids, Inc. in the U.S. and other countries.

Library of Congress Control Number: 2022933309

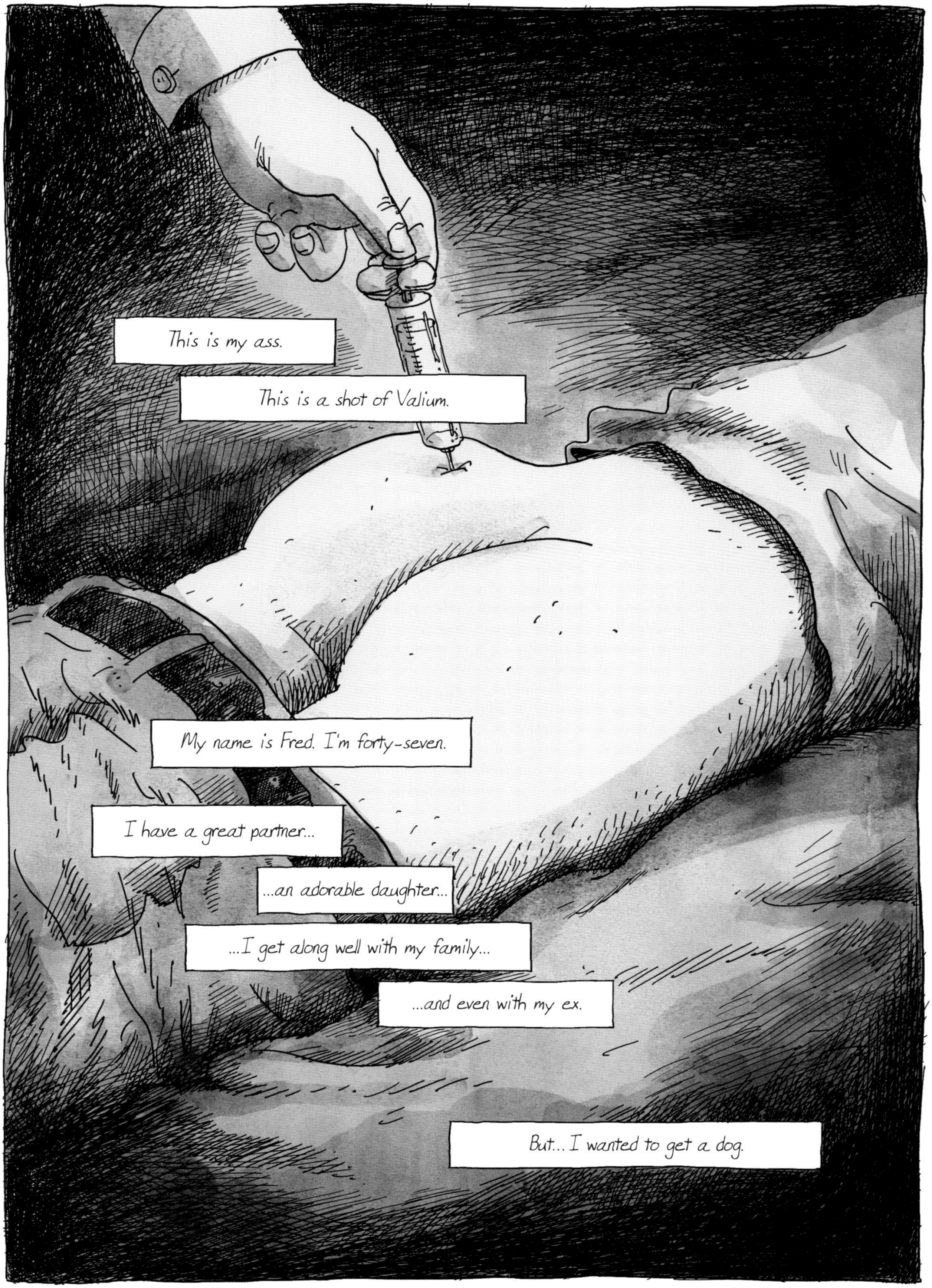
This is my ass.
This is a shot of Valium.
My name is Fred. I'm forty-seven.
I have a great partner...
...an adorable daughter...
...I get along well with my family...
...and even with my ex.
But... I wanted to get a dog.

Chapter One

Dog Dreams

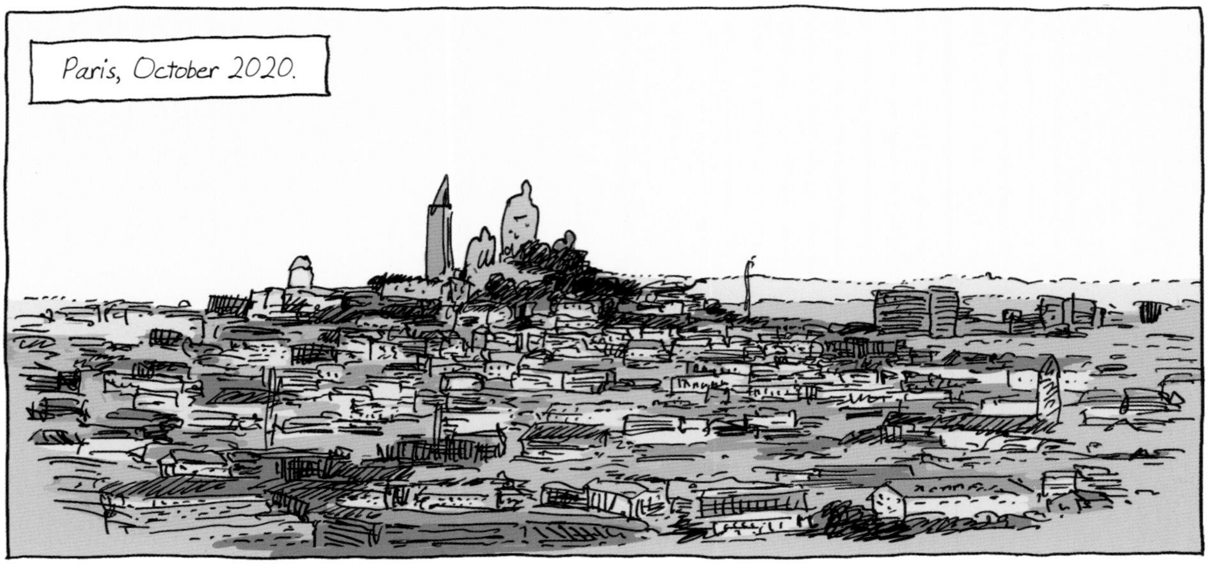
Paris, October 2020.

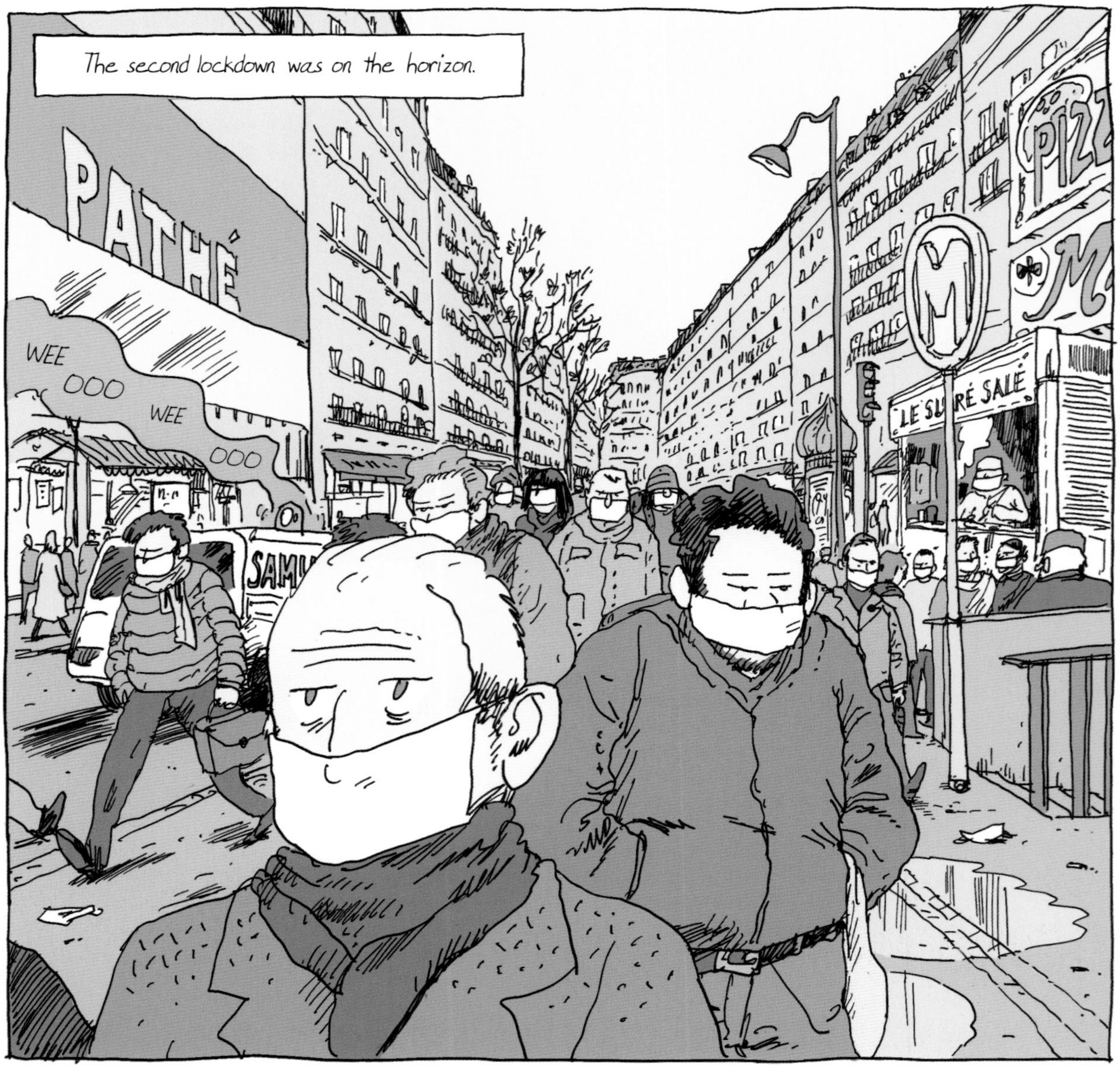
The second lockdown was on the horizon.
PATHÉ
WEE
OOO
WEE
OOO

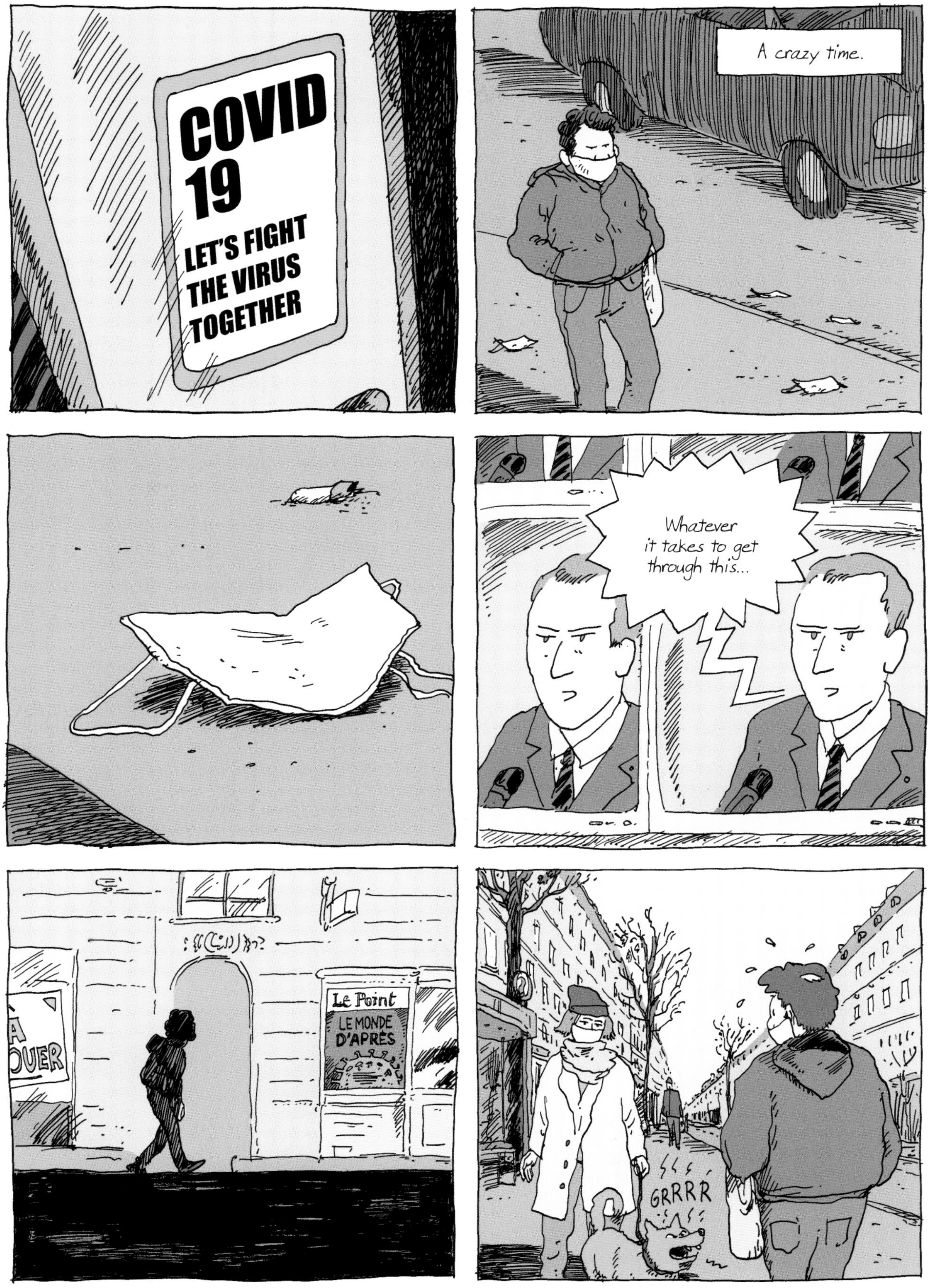
COVID 19
LET'S FIGHT THE VIRUS TOGETHER
A crazy time.
Whatever it takes to get through this...
Le Point
LE MONDE D'APRÈS
GRRRR

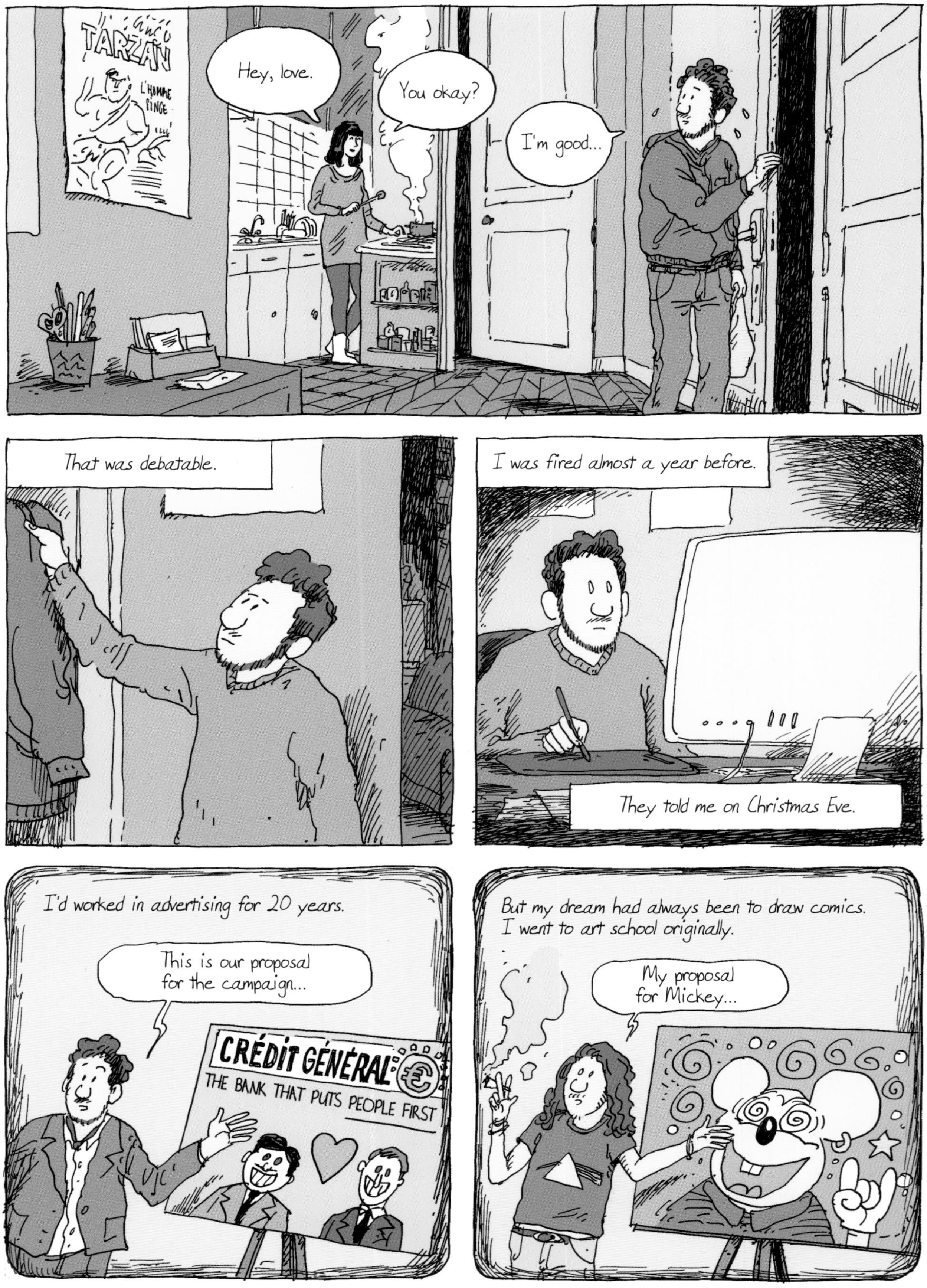
TARZAN
L'HOMME SINGE
Hey, love.
You okay?
I'm good...
That was debatable.
I was fired almost a year before.
They told me on Christmas Eve.
I'd worked in advertising for 20 years.
This is our proposal for the campaign...
CRÉDIT GÉNÉRAL
THE BANK THAT PUTS PEOPLE FIRST
But my dream had always been to draw comics. I went to art school originally.
My proposal for Mickey...

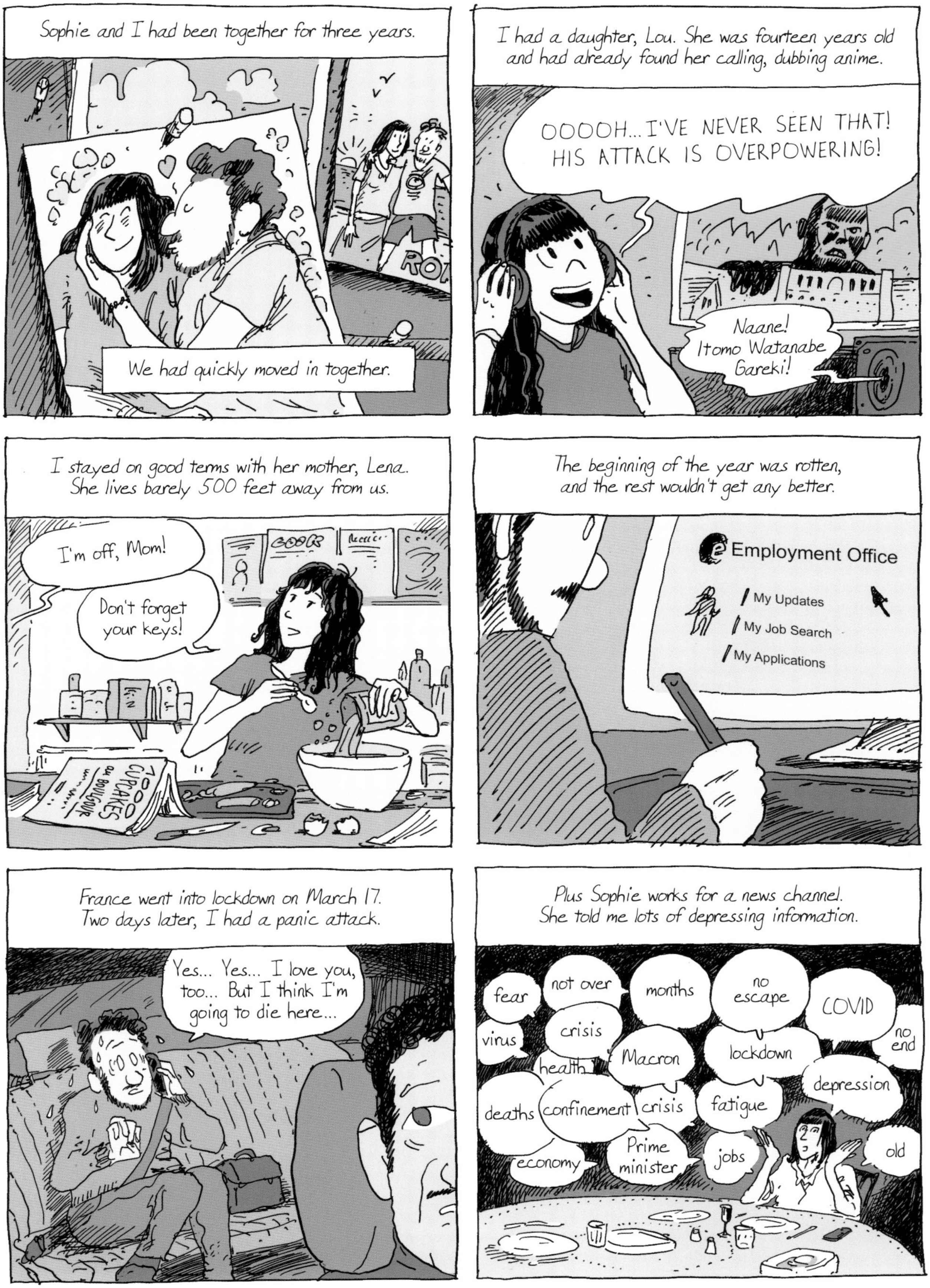
Sophie and I had been together for three years.
We had quickly moved in together.
I had a daughter, Lou. She was fourteen years old and had already found her calling, dubbing anime.
OOOOH... I'VE NEVER SEEN THAT! HIS ATTACK IS OVERPOWERING!
Naane! Itomo Watanabe Gareki!
I stayed on good terms with her mother, Lena. She lives barely 500 feet away from us.
I'm off, Mom!
Don't forget your keys!
1000 CUPCAKES au BOULGOUR
The beginning of the year was rotten, and the rest wouldn't get any better.
Employment Office
My Updates
My Job Search
My Applications
France went into lockdown on March 17. Two days later, I had a panic attack.
Yes... Yes... I love you, too... But I think I'm going to die here...
Plus Sophie works for a news channel. She told me lots of depressing information.
fear
not over
months
no escape
COVID
virus
crisis
no end
health
Macron
lockdown
depression
deaths
confinement
crisis
fatigue
economy
Prime minister
jobs
old

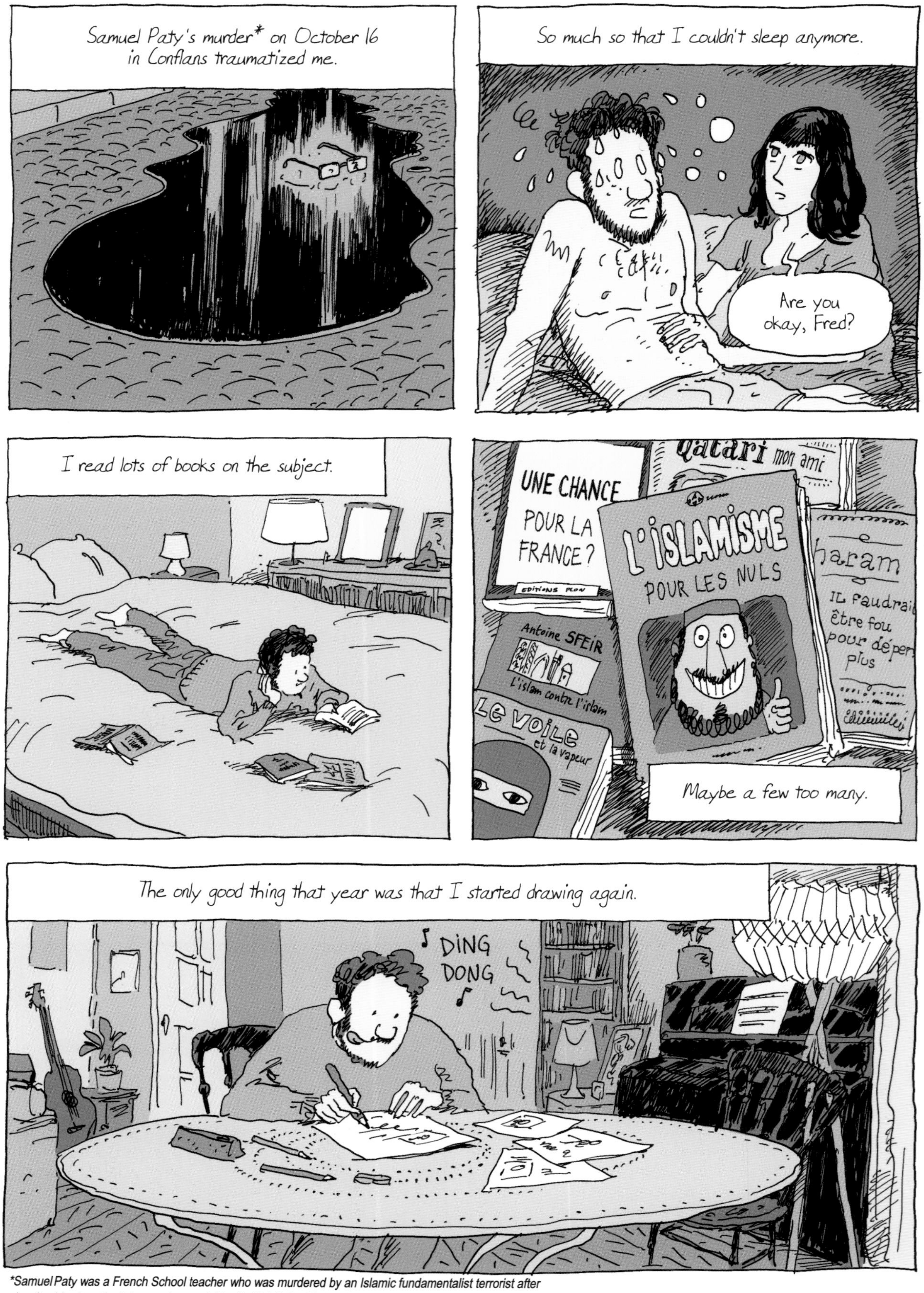
Samuel Paty's murder* on October 16 in Conflans traumatized me.
So much so that I couldn't sleep anymore.
Are you okay, Fred?
I read lots of books on the subject.
Qatari mon ami
UNE CHANCE POUR LA FRANCE?
EDITIONS PLON
L'ISLAMISME POUR LES NULS
Antoine SFEIR
L'islam contre l'islam
LE VOILE et la vapeur
Maybe a few too many.
The only good thing that year was that I started drawing again.
DING DONG

*Samuel Paty was a French School teacher who was murdered by an Islamic fundamentalist terrorist after showing his class the infamous issue of *Charlie Hebdo* that featured cartoons depicting the prophet Muhammad.

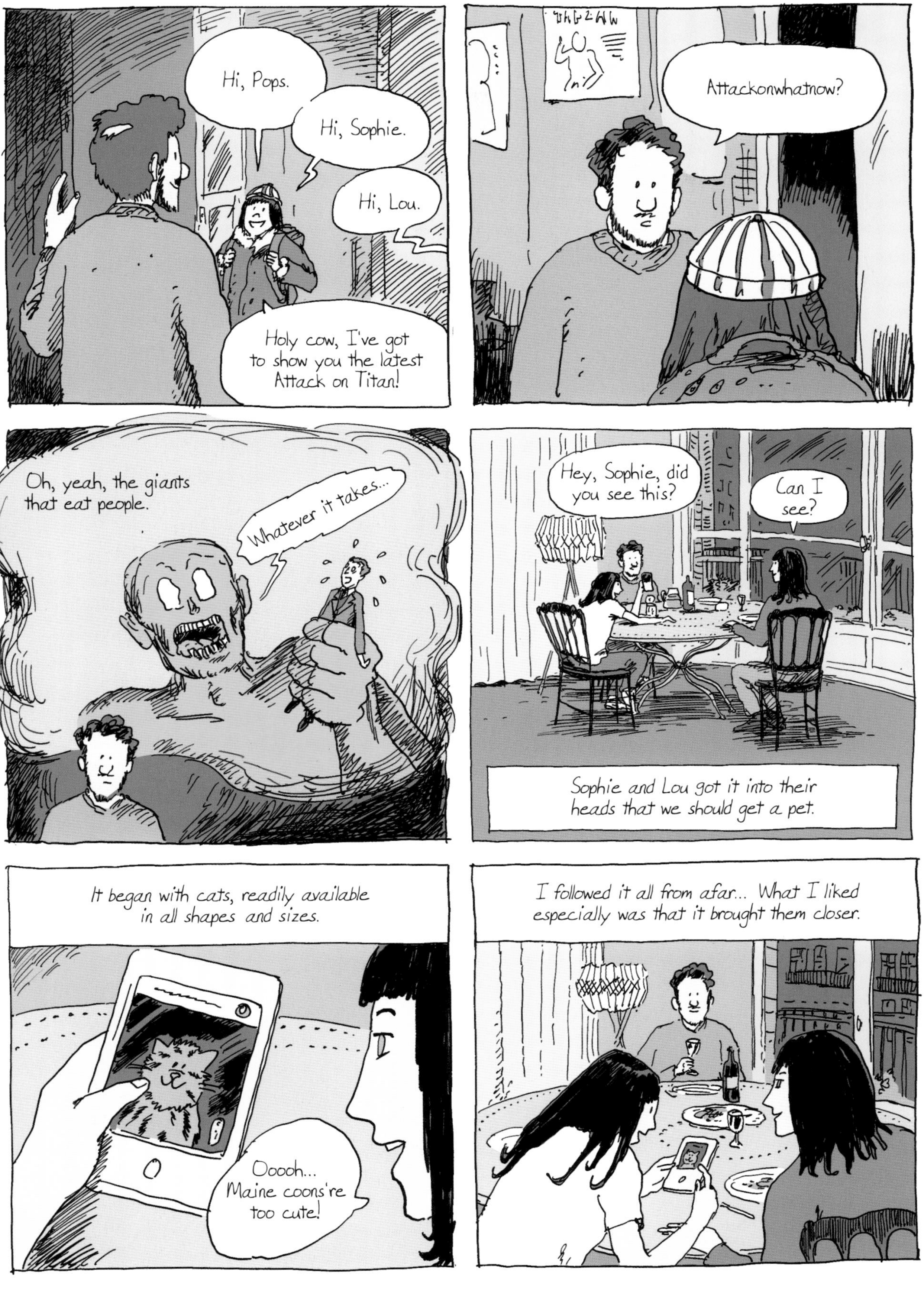
Hi, Pops.
Hi, Sophie.
Hi, Lou.
Holy cow, I've got to show you the latest Attack on Titan!
Attackonwhatnow?
Oh, yeah, the giants that eat people.
Whatever it takes...
Hey, Sophie, did you see this?
Can I see?
Sophie and Lou got it into their heads that we should get a pet.
It began with cats, readily available in all shapes and sizes.
Ooooh... Maine coons're too cute!
I followed it all from afar... What I liked especially was that it brought them closer.

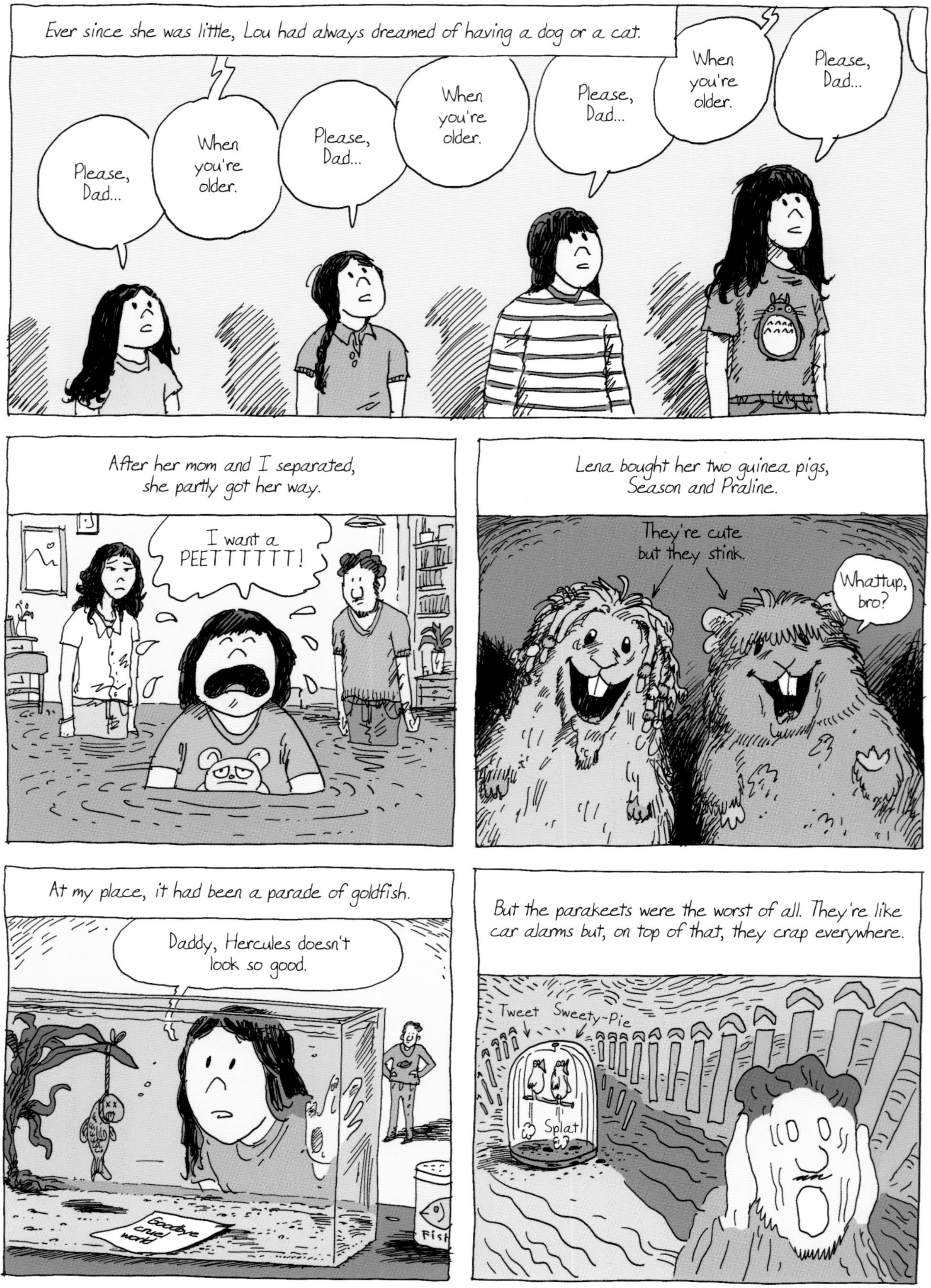
Ever since she was little, Lou had always dreamed of having a dog or a cat.
Please, Dad...
When you're older.
Please, Dad...
When you're older.
Please, Dad...
When you're older.
Please, Dad...
After her mom and I separated, she partly got her way.
I want a PEETTTTTTT!
Lena bought her two guinea pigs, Season and Praline.
They're cute but they stink.
Whattup, bro?
At my place, it had been a parade of goldfish.
Daddy, Hercules doesn't look so good.
Goodbye cruel world
Fish
But the parakeets were the worst of all. They're like car alarms but, on top of that, they crap everywhere.
Tweet
Sweety-Pie
Splat

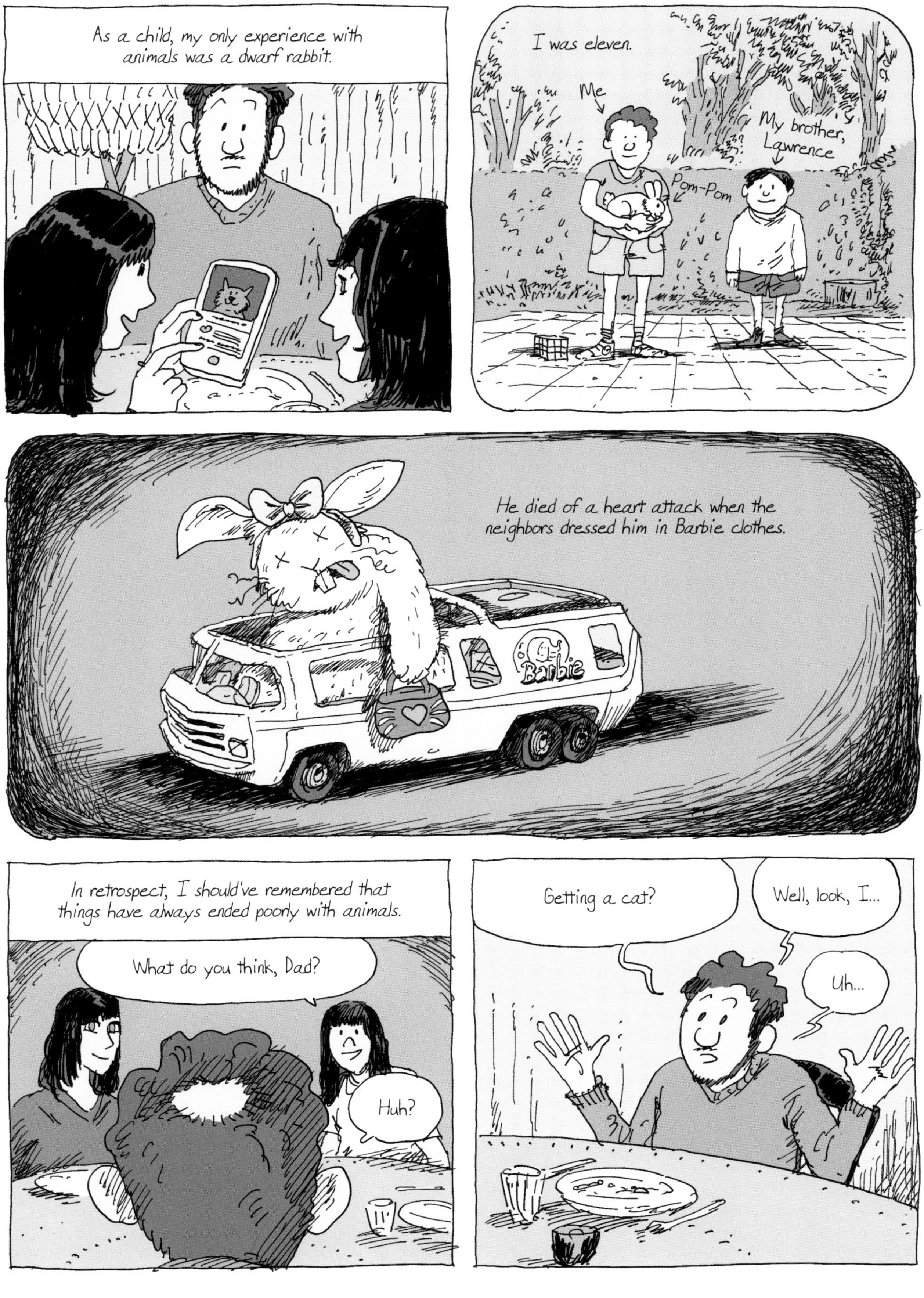
As a child, my only experience with animals was a dwarf rabbit.
I was eleven.
Me
My brother, Lawrence
Pom-Pom
He died of a heart attack when the neighbors dressed him in Barbie clothes.
Barbie
In retrospect, I should've remembered that things have always ended poorly with animals.
What do you think, Dad?
Huh?
Getting a cat?
Well, look, I...
Uh...

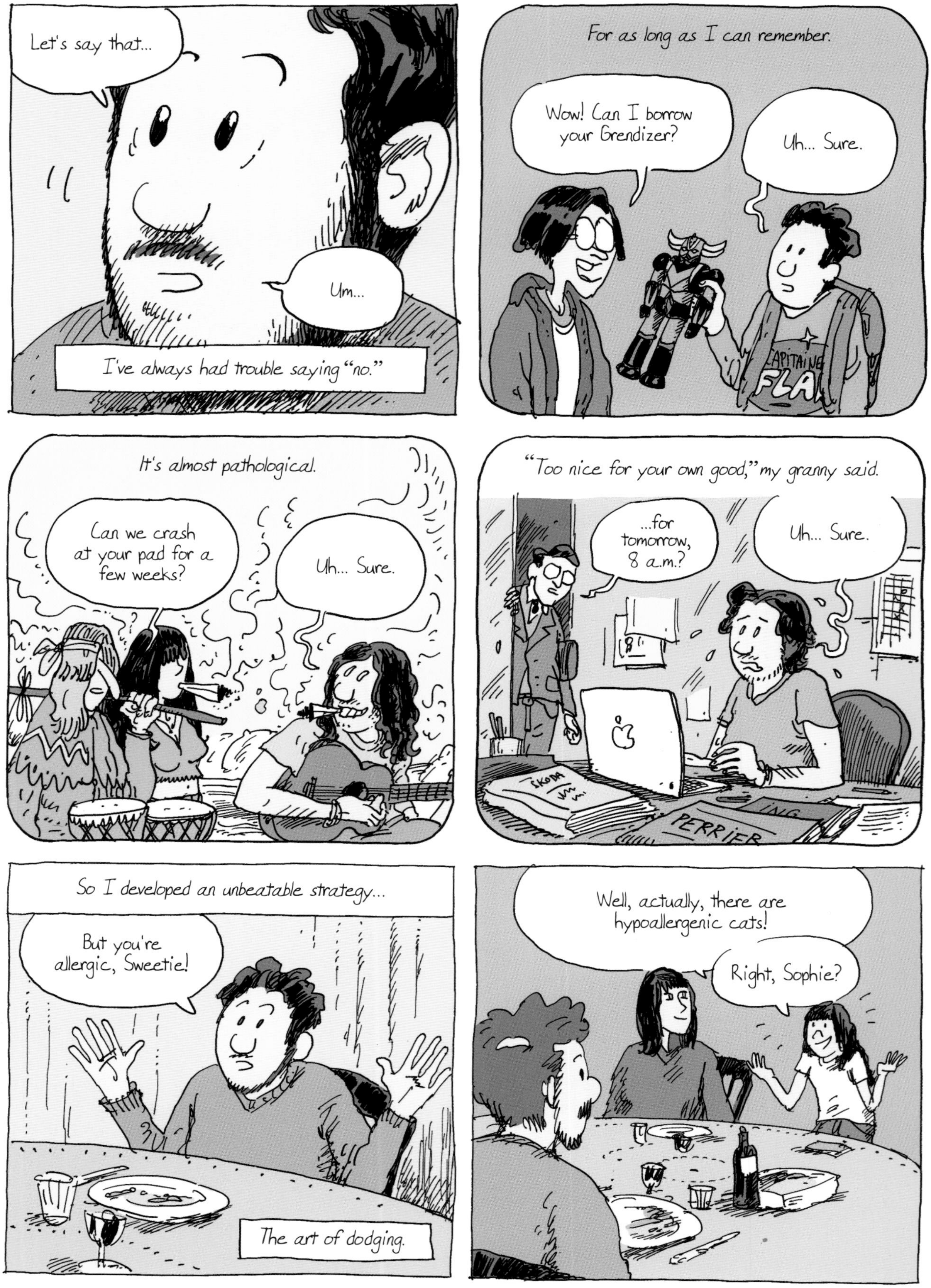
Let's say that...
Um...
I've always had trouble saying "no."
For as long as I can remember.
Wow! Can I borrow your Grendizer?
Uh... Sure.
CAPITAINE FLA
It's almost pathological.
Can we crash at your pad for a few weeks?
Uh... Sure.
"Too nice for your own good," my granny said.
...for tomorrow, 8 a.m.?
Uh... Sure.
SKODA
PERRIER
So I developed an unbeatable strategy...
But you're allergic, Sweetie!
The art of dodging.
Well, actually, there are hypoallergenic cats!
Right, Sophie?

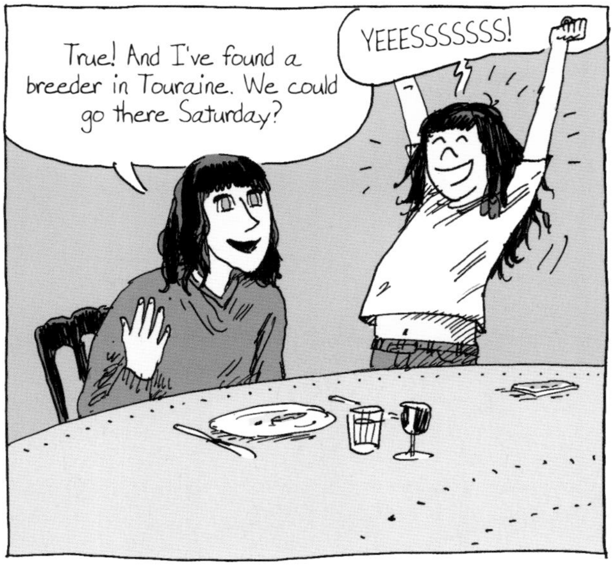
True! And I've found a breeder in Touraine. We could go there Saturday?
YEEESSSSSSS!

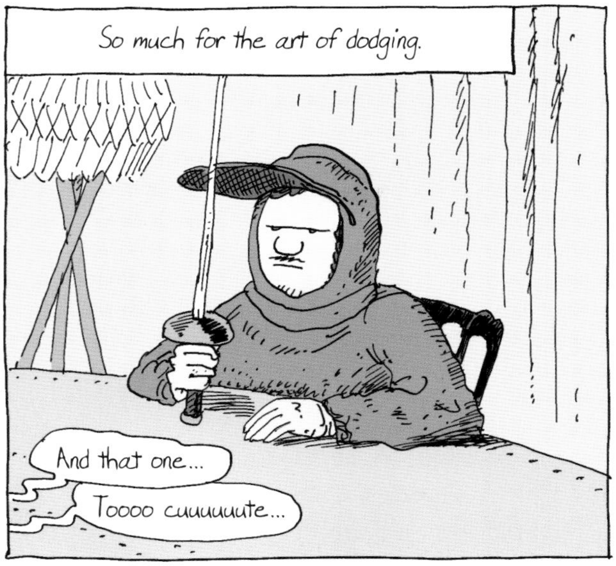
So much for the art of dodging.
And that one...
Toooo cuuuuuute...

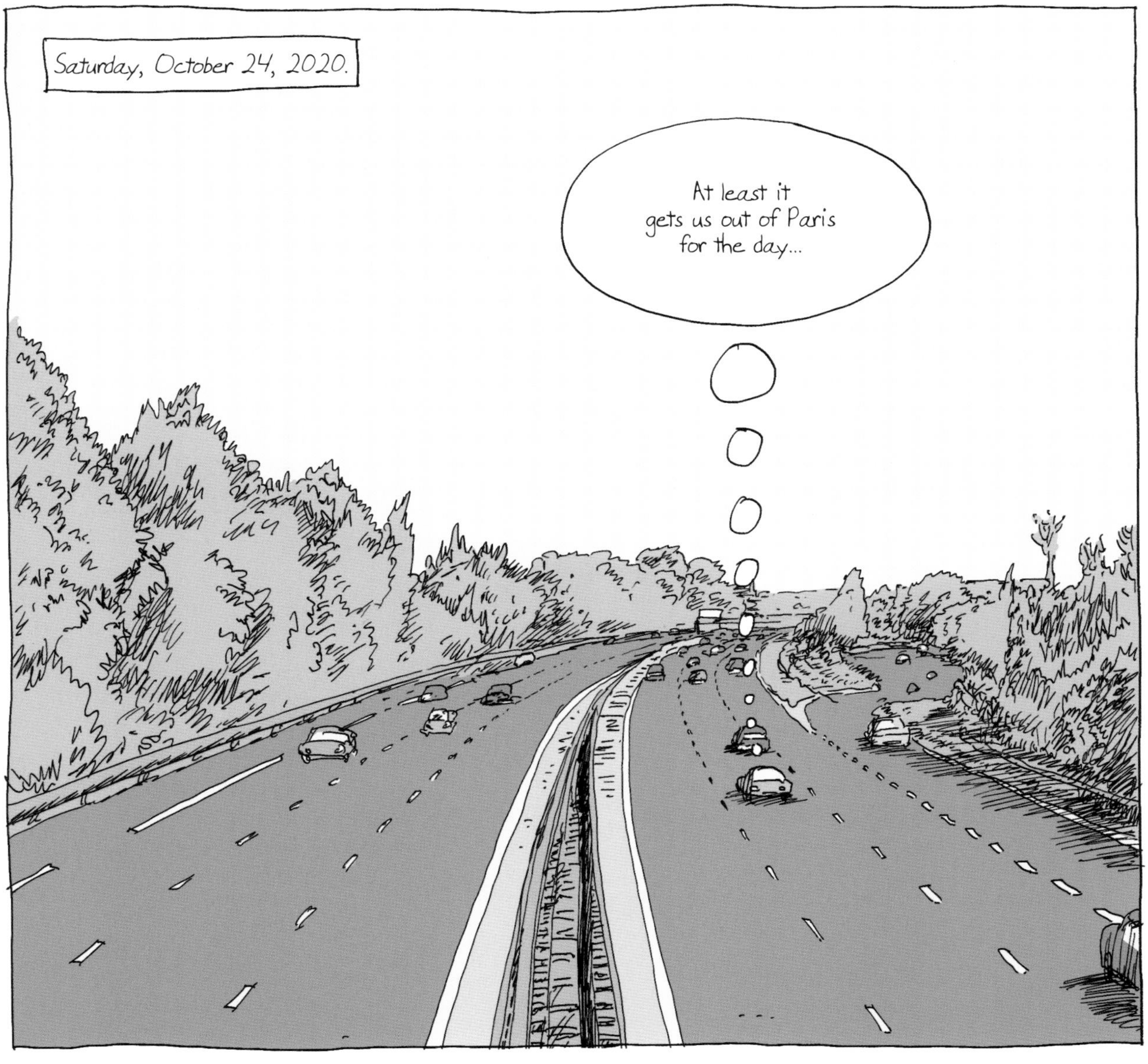
Saturday, October 24, 2020.
At least it gets us out of Paris for the day...

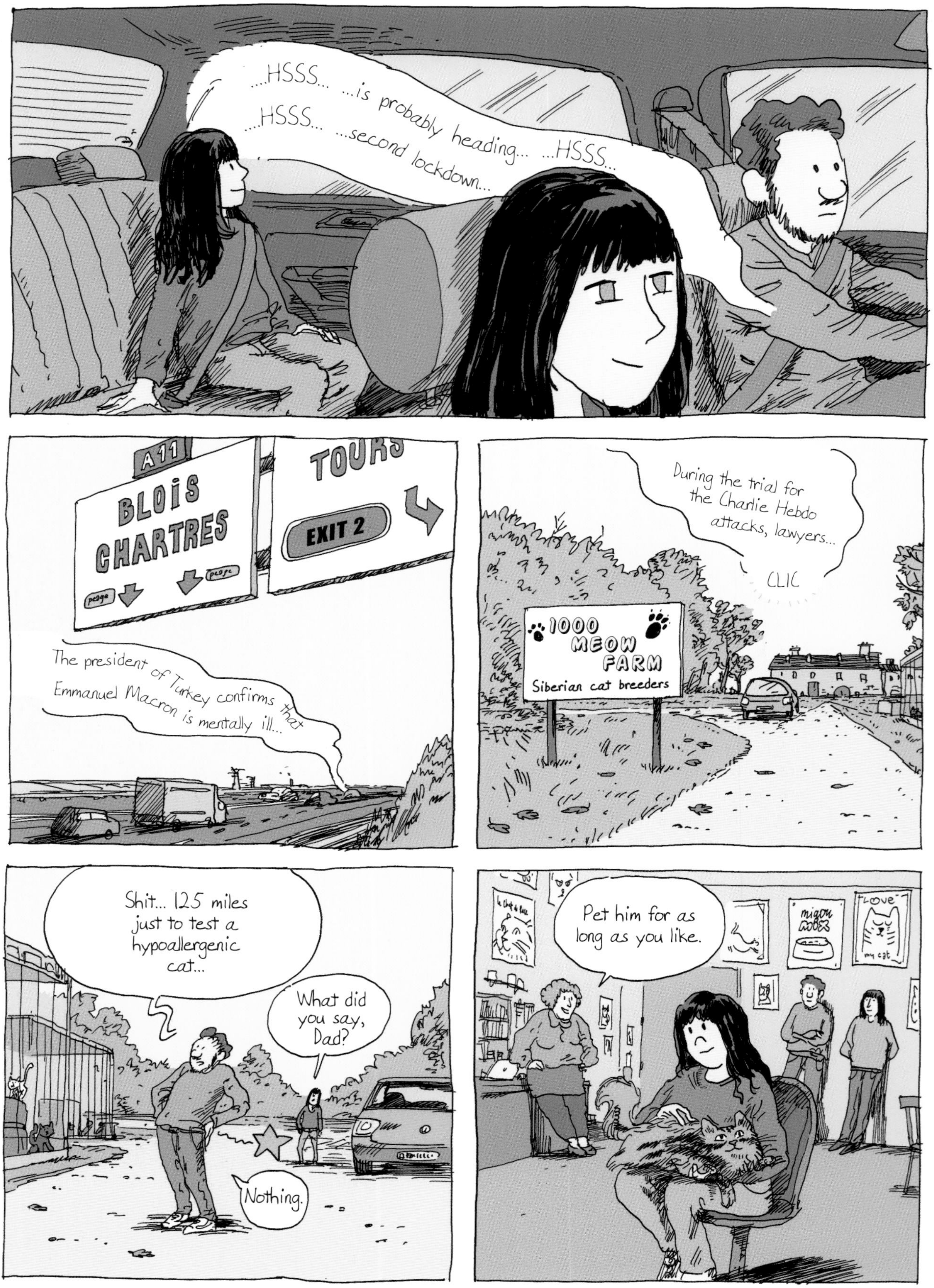
...HSSS... ...is probably heading... ...HSSS...
...HSSS... ...second lockdown...
A11
BLOIS
CHARTRES
péage
TOURS
EXIT 2
The president of Turkey confirms that Emmanuel Macron is mentally ill...
During the trial for the Charlie Hebdo attacks, lawyers...
CLIC
1000 MEOW FARM
Siberian cat breeders
Shit... 125 miles just to test a hypoallergenic cat...
What did you say, Dad?
Nothing.
Pet him for as long as you like.
LOVE
my cat

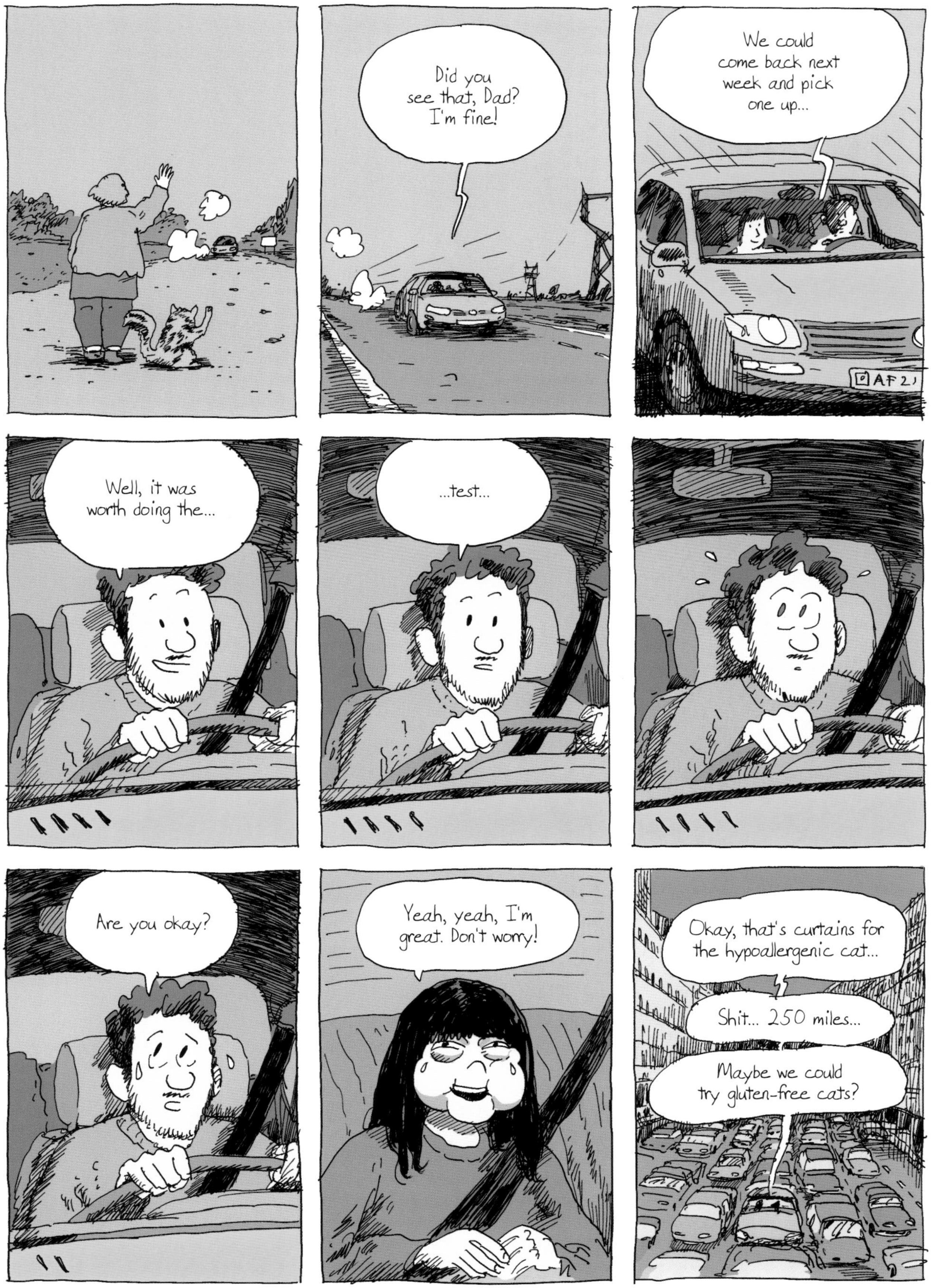
Did you see that, Dad? I'm fine!
We could come back next week and pick one up...
AF 2
Well, it was worth doing the...
...test...
Are you okay?
Yeah, yeah, I'm great. Don't worry!
Okay, that's curtains for the hypoallergenic cat...
Shit... 250 miles...
Maybe we could try gluten-free cats?

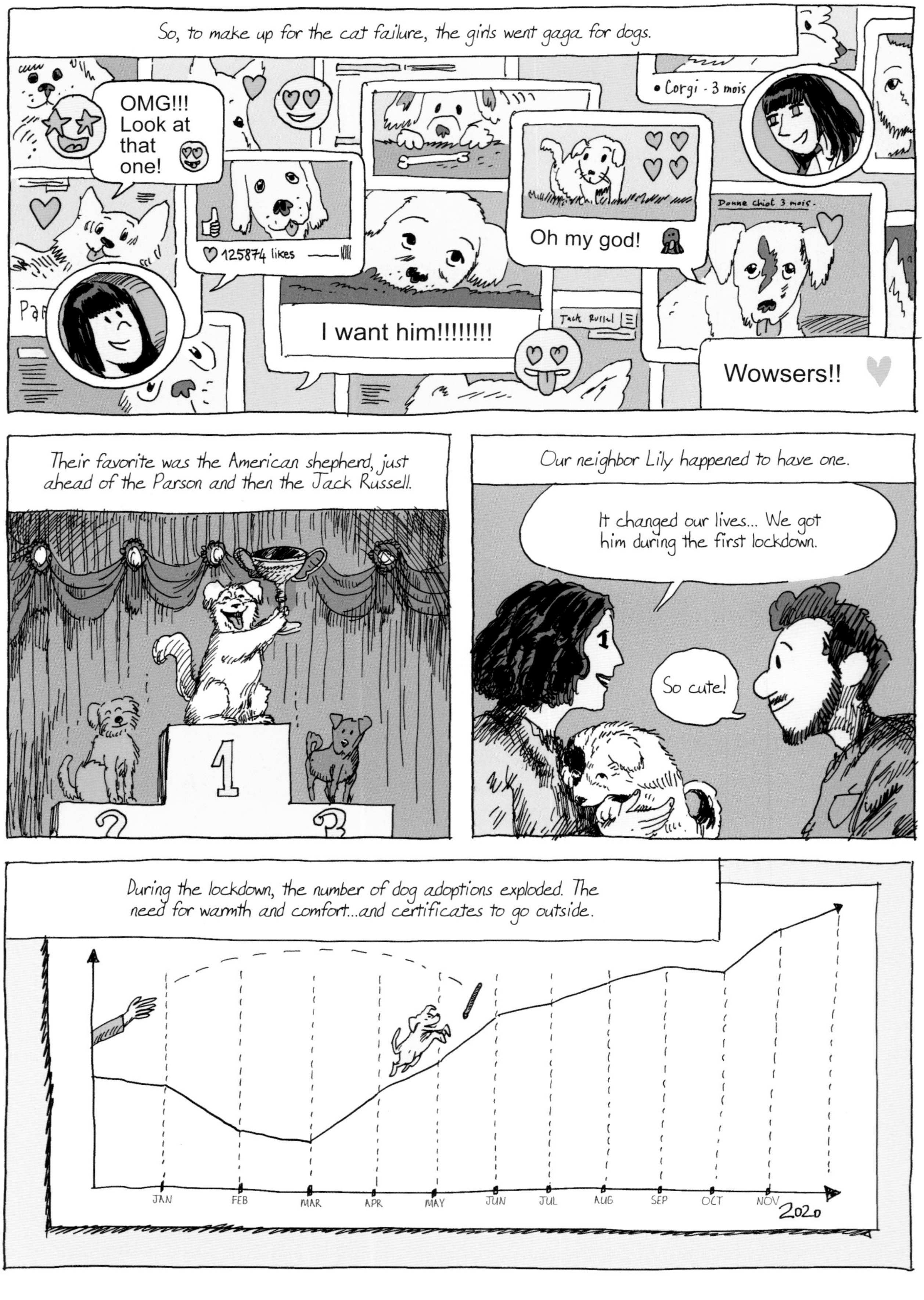
So, to make up for the cat failure, the girls went gaga for dogs.
OMG!!! Look at that one!
125874 likes
• Corgi - 3 mois
Oh my god!
Donne chiot 3 mois.
I want him!!!!!!!!
Jack Russel
Wowsers!!
Their favorite was the American shepherd, just ahead of the Parson and then the Jack Russell.
1
2
3
Our neighbor Lily happened to have one.
It changed our lives... We got him during the first lockdown.
So cute!
During the lockdown, the number of dog adoptions exploded. The need for warmth and comfort...and certificates to go outside.
JAN
FEB
MAR
APR
MAY
JUN
JUL
AUG
SEP
OCT
NOV
2020

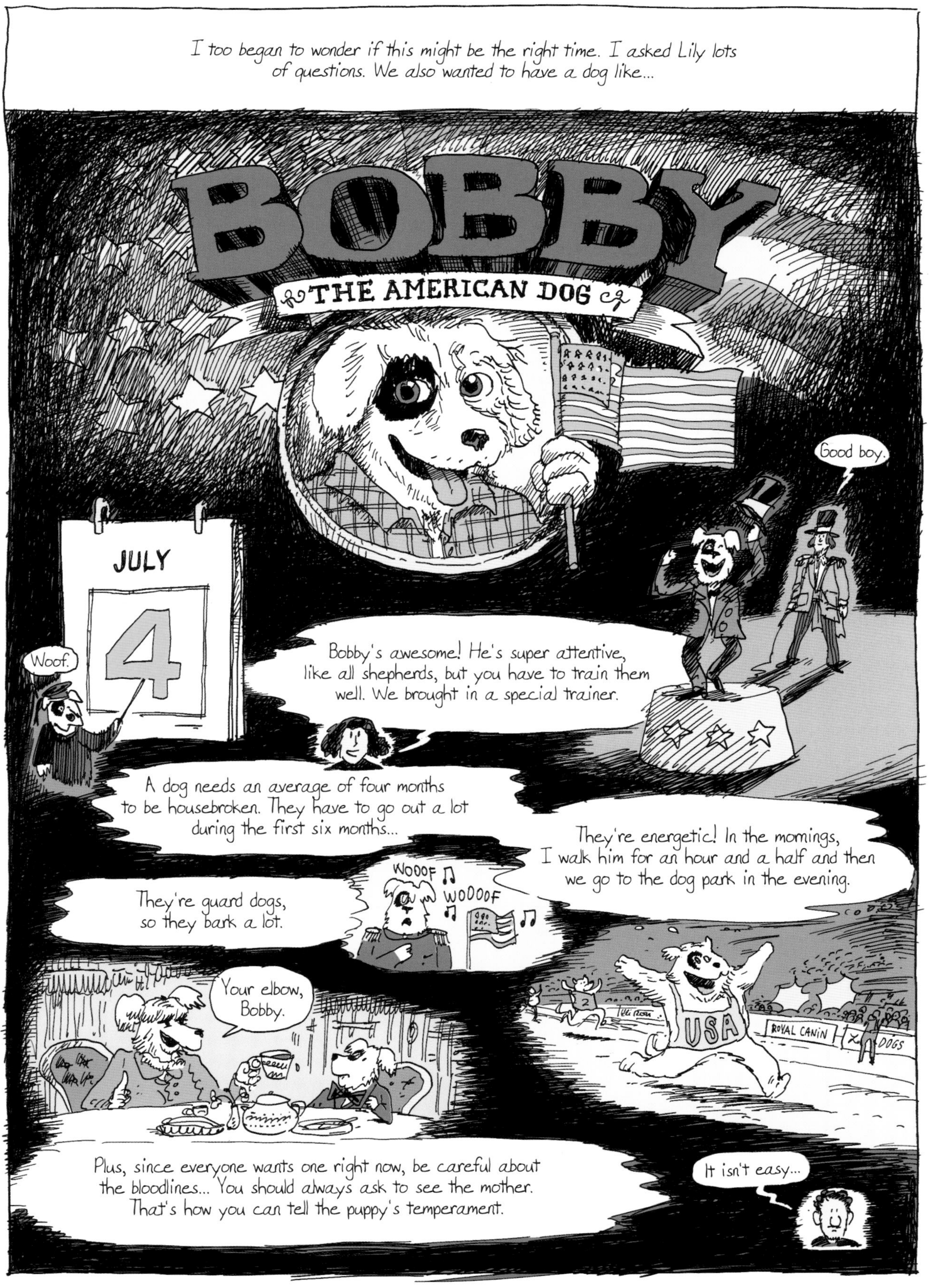
I too began to wonder if this might be the right time. I asked Lily lots of questions. We also wanted to have a dog like...
BOBBY
THE AMERICAN DOG
JULY
4
Woof.
Good boy.
Bobby's awesome! He's super attentive, like all shepherds, but you have to train them well. We brought in a special trainer.
A dog needs an average of four months to be housebroken. They have to go out a lot during the first six months...
They're energetic! In the mornings, I walk him for an hour and a half and then we go to the dog park in the evening.
They're guard dogs, so they bark a lot.
WOOOF
WOOOOF
Your elbow, Bobby.
USA
ROYAL CANIN
DOGS
Plus, since everyone wants one right now, be careful about the bloodlines... You should always ask to see the mother. That's how you can tell the puppy's temperament.
It isn't easy...

Still, the idea of having a dog wormed its way into our minds.

Okay...

You'll get a dog for your birthday AND Christmas. But only if you get straight As.

YES!

I've already got a name...

Tiki.

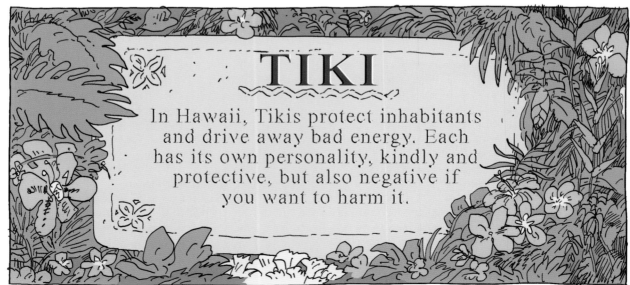

TIKI

In Hawaii, Tikis protect inhabitants and drive away bad energy. Each has its own personality, kindly and protective, but also negative if you want to harm it.

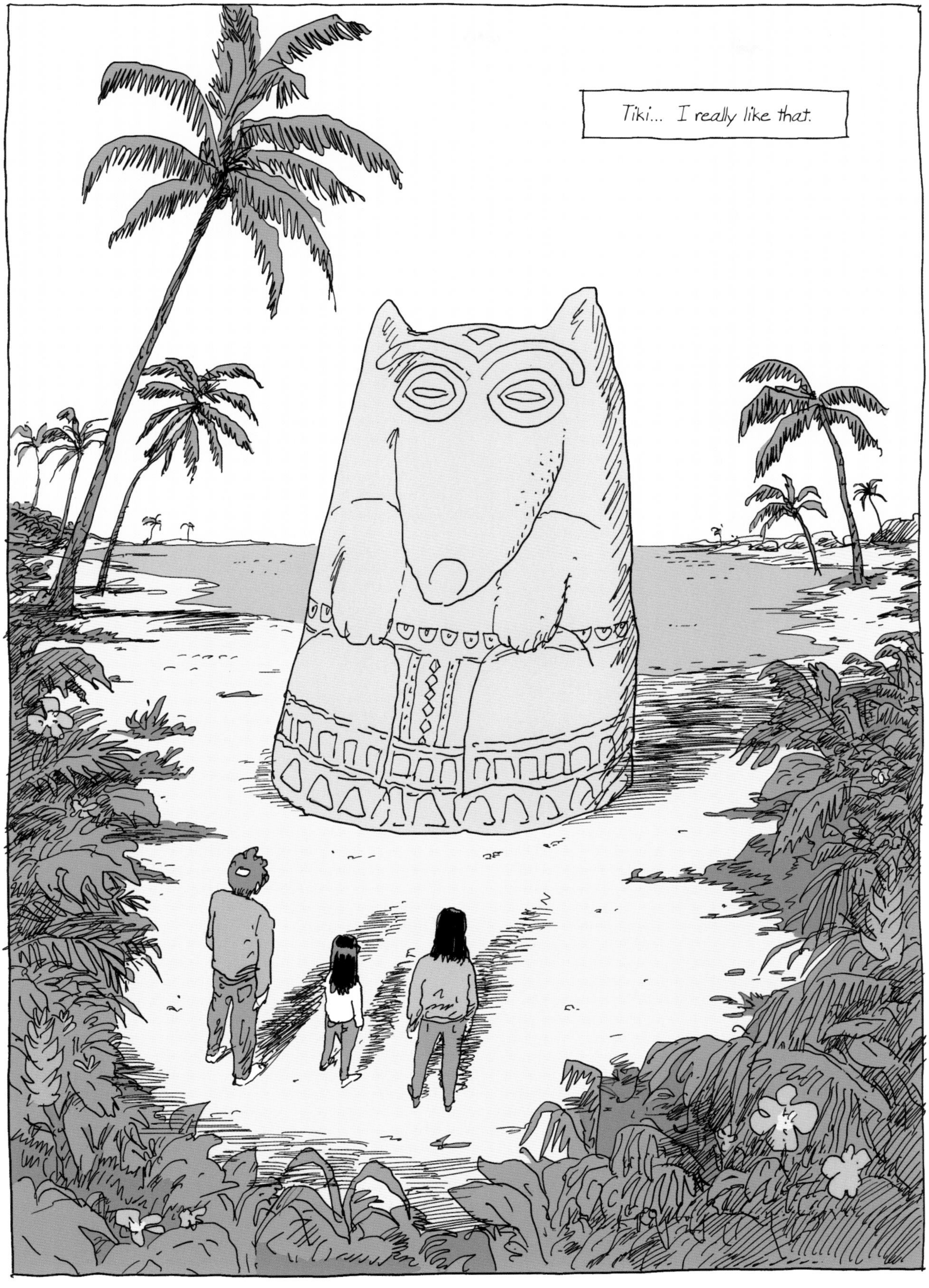
Tiki... I really like that.

Chapter Two

The Meeting

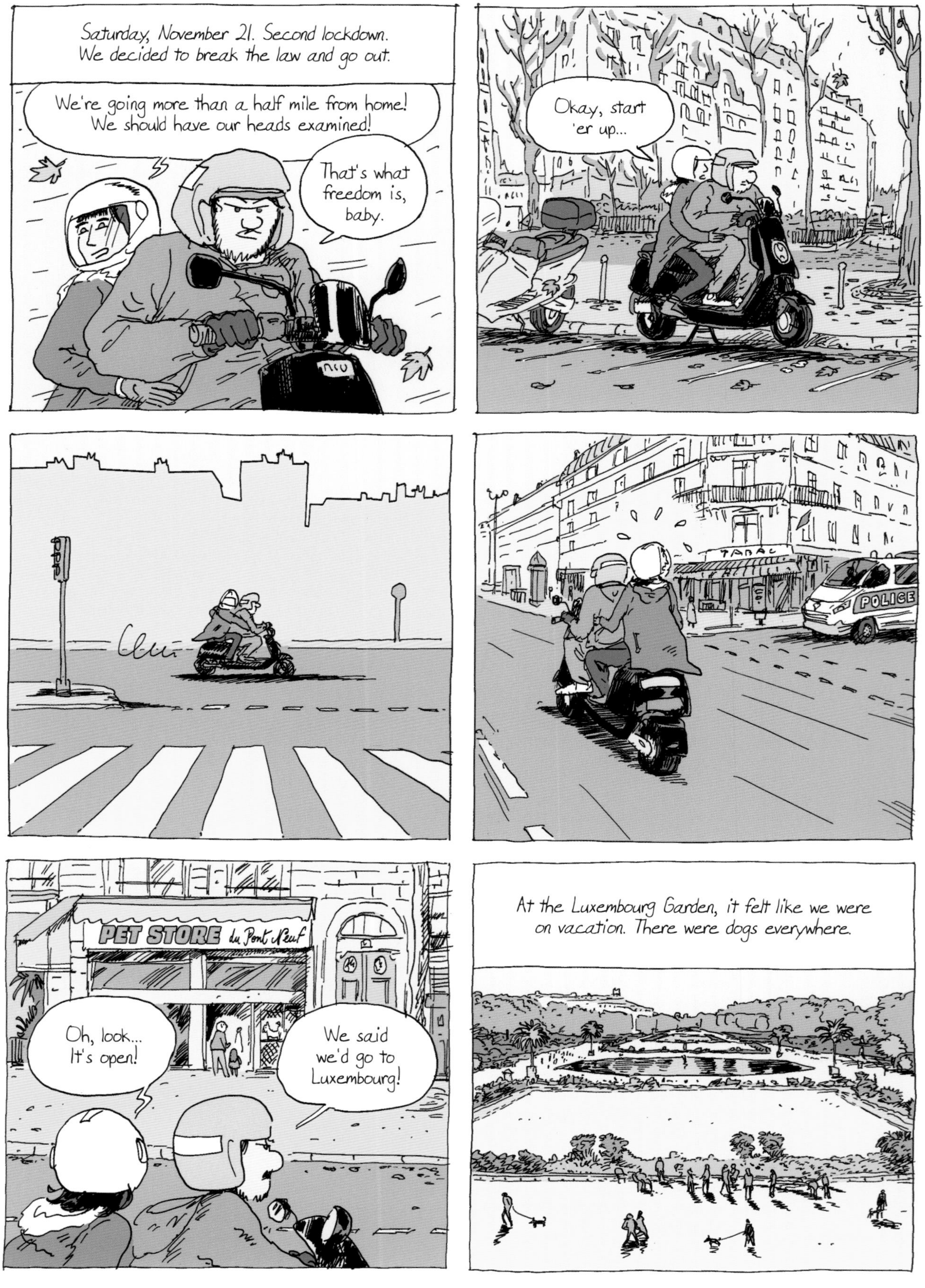
Saturday, November 21. Second lockdown. We decided to break the law and go out.
We're going more than a half mile from home! We should have our heads examined!
That's what freedom is, baby.
Okay, start 'er up...
POLICE
PET STORE du Pont Neuf
Oh, look... It's open!
We said we'd go to Luxembourg!
At the Luxembourg Garden, it felt like we were on vacation. There were dogs everywhere.

Two hours later...

Turn left!

But I turned right. It was fate.

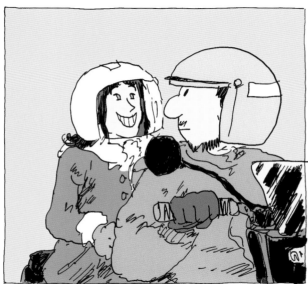

Come on, let's go look.

I know the Pont Neuf Pet Store well. That's where I'd bought food for the parakeets and goldfish.

It smells of beasts and confinement. It's like a nursing home, but for animals.

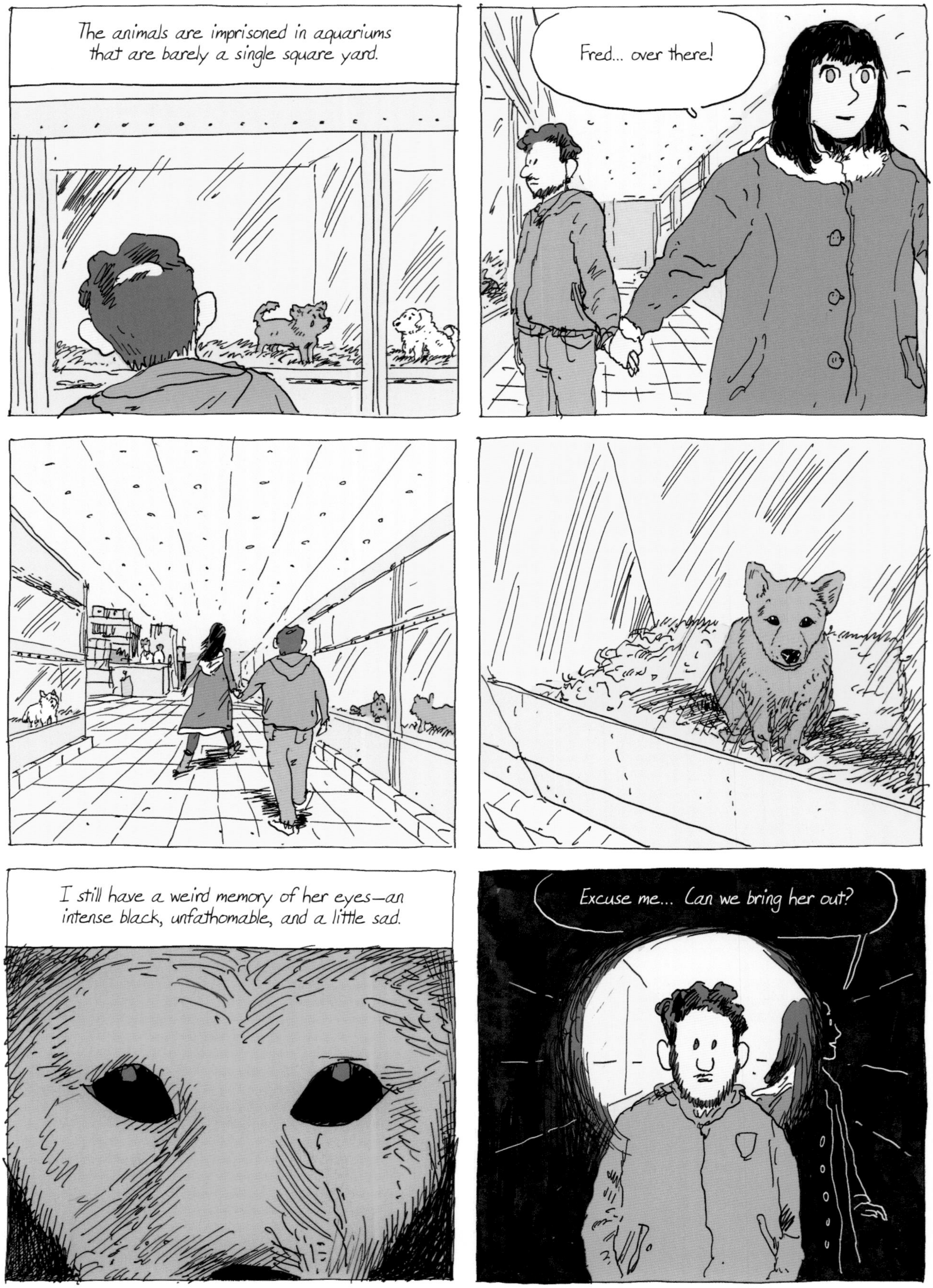

The animals are imprisoned in aquariums that are barely a single square yard.
Fred... over there!
I still have a weird memory of her eyes—an intense black, unfathomable, and a little sad.
Excuse me... Can we bring her out?

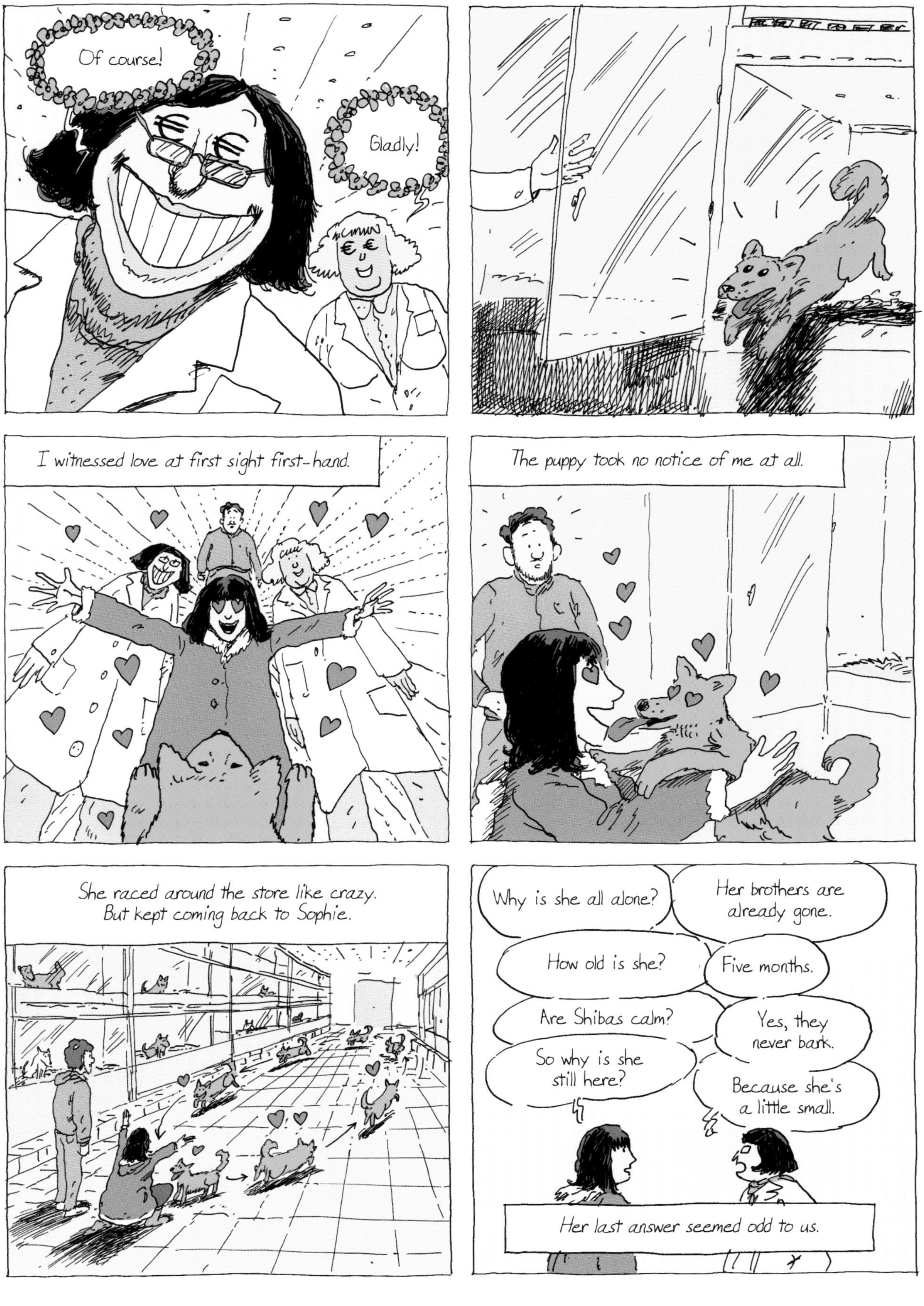
Of course!
Gladly!
I witnessed love at first sight first-hand.
The puppy took no notice of me at all.
She raced around the store like crazy. But kept coming back to Sophie.
Why is she all alone?
Her brothers are already gone.
How old is she?
Five months.
Are Shibas calm?
Yes, they never bark.
So why is she still here?
Because she's a little small.
Her last answer seemed odd to us.

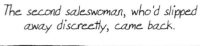

The second saleswoman, who'd slipped away discreetly, came back.

Heeeeere...

Here what?

Well...her leash. You can leave with it.

But...my daughter... Doesn't she have to see her? It's my gift to her after all...

We'll come back with her tomorrow!

But, sir, imagine when she finds the surprise! It'll be the best day of her life! What better present for a child?

If you come back tomorrow, it won't be the same.

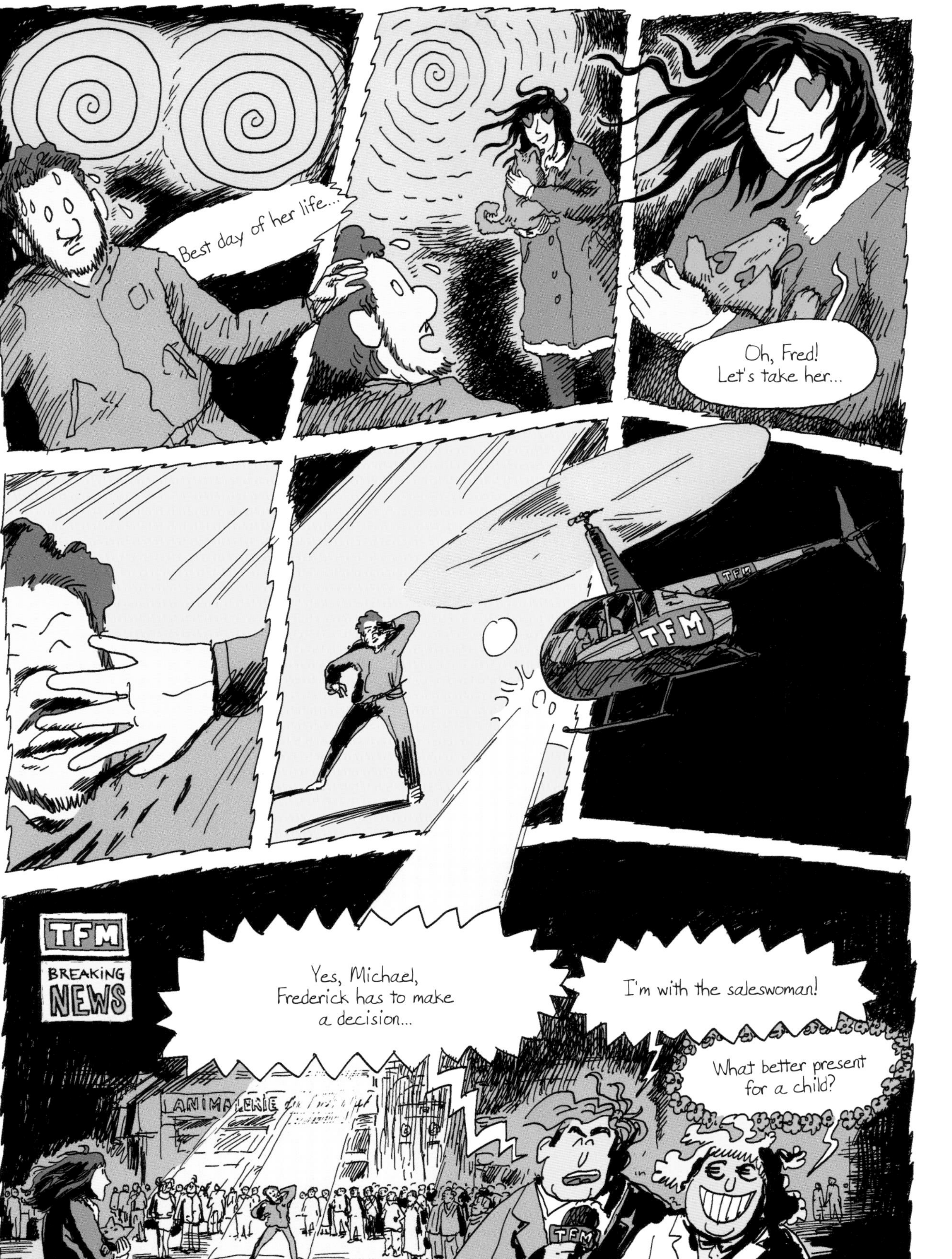
Best day of her life...
Oh, Fred!
Let's take her...
TFM
TFM
TFM
BREAKING
NEWS
Yes, Michael,
Frederick has to make
a decision...
I'm with the saleswoman!
What better present
for a child?
ANIMALERIE
TFM

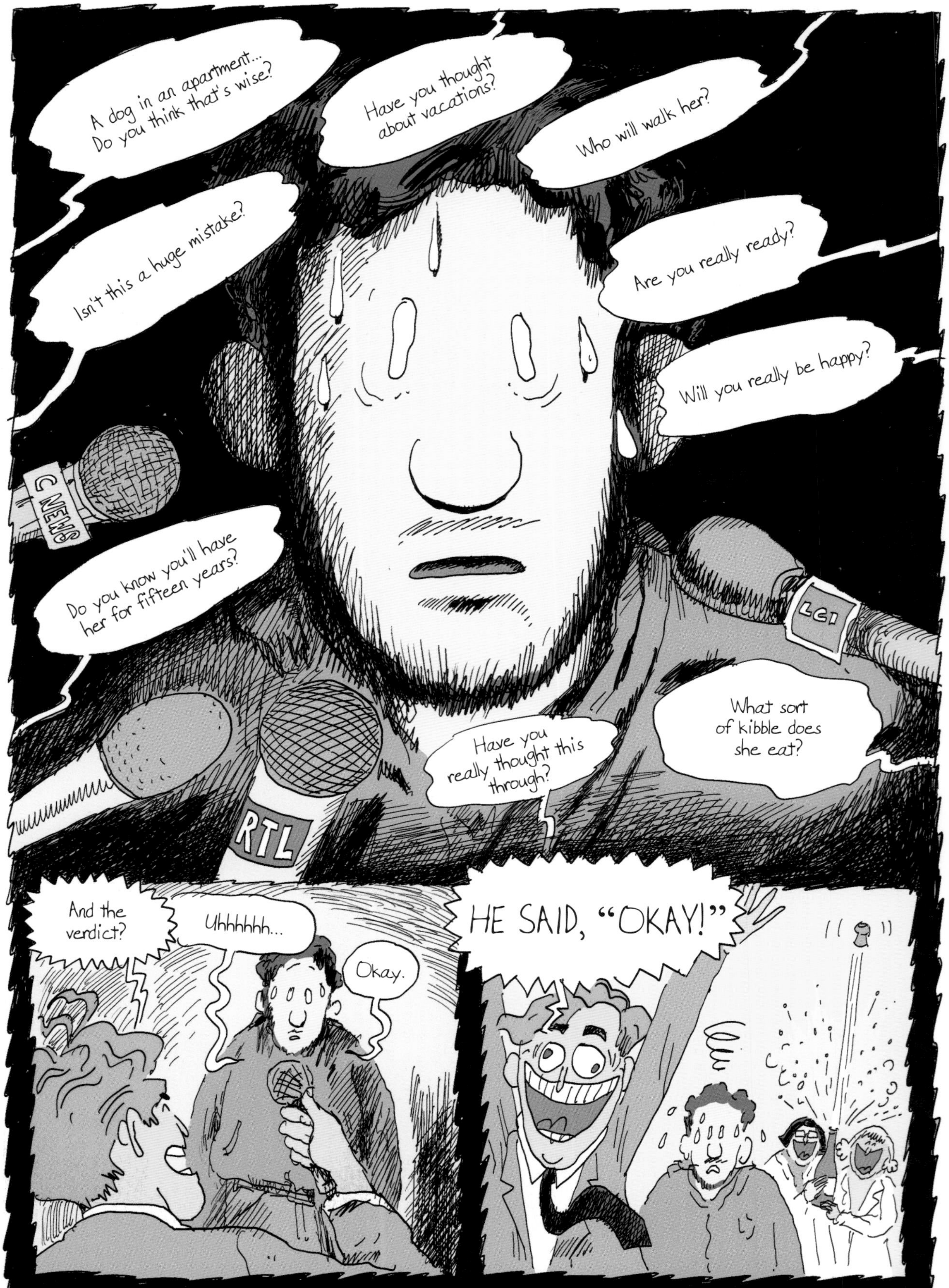
A dog in an apartment... Do you think that's wise?
Have you thought about vacations?
Who will walk her?
Isn't this a huge mistake?
Are you really ready?
Will you really be happy?
C NEWS
Do you know you'll have her for fifteen years?
LCI
What sort of kibble does she eat?
Have you really thought this through?
RTL
And the verdict?
Uhhhhhh...
Okay.
HE SAID, "OKAY!"

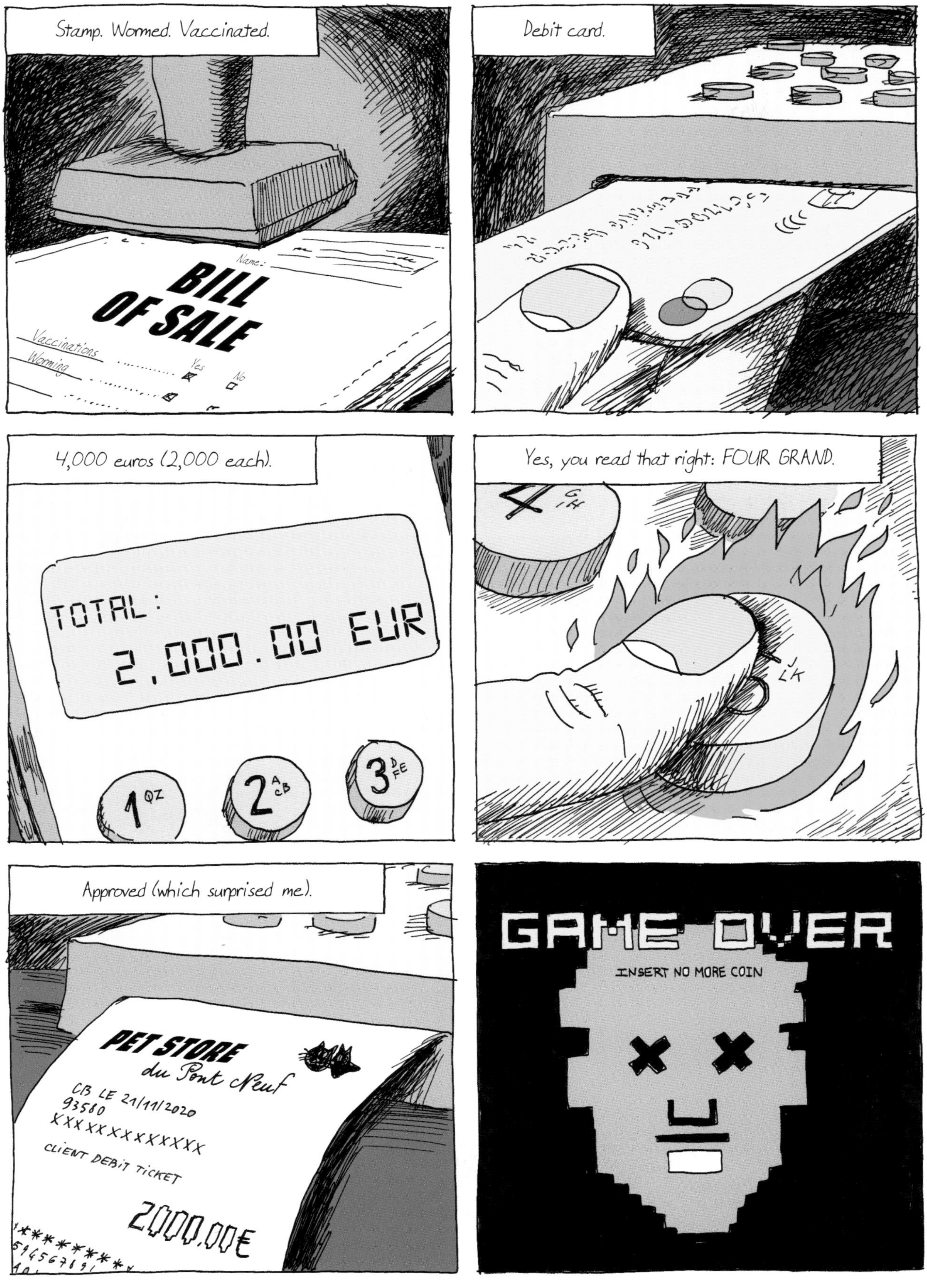
Stamp. Wormed. Vaccinated.
Name:
BILL OF SALE
Vaccinations
Worming
Yes
No
Debit card.
4,000 euros (2,000 each).
TOTAL :
2.000.00 EUR
Yes, you read that right: FOUR GRAND.
Approved (which surprised me).
PET STORE
du Pont Neuf
CB LE 21/11/2020
93580
XXXXXXXXXXXX
CLIENT DEBIT TICKET
2000,00€
GAME OVER
INSERT NO MORE COIN

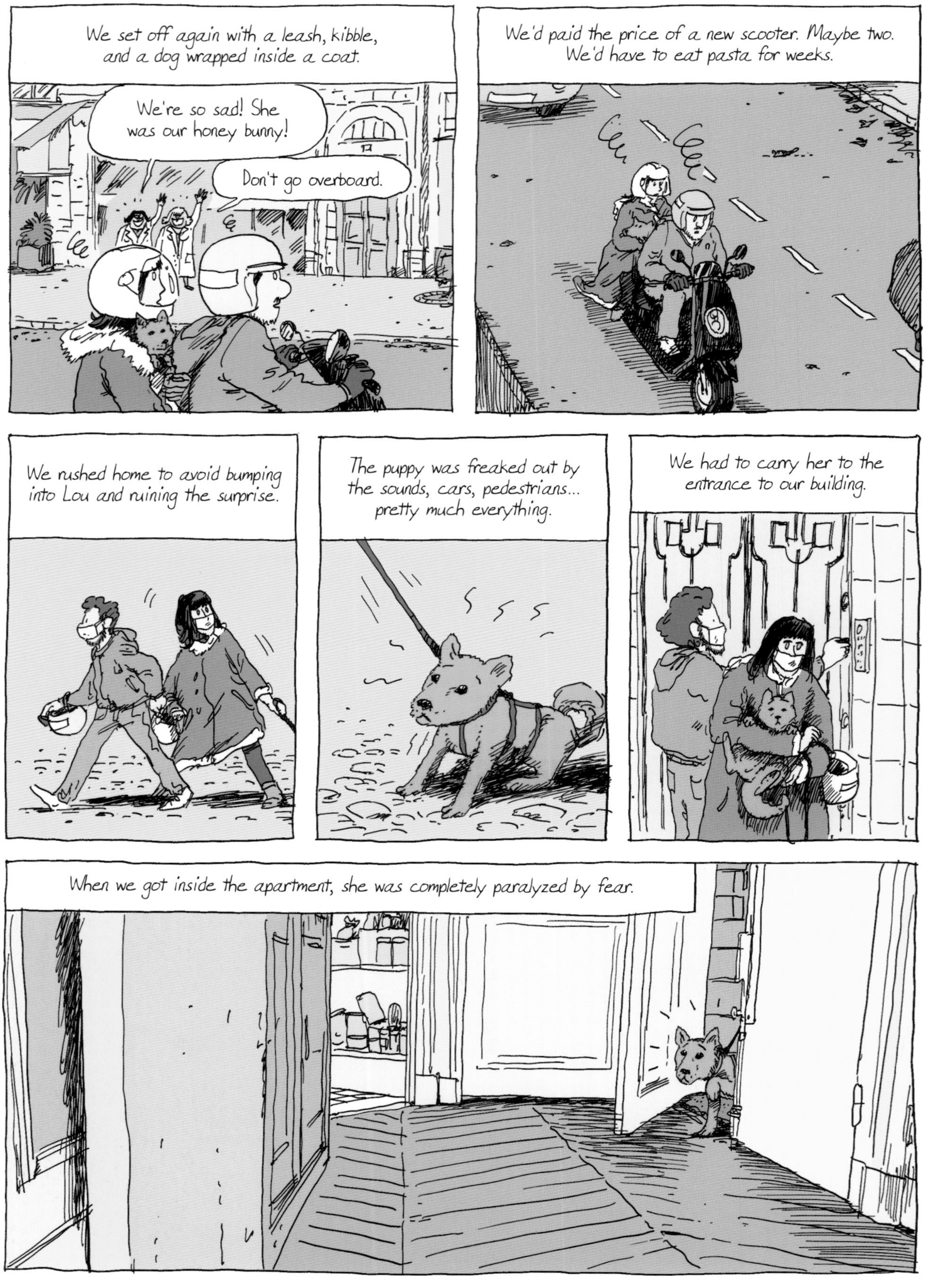
We set off again with a leash, kibble, and a dog wrapped inside a coat.
We're so sad! She was our honey bunny!
Don't go overboard.
We'd paid the price of a new scooter. Maybe two. We'd have to eat pasta for weeks.
We rushed home to avoid bumping into Lou and ruining the surprise.
The puppy was freaked out by the sounds, cars, pedestrians... pretty much everything.
We had to carry her to the entrance to our building.
When we got inside the apartment, she was completely paralyzed by fear.

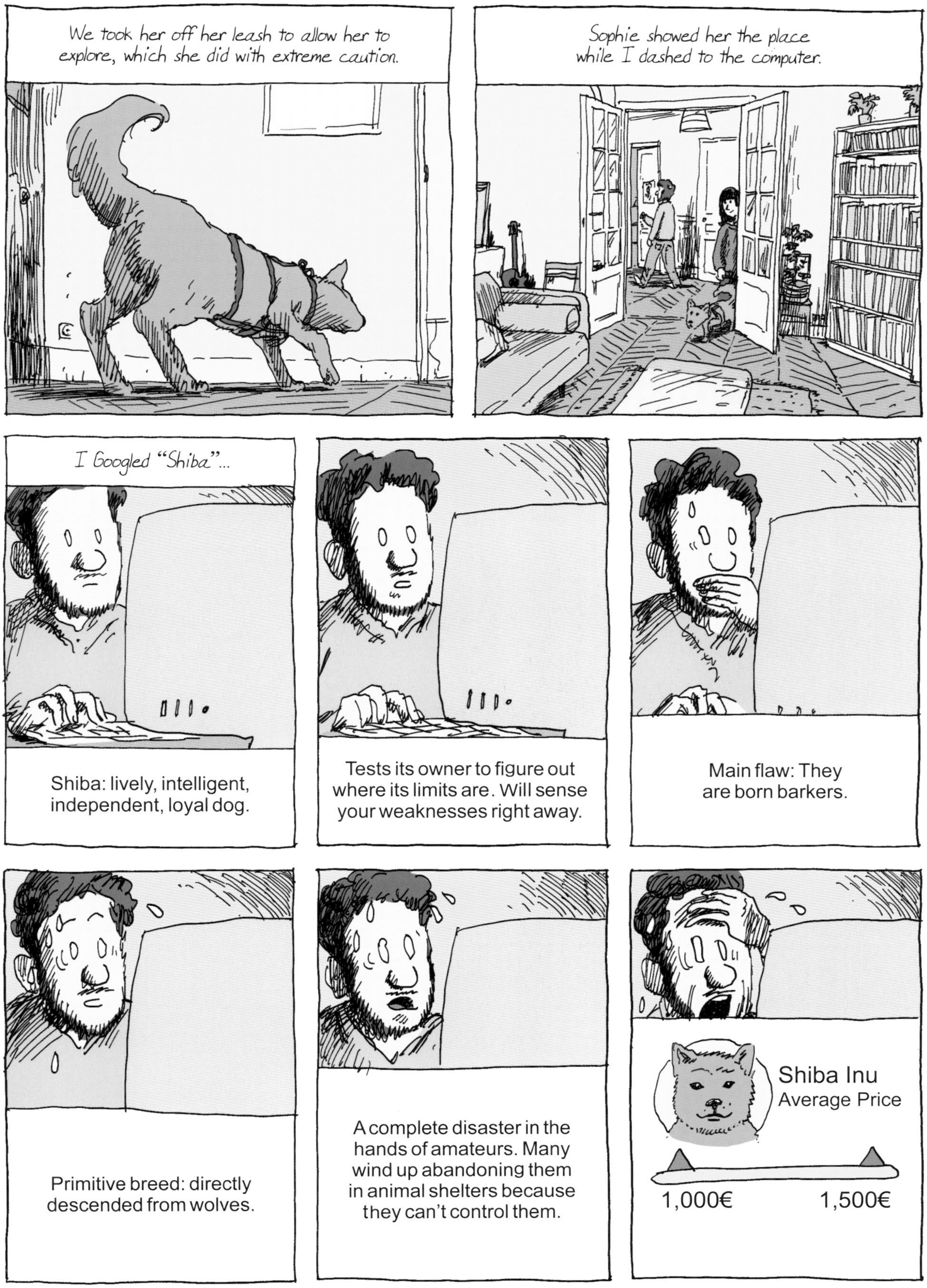
We took her off her leash to allow her to explore, which she did with extreme caution.
Sophie showed her the place while I dashed to the computer.
I Googled "Shiba"...
Shiba: lively, intelligent, independent, loyal dog.
Tests its owner to figure out where its limits are. Will sense your weaknesses right away.
Main flaw: They are born barkers.
Primitive breed: directly descended from wolves.
A complete disaster in the hands of amateurs. Many wind up abandoning them in animal shelters because they can't control them.
Shiba Inu
Average Price
1,000€
1,500€

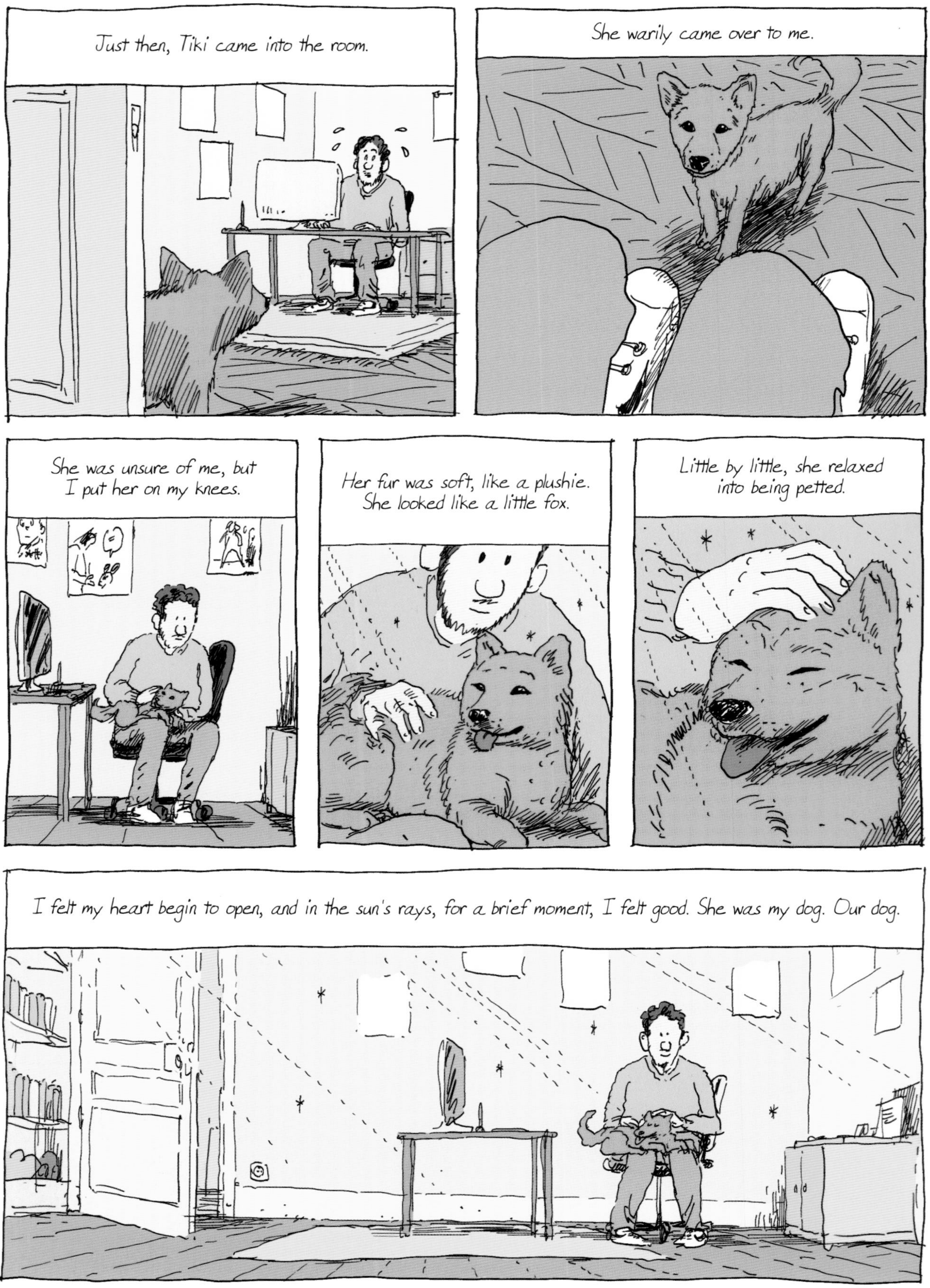
Just then, Tiki came into the room.
She warily came over to me.
She was unsure of me, but I put her on my knees.
Her fur was soft, like a plushie. She looked like a little fox.
Little by little, she relaxed into being petted.
I felt my heart begin to open, and in the sun's rays, for a brief moment, I felt good. She was my dog. Our dog.

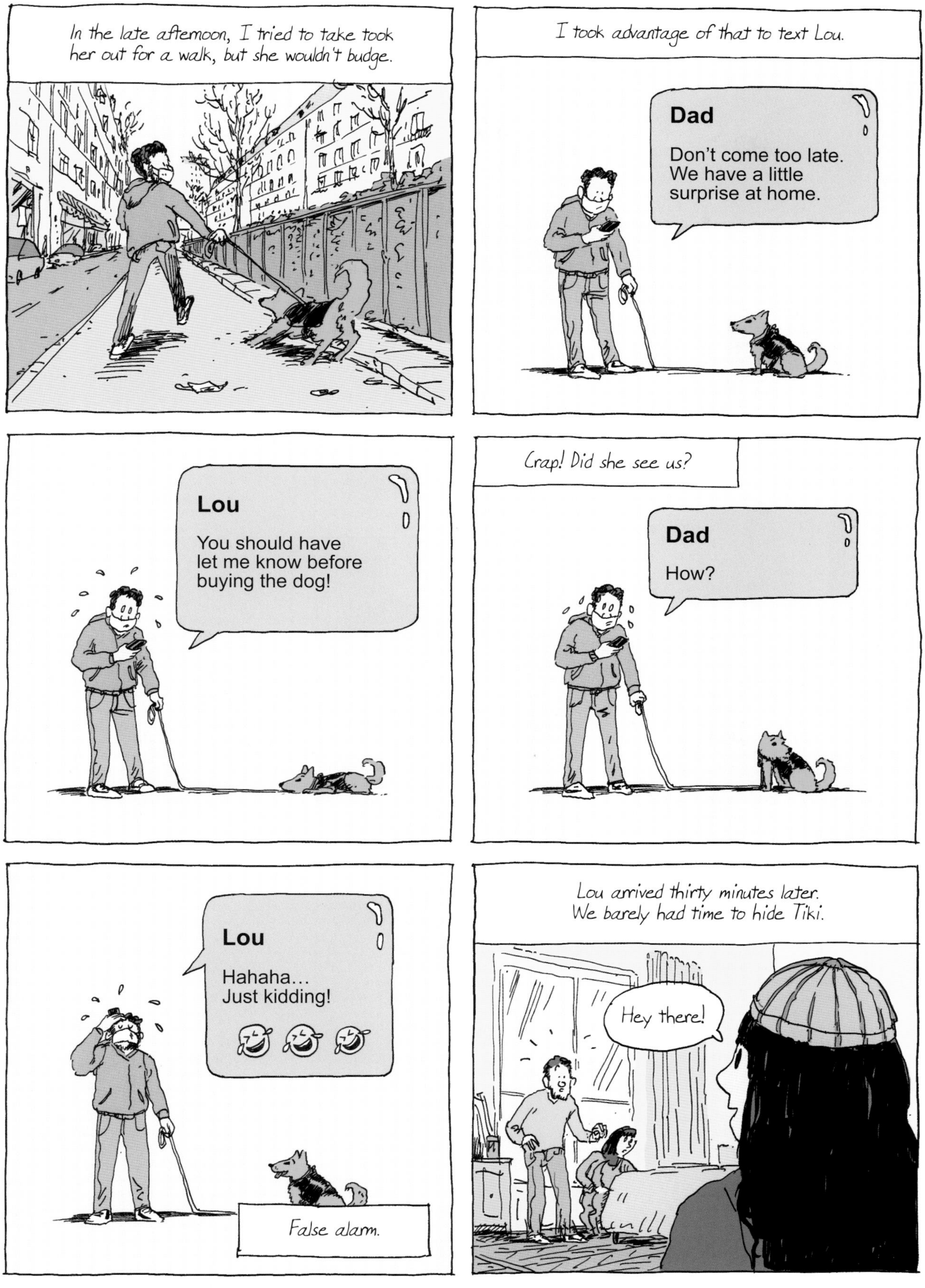
In the late afternoon, I tried to take took her out for a walk, but she wouldn't budge.
I took advantage of that to text Lou.
Dad
Don't come too late. We have a little surprise at home.
Lou
You should have let me know before buying the dog!
Crap! Did she see us?
Dad
How?
Lou
Hahaha... Just kidding!
False alarm.
Lou arrived thirty minutes later. We barely had time to hide Tiki.
Hey there!

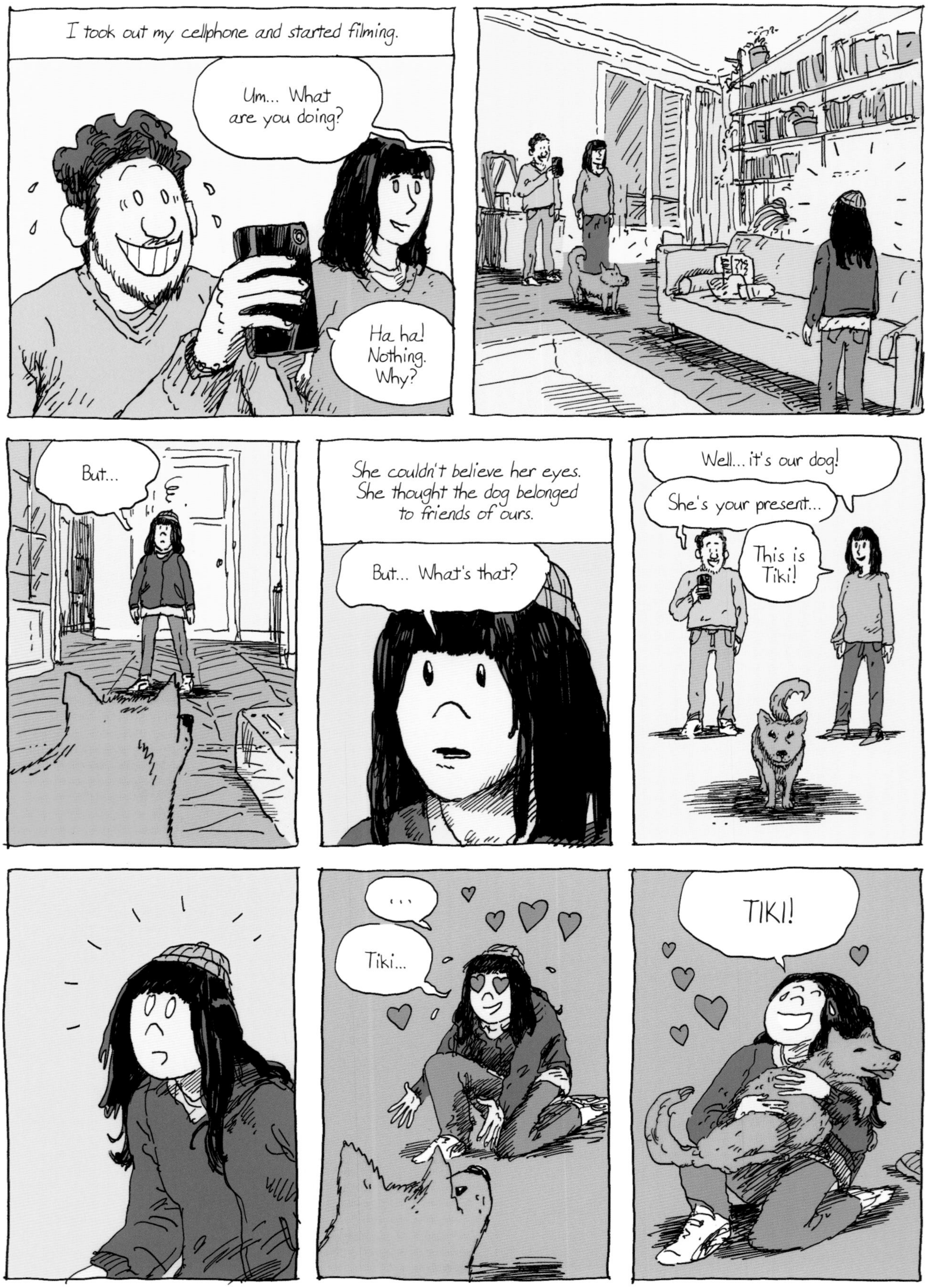
I took out my cellphone and started filming.
Um... What are you doing?
Ha ha! Nothing. Why?
But...
She couldn't believe her eyes. She thought the dog belonged to friends of ours.
But... What's that?
Well... it's our dog!
She's your present...
This is Tiki!
...
Tiki...
TIKI!

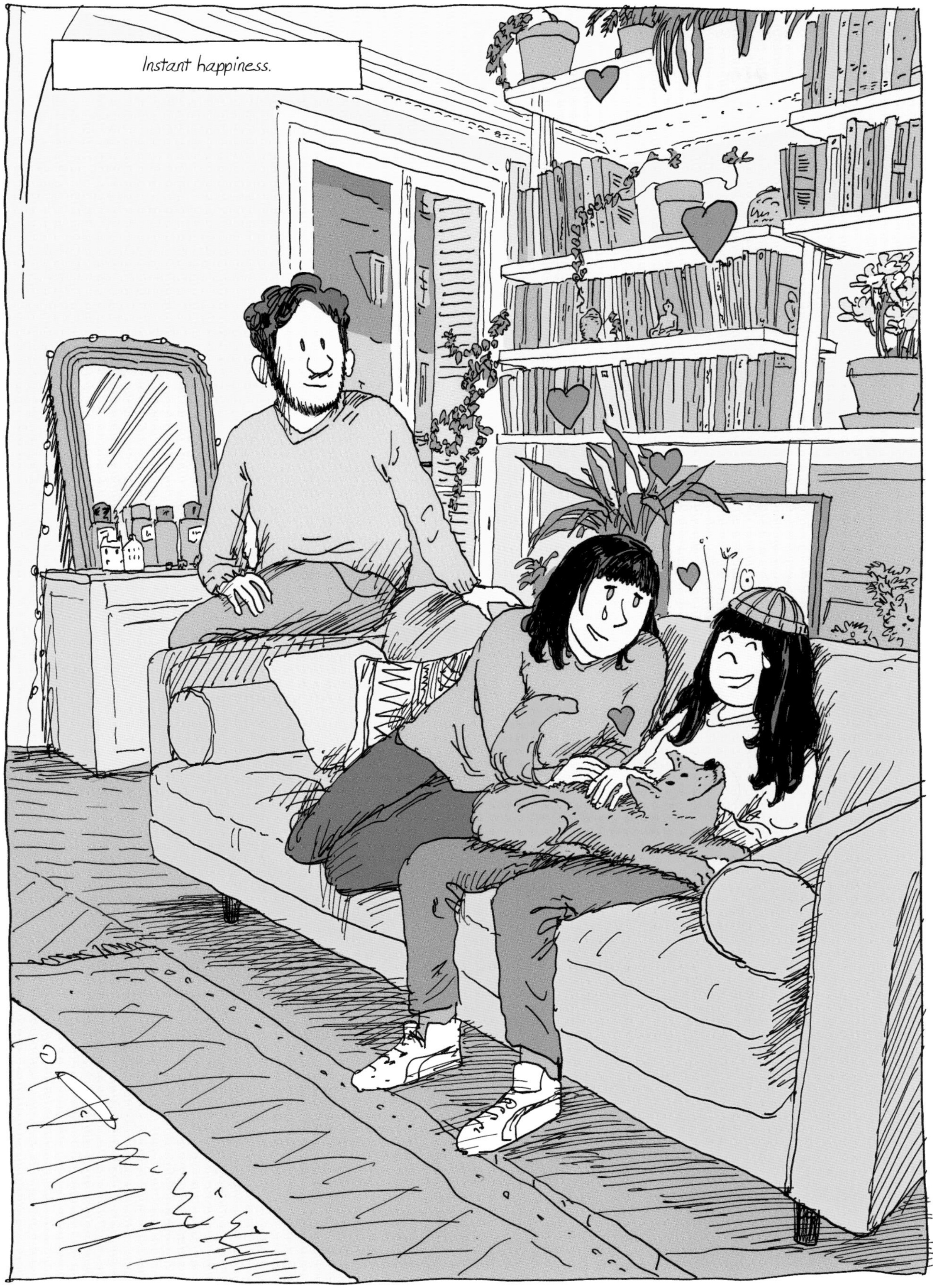
Instant happiness.

Chapter Three

First Days

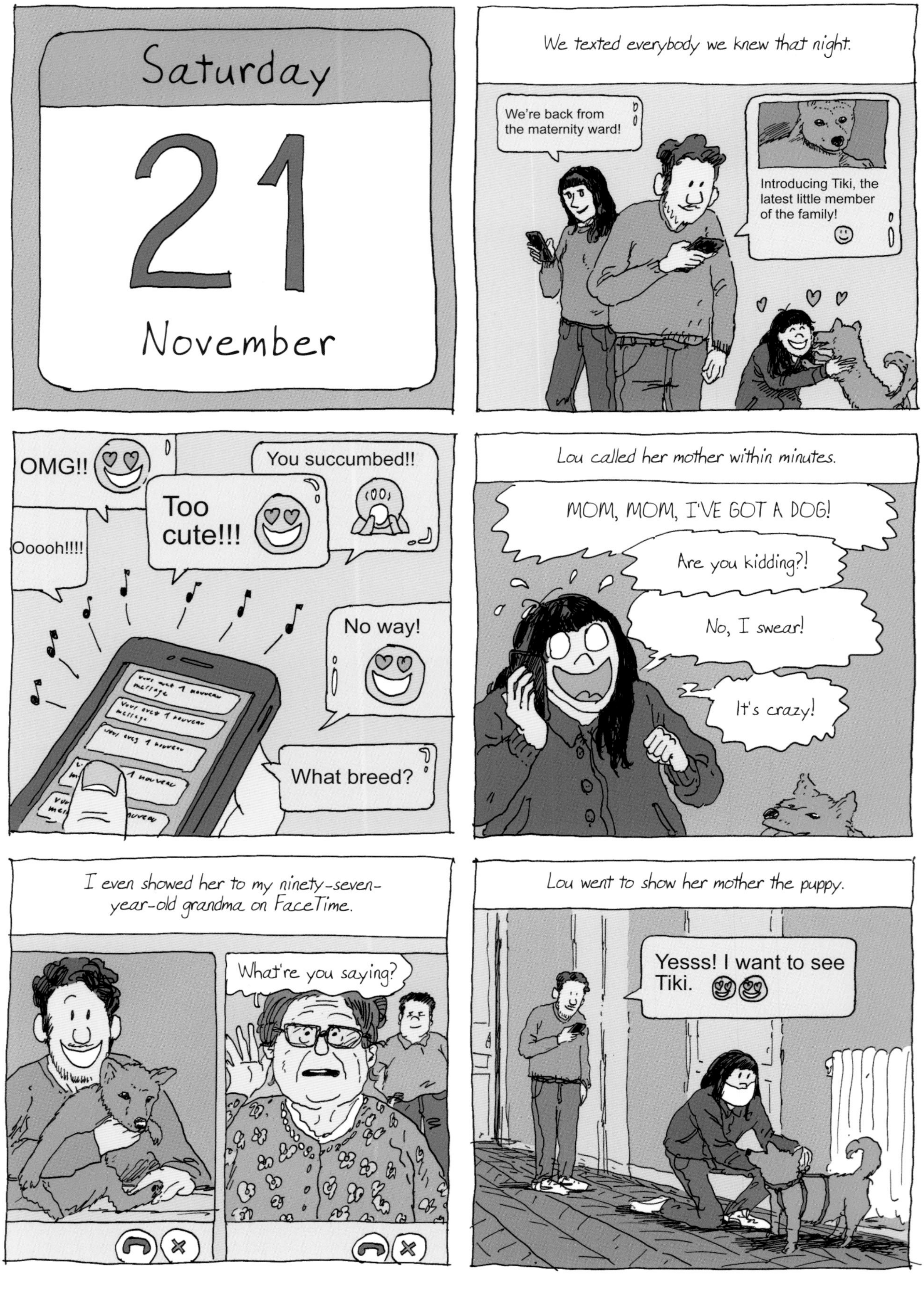
Saturday
21
November
We texted everybody we knew that night.
We're back from the maternity ward!
Introducing Tiki, the latest little member of the family!
OMG!!
You succumbed!!
Too cute!!!
Ooooh!!!!
No way!
What breed?
Lou called her mother within minutes.
MOM, MOM, I'VE GOT A DOG!
Are you kidding?!
No, I swear!
It's crazy!
I even showed her to my ninety-seven-year-old grandma on FaceTime.
What're you saying?
Lou went to show her mother the puppy.
Yesss! I want to see Tiki.

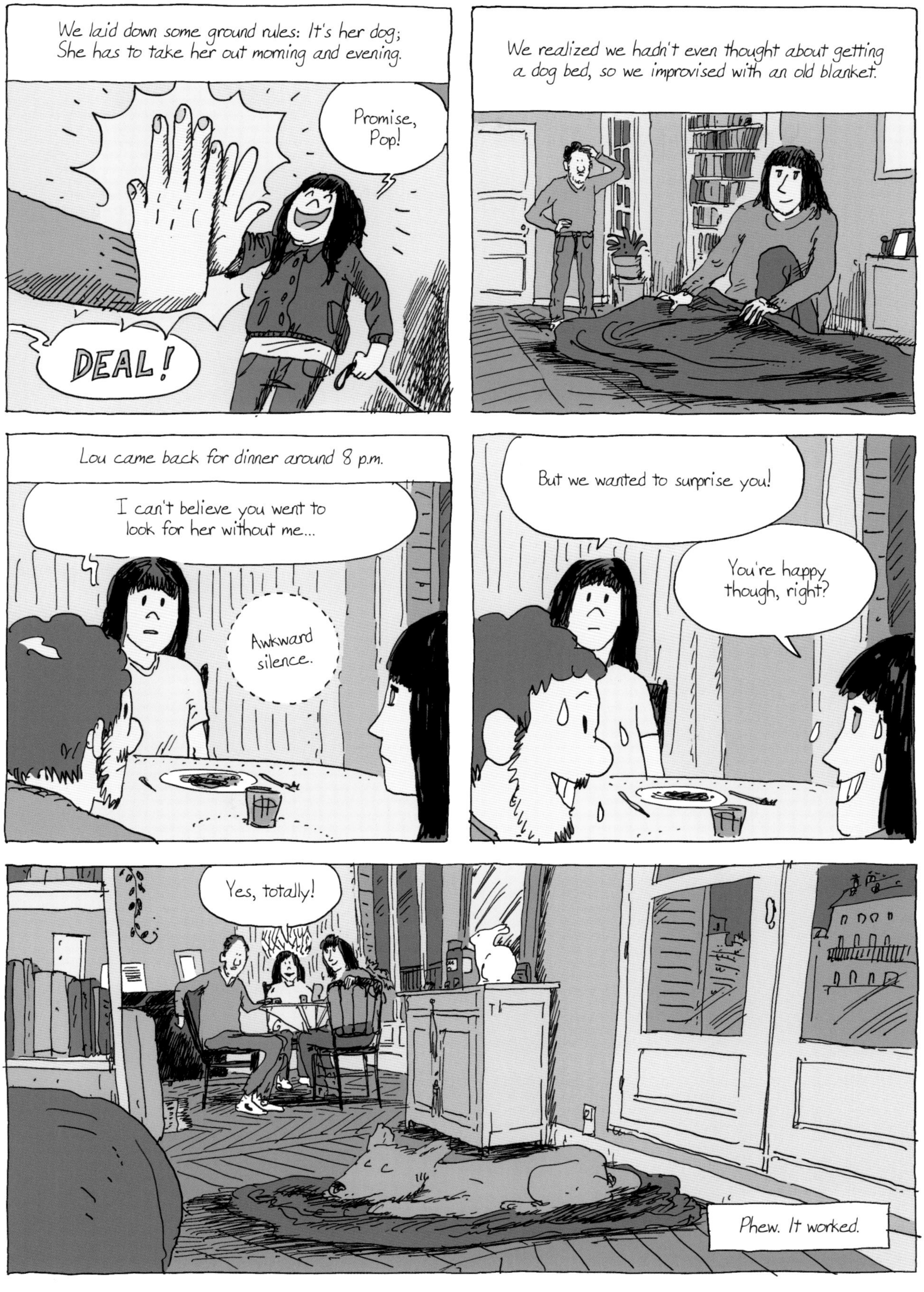
We laid down some ground rules: It's her dog; She has to take her out morning and evening.
Promise, Pop!
DEAL!
We realized we hadn't even thought about getting a dog bed, so we improvised with an old blanket.
Lou came back for dinner around 8 p.m.
I can't believe you went to look for her without me...
Awkward silence.
But we wanted to surprise you!
You're happy though, right?
Yes, totally!
Phew. It worked.

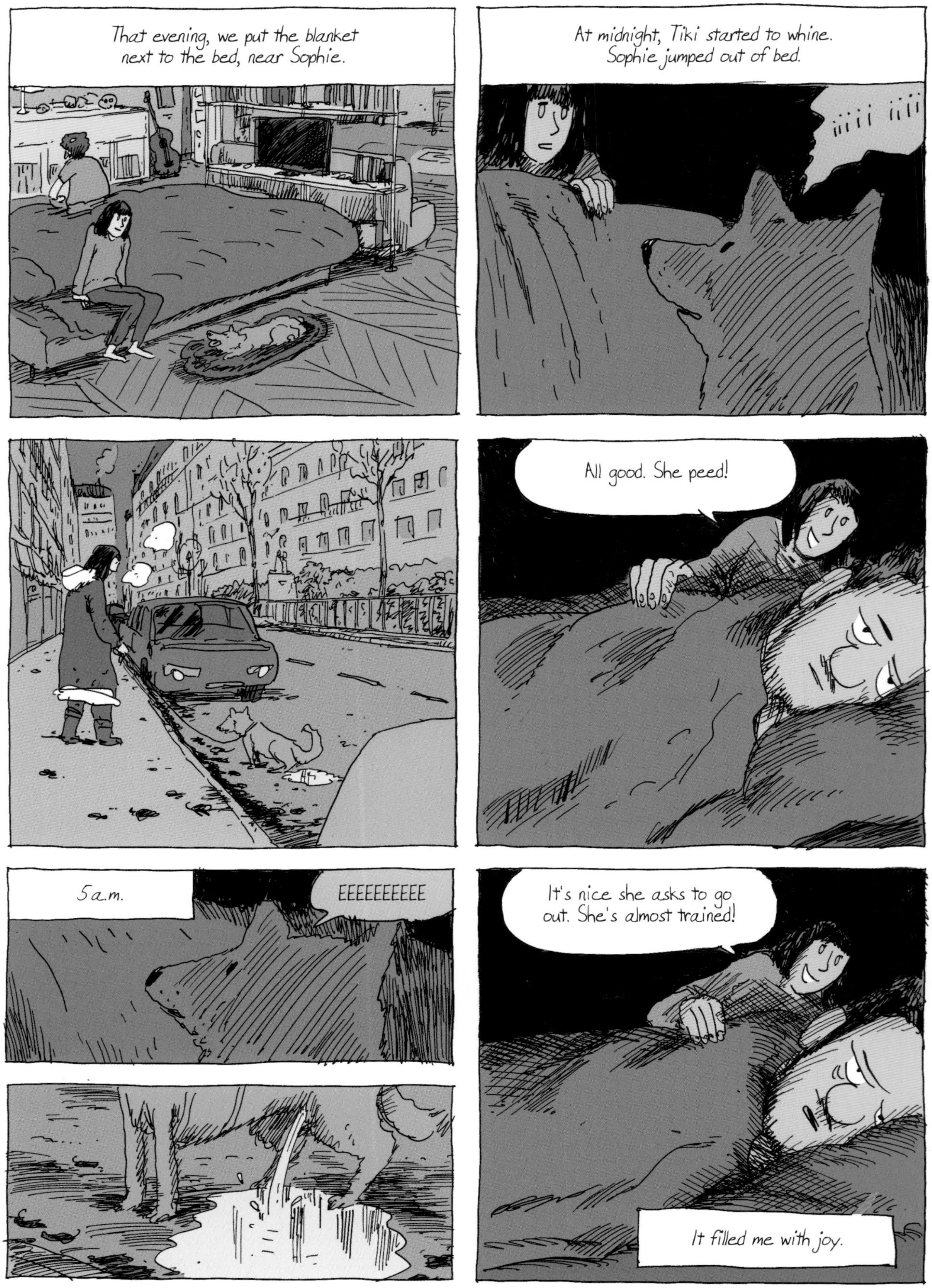
That evening, we put the blanket next to the bed, near Sophie.
At midnight, Tiki started to whine. Sophie jumped out of bed.
iiiii iiiii
All good. She peed!
5 a.m.
EEEEEEEEEE
It's nice she asks to go out. She's almost trained!
It filled me with joy.

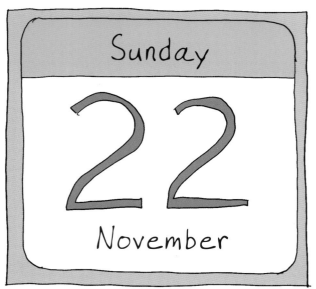

Sunday

22

November

Lou took her out again at 7 a.m. Around 8 a.m., Tiki started barking for the first time.

WOOF

SHHH!

TIKI!

During breakfast, Tiki was all we talked about.

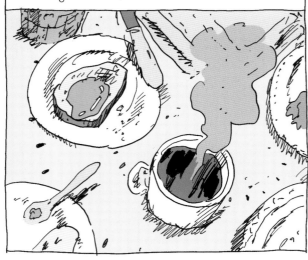

She gradually began to feel more comfortable in the apartment.

SNIF
SNIF

Then we ran some errands.

Come on, Tiki!

She was afraid of everything.

Come on! Tiki!

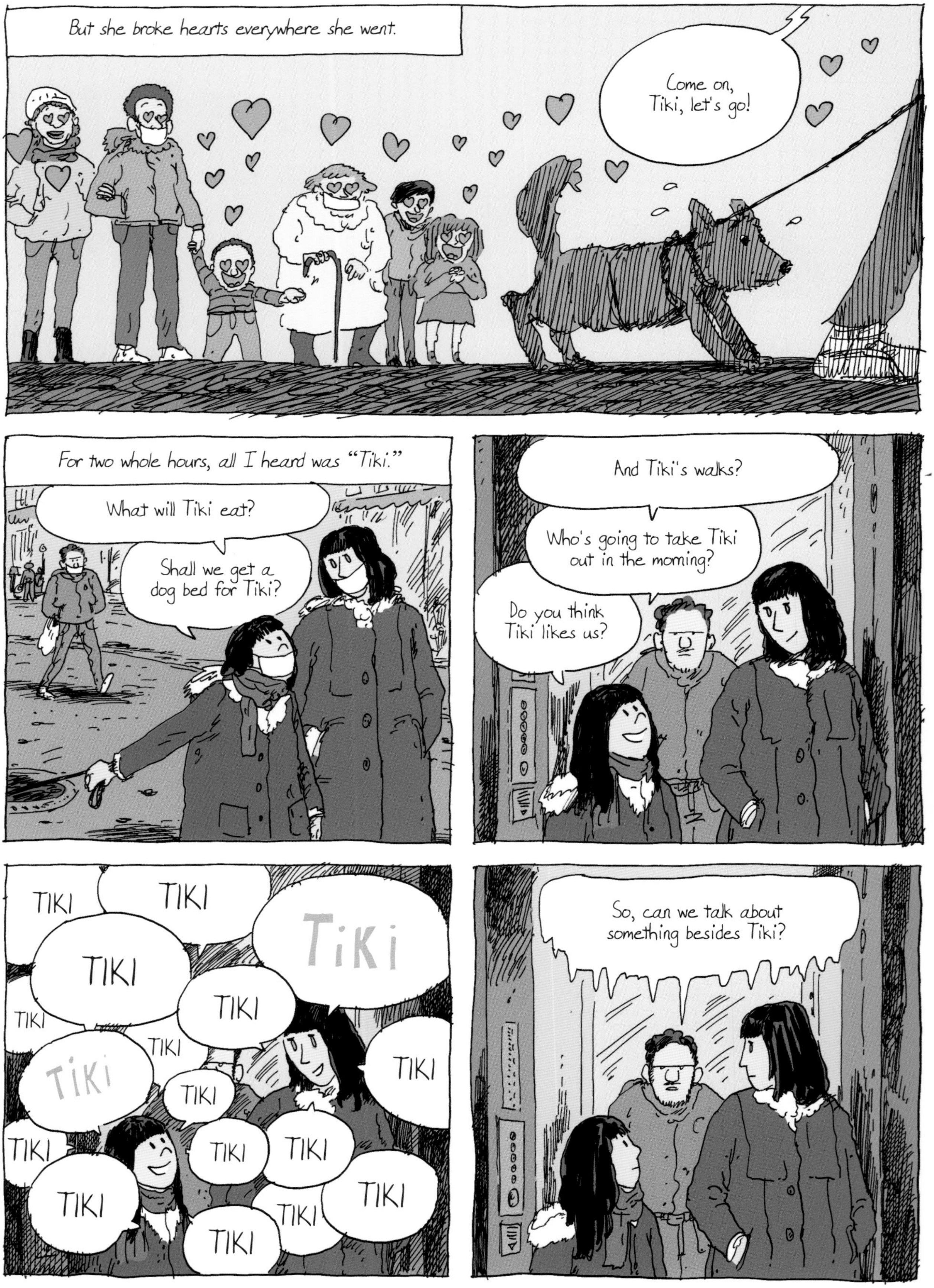
But she broke hearts everywhere she went.
Come on, Tiki, let's go!
For two whole hours, all I heard was "Tiki."
What will Tiki eat?
Shall we get a dog bed for Tiki?
And Tiki's walks?
Who's going to take Tiki out in the morning?
Do you think Tiki likes us?
TIKI
TIKI
TIKI
TiKi
TIKI
TIKI
TIKI
TiKi
TIKI
TIKI
TIKI
TIKI
TIKI
TIKI
TIKI
TIKI
TIKI
So, can we talk about something besides Tiki?

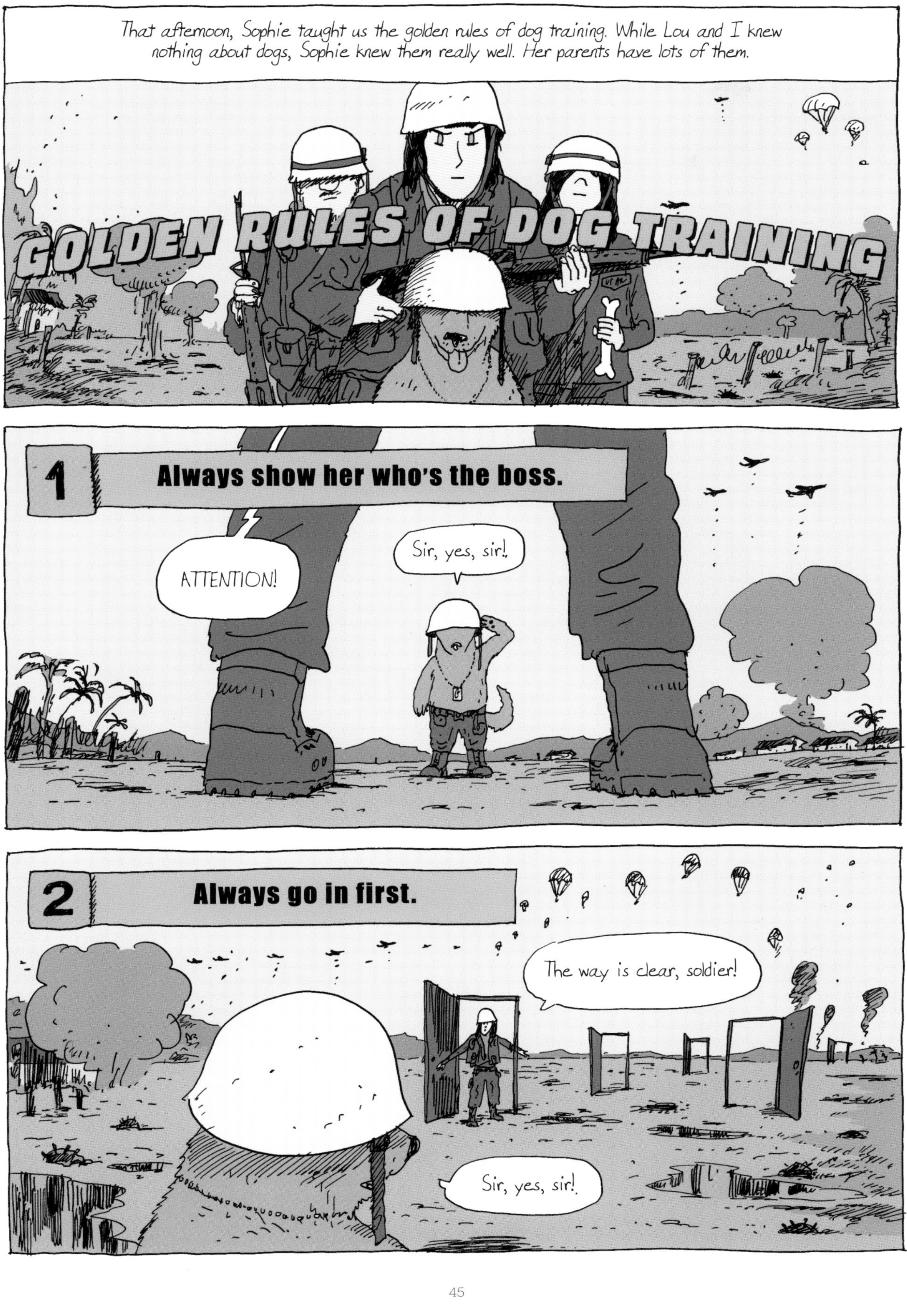
That afternoon, Sophie taught us the golden rules of dog training. While Lou and I knew nothing about dogs, Sophie knew them really well. Her parents have lots of them.
GOLDEN RULES OF DOG TRAINING
1
Always show her who's the boss.
ATTENTION!
Sir, yes, sir!
2
Always go in first.
The way is clear, soldier!
Sir, yes, sir!

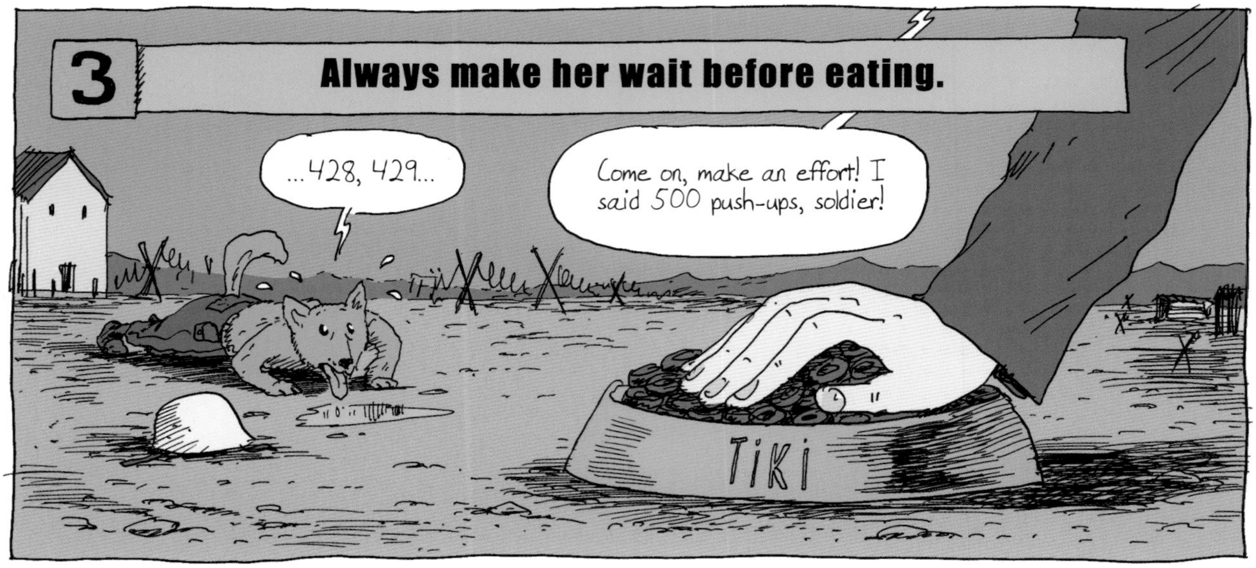
3
Always make her wait before eating.
...428, 429...
Come on, make an effort! I said 500 push-ups, soldier!
TiKi

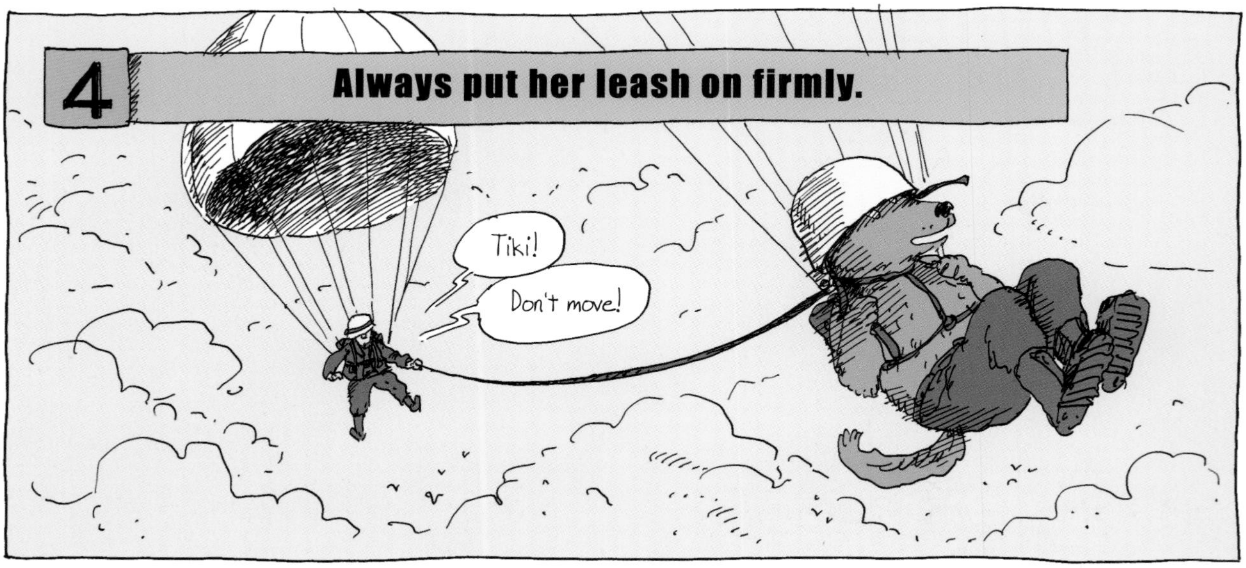
4
Always put her leash on firmly.
Tiki!
Don't move!

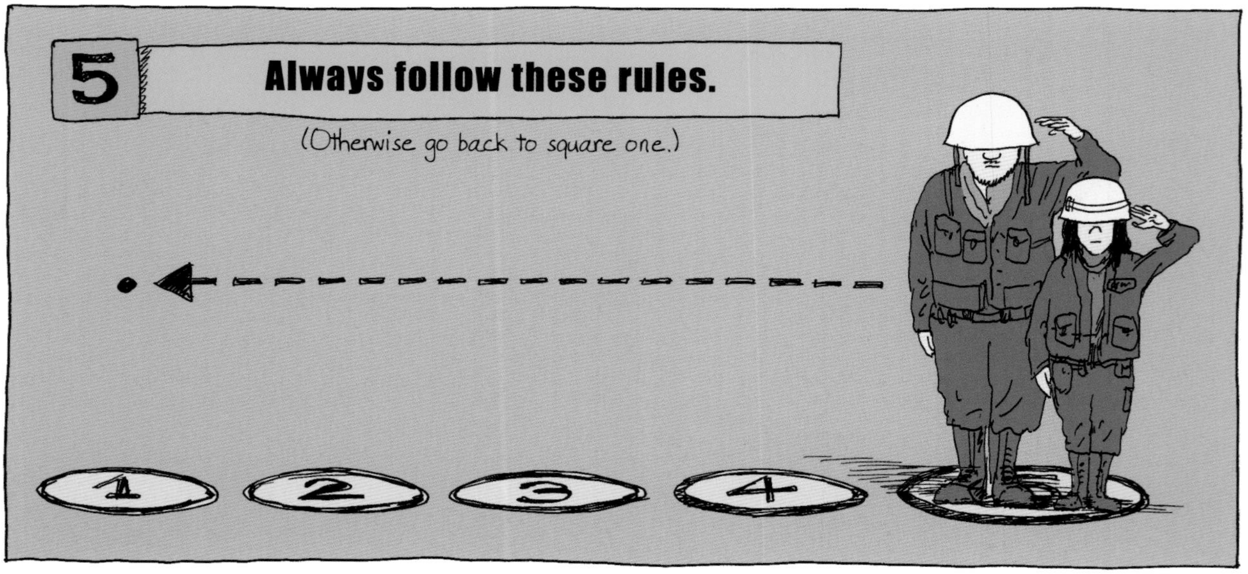
5
Always follow these rules.
(Otherwise go back to square one.)
1
2
3
4

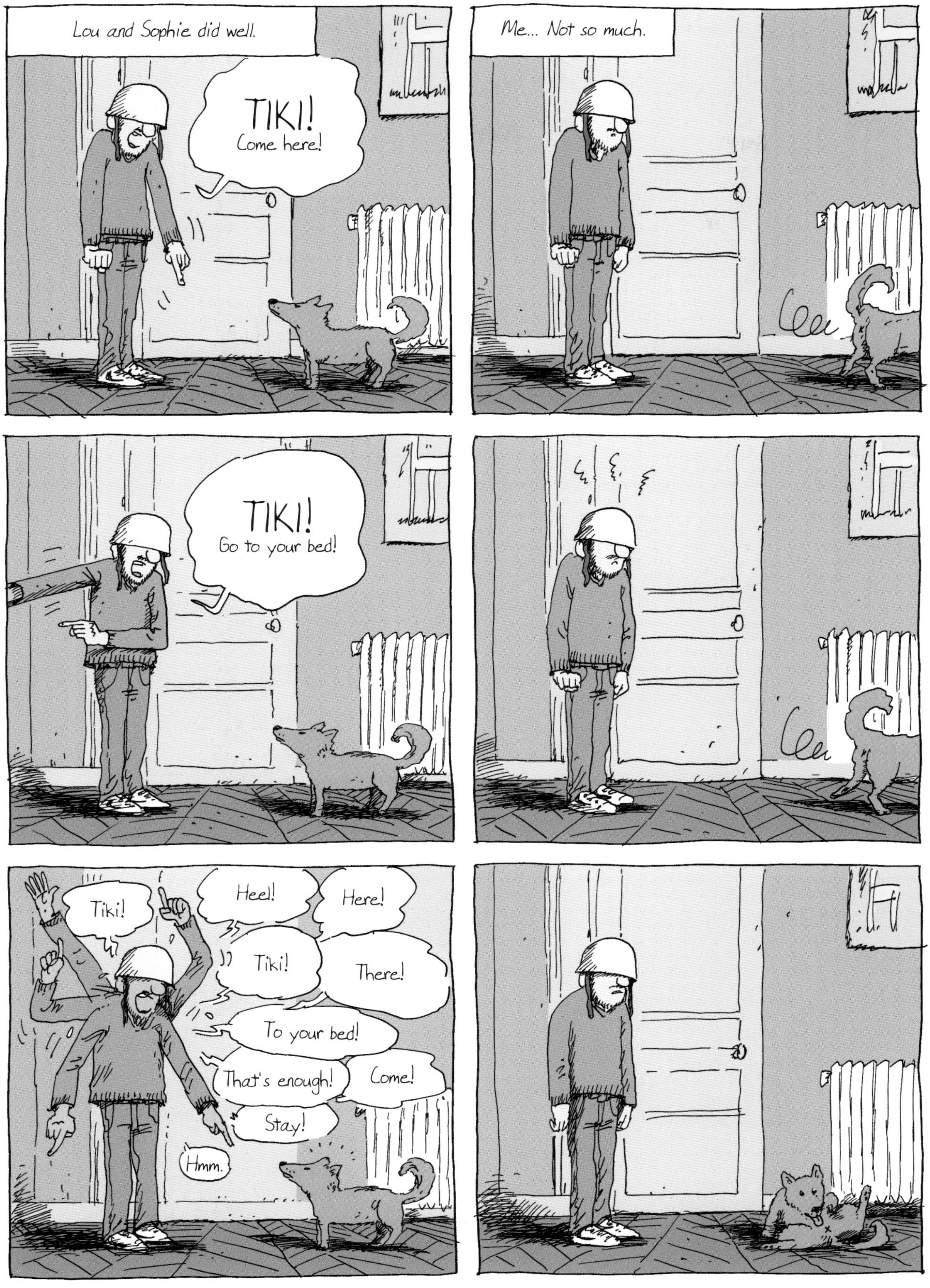
Lou and Sophie did well.
TIKI! Come here!
Me... Not so much.
TIKI! Go to your bed!
Tiki!
Heel!
Here!
Tiki!
There!
To your bed!
That's enough!
Come!
Stay!
Hmm.

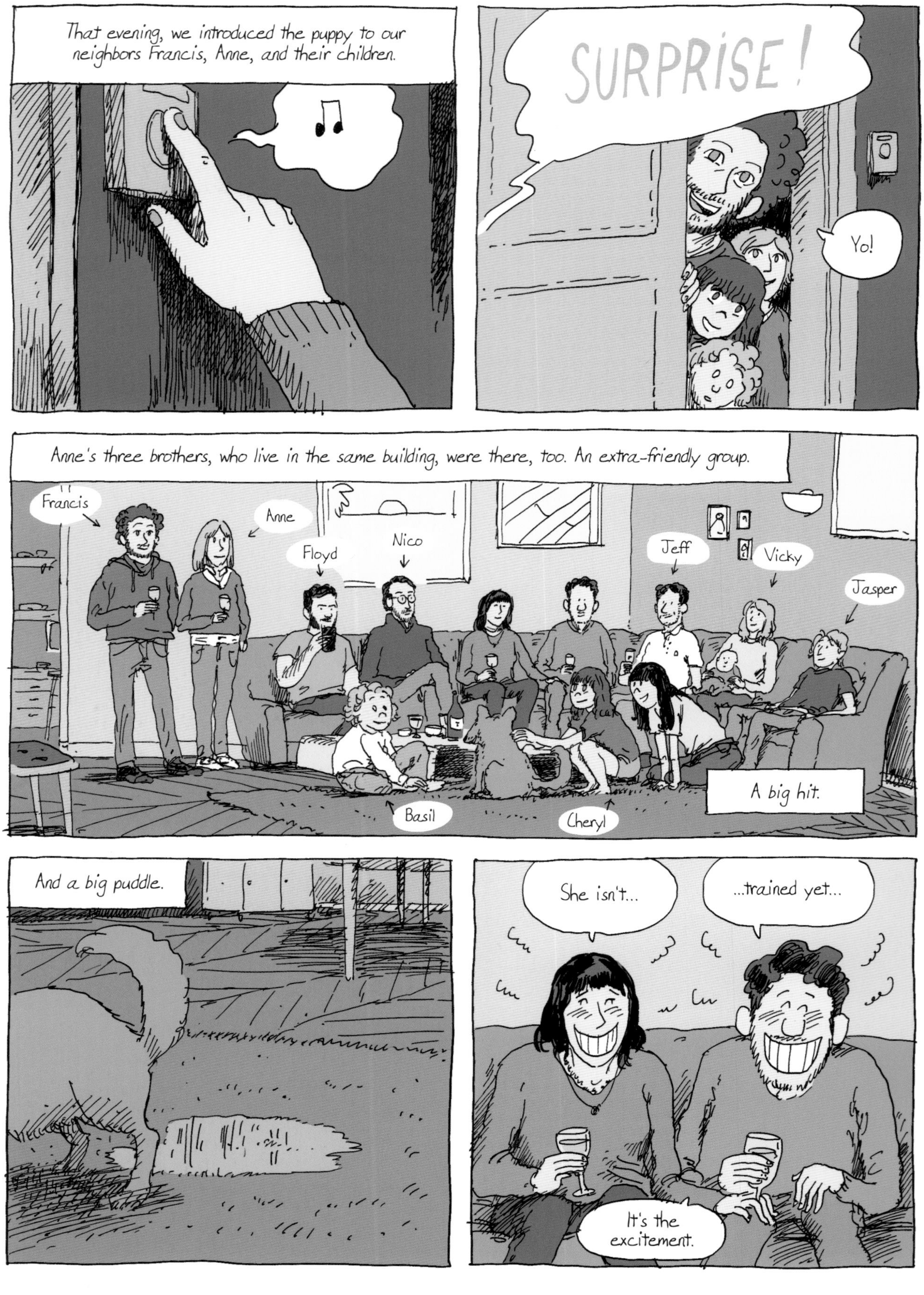
That evening, we introduced the puppy to our neighbors Francis, Anne, and their children.
SURPRISE!
Yo!
Anne's three brothers, who live in the same building, were there, too. An extra-friendly group.
Francis
Anne
Floyd
Nico
Jeff
Vicky
Jasper
Basil
Cheryl
A big hit.
And a big puddle.
She isn't...
...trained yet...
It's the excitement.

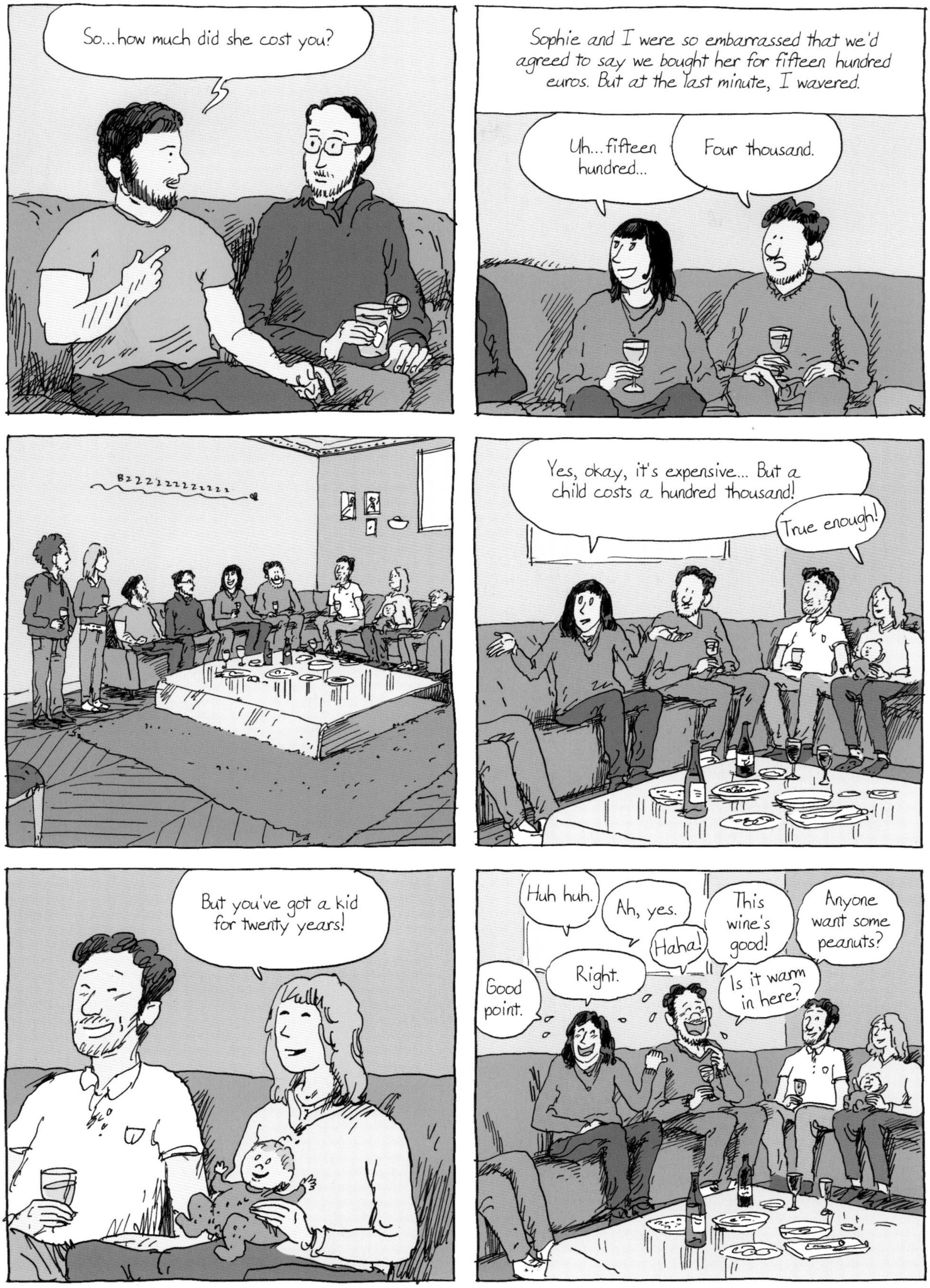
So... how much did she cost you?
Sophie and I were so embarrassed that we'd agreed to say we bought her for fifteen hundred euros. But at the last minute, I wavered.
Uh... fifteen hundred...
Four thousand.
Bzzzzzzzzzzzz
Yes, okay, it's expensive... But a child costs a hundred thousand!
True enough!
But you've got a kid for twenty years!
Huh huh.
Ah, yes.
Haha!
This wine's good!
Anyone want some peanuts?
Good point.
Right.
Is it warm in here?

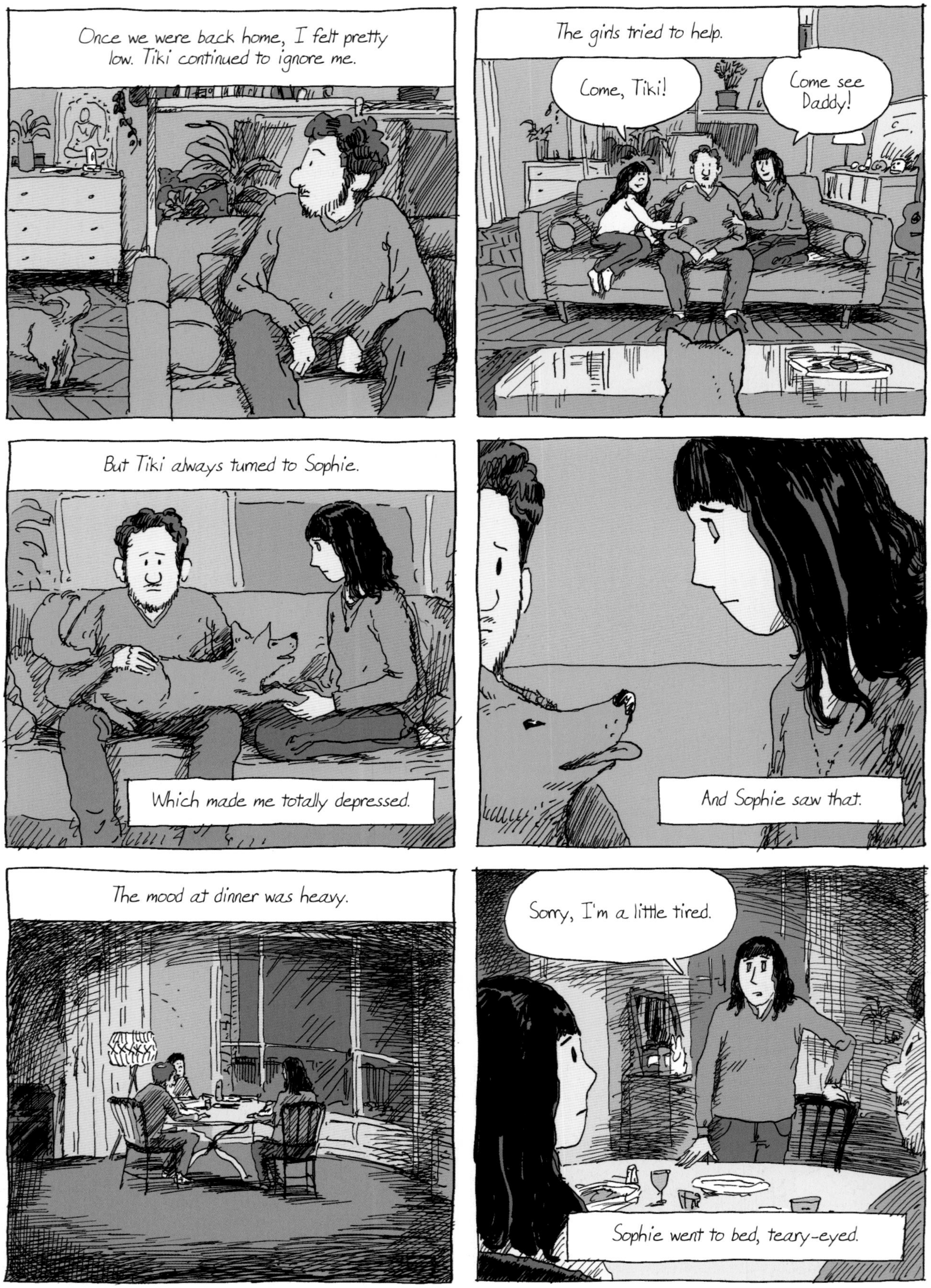
Once we were back home, I felt pretty low. Tiki continued to ignore me.
The girls tried to help.
Come, Tiki!
Come see Daddy!
But Tiki always turned to Sophie.
Which made me totally depressed.
And Sophie saw that.
The mood at dinner was heavy.
Sorry, I'm a little tired.
Sophie went to bed, teary-eyed.

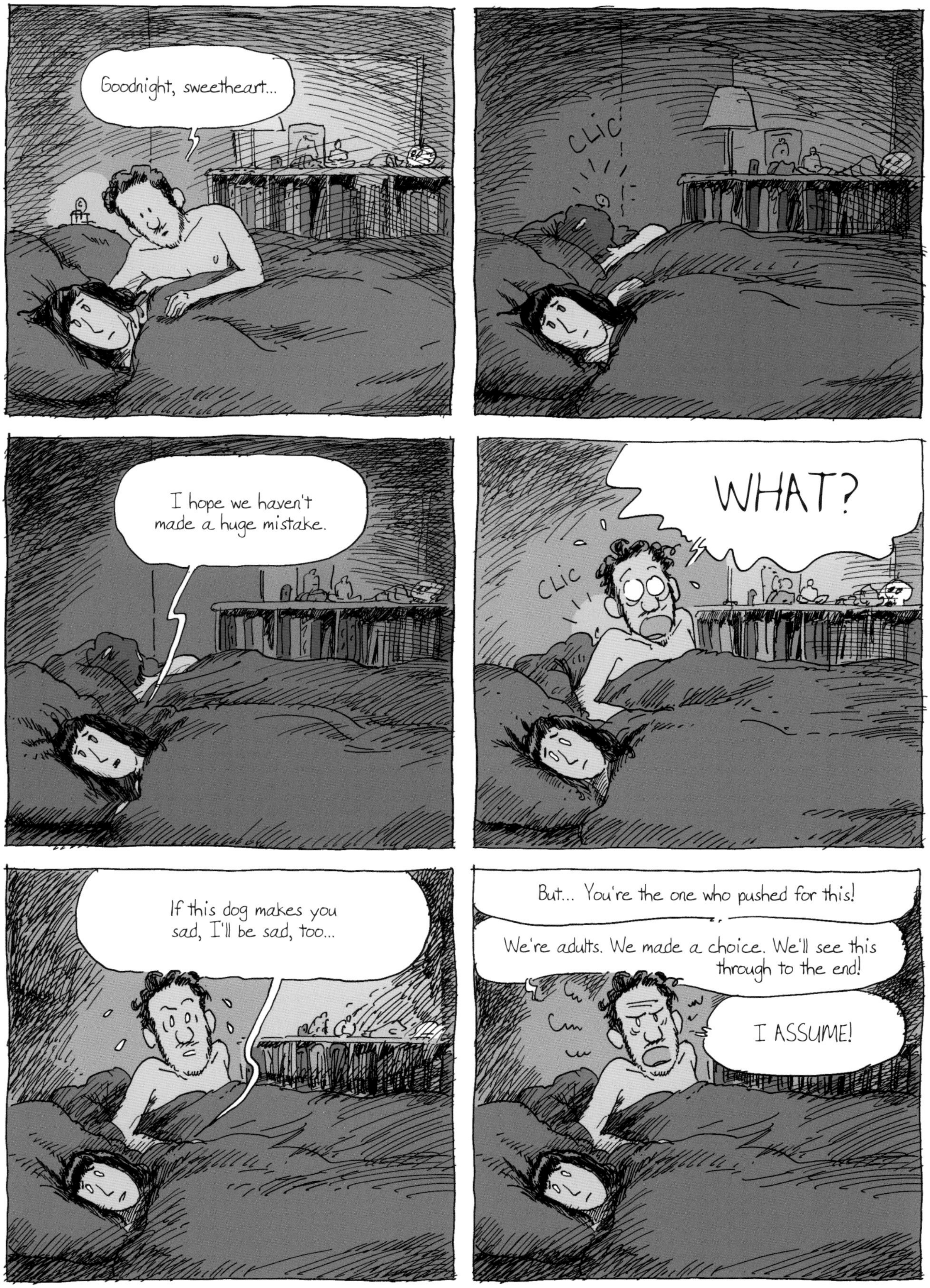
Goodnight, sweetheart...
CLIC
I hope we haven't made a huge mistake.
WHAT?
CLIC
If this dog makes you sad, I'll be sad, too...
But... You're the one who pushed for this!
We're adults. We made a choice. We'll see this through to the end!
I ASSUME!

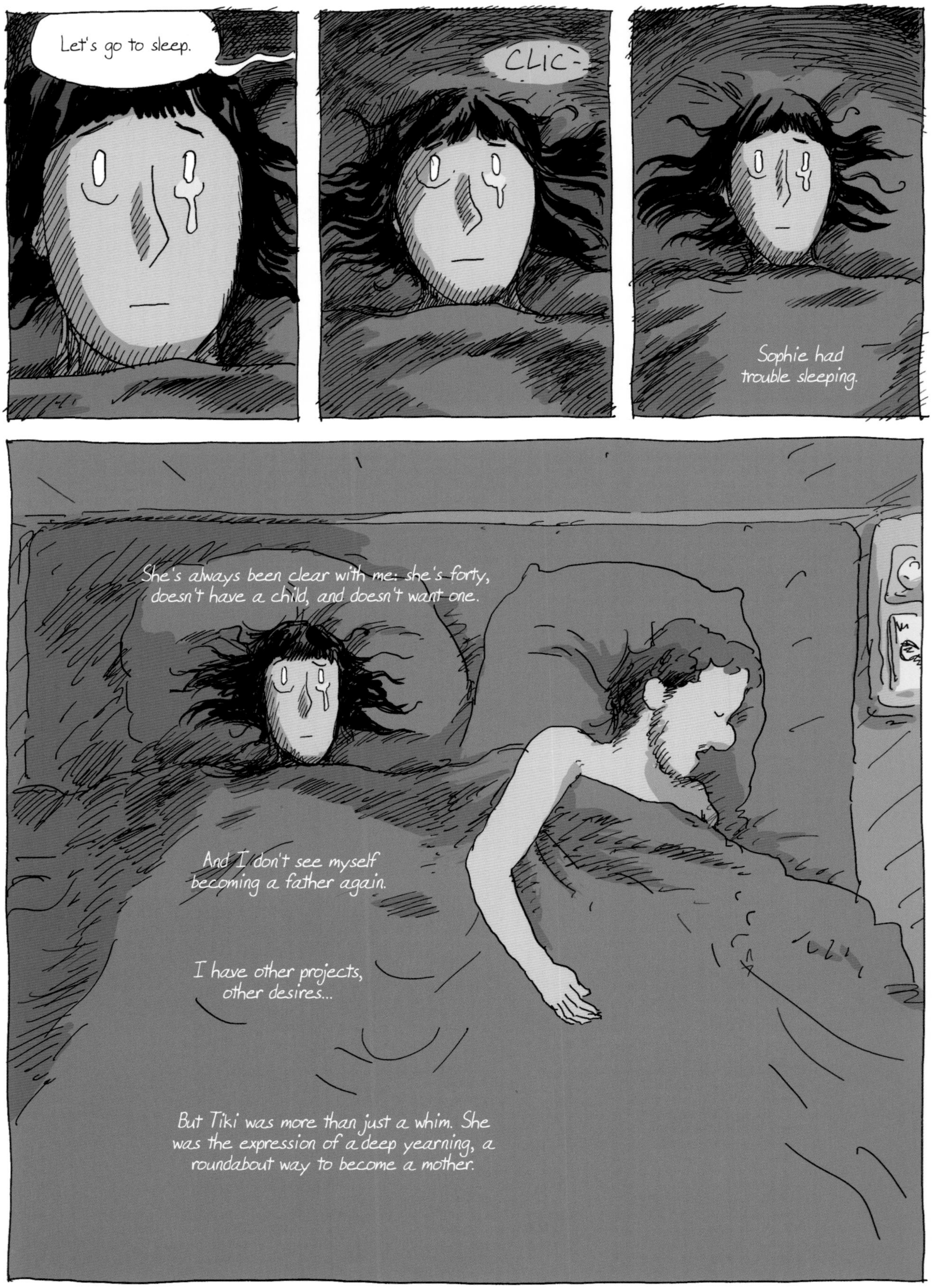

Let's go to sleep.
CLIC
Sophie had trouble sleeping.
She's always been clear with me: she's forty, doesn't have a child, and doesn't want one.
And I don't see myself becoming a father again.
I have other projects, other desires...
But Tiki was more than just a whim. She was the expression of a deep yearning, a roundabout way to become a mother.

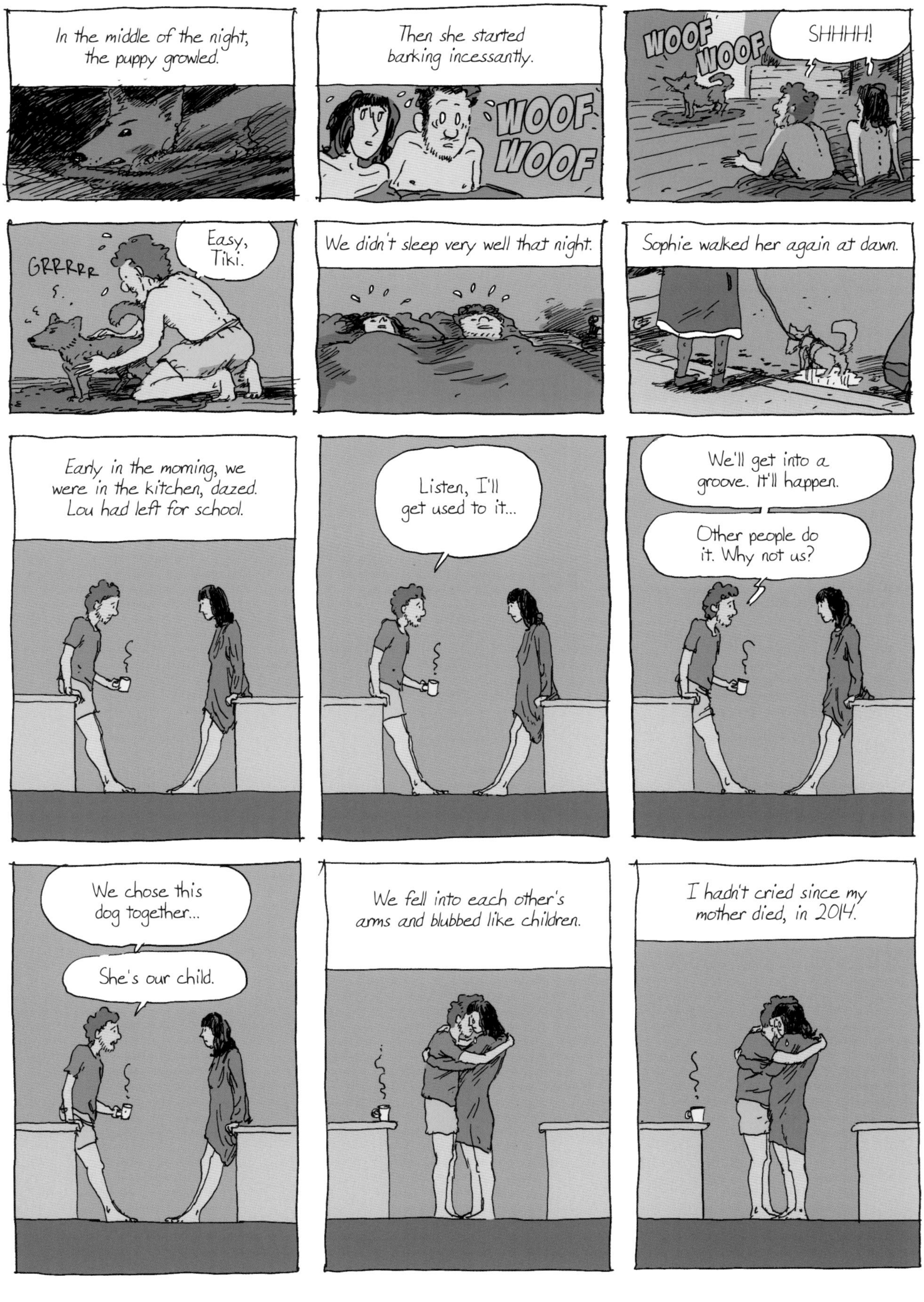
In the middle of the night, the puppy growled.
Then she started barking incessantly.
WOOF WOOF
WOOF WOOF
SHHHH!
GRRRRR
Easy, Tiki.
We didn't sleep very well that night.
Sophie walked her again at dawn.
Early in the morning, we were in the kitchen, dazed. Lou had left for school.
Listen, I'll get used to it...
We'll get into a groove. It'll happen.
Other people do it. Why not us?
We chose this dog together...
She's our child.
We fell into each other's arms and blubbed like children.
I hadn't cried since my mother died, in 2014.

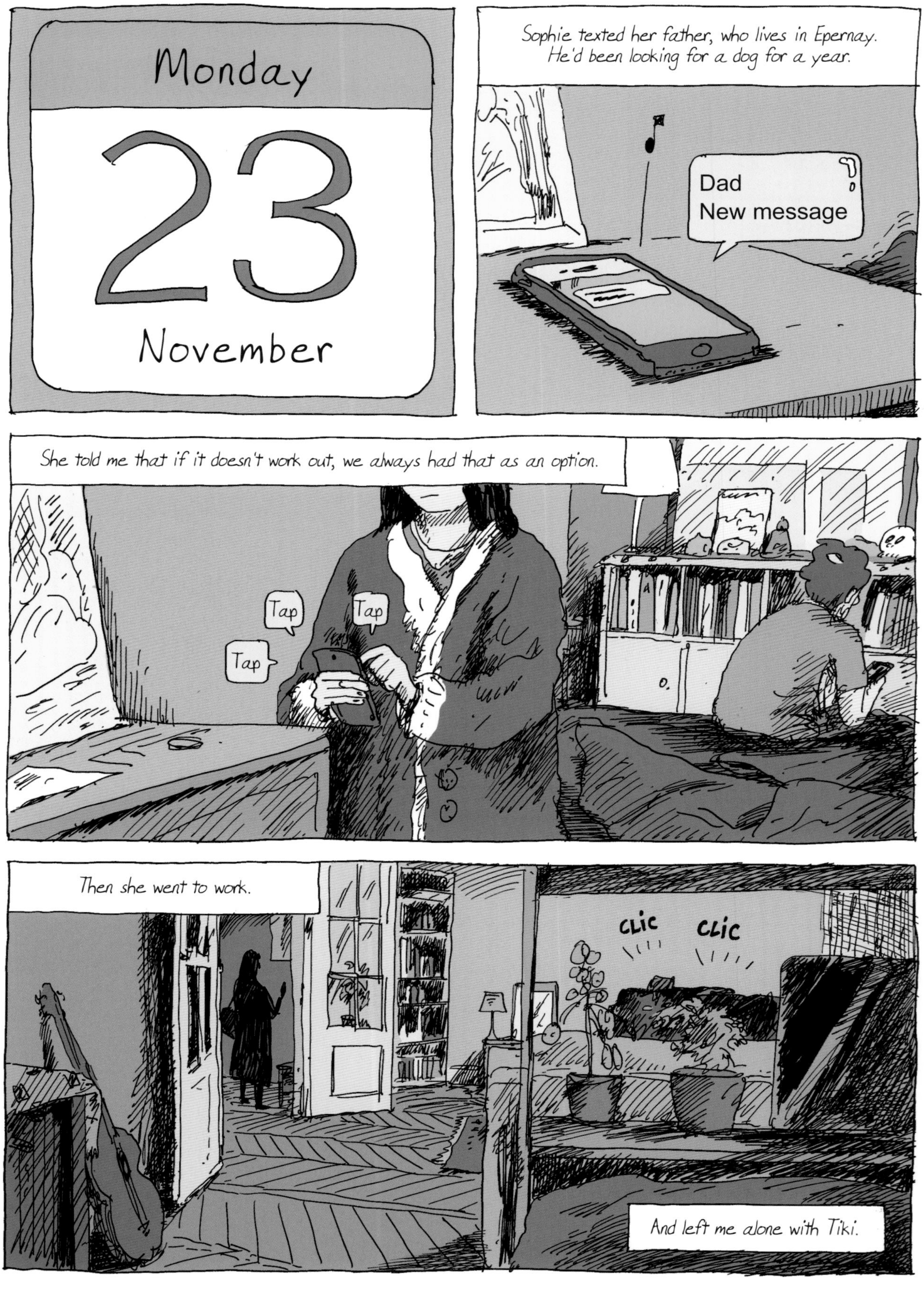
Monday
23
November
Sophie texted her father, who lives in Epernay. He'd been looking for a dog for a year.
Dad
New message
She told me that if it doesn't work out, we always had that as an option.
Tap
Tap
Tap
Then she went to work.
CLIC
CLIC
And left me alone with Tiki.

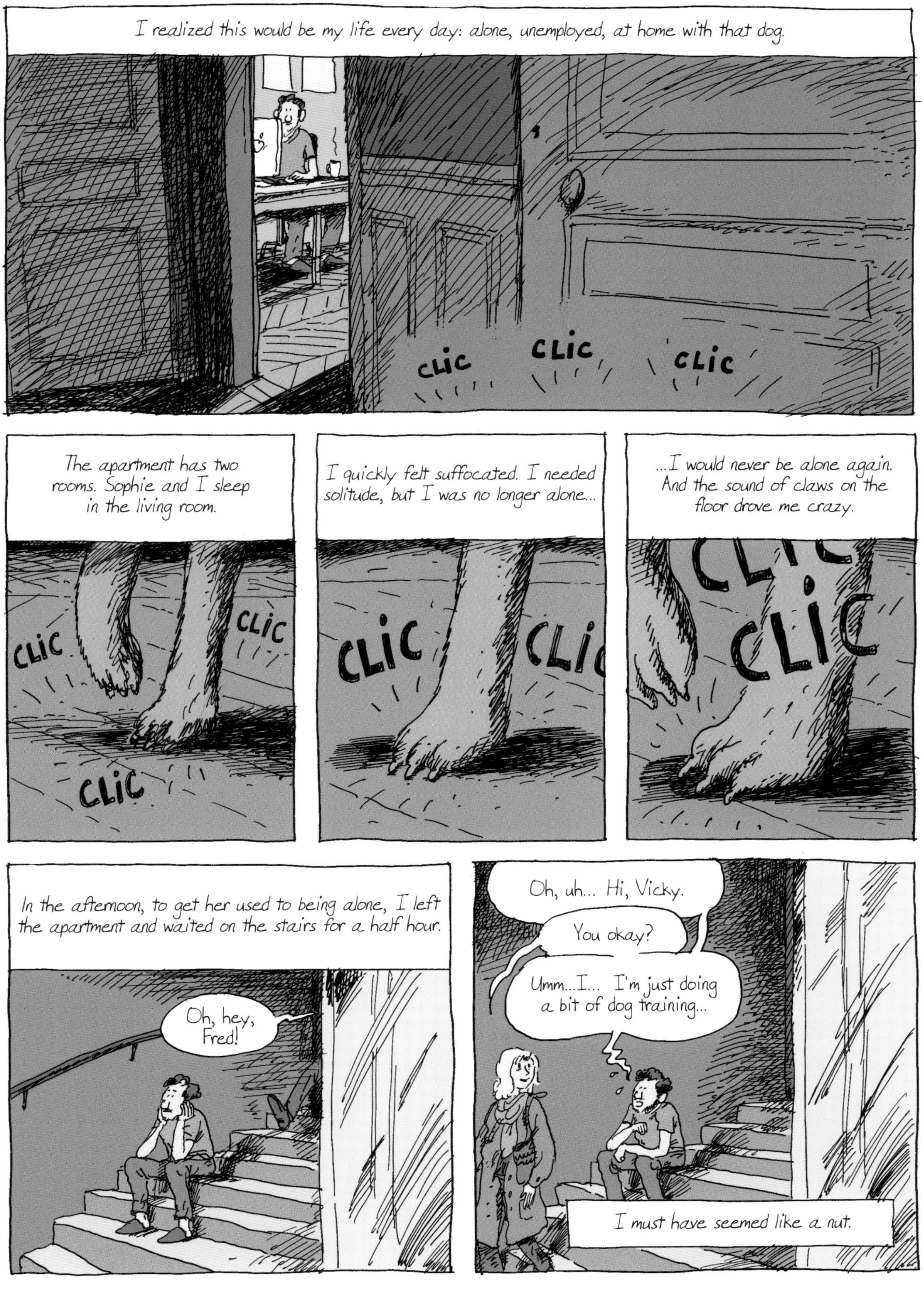

I realized this would be my life every day: alone, unemployed, at home with that dog.
CLIC
CLIC
CLIC
The apartment has two rooms. Sophie and I sleep in the living room.
CLIC
CLIC
CLIC
I quickly felt suffocated. I needed solitude, but I was no longer alone...
CLIC
CLIC
...I would never be alone again. And the sound of claws on the floor drove me crazy.
CLIC
In the afternoon, to get her used to being alone, I left the apartment and waited on the stairs for a half hour.
Oh, hey, Fred!
Oh, uh... Hi, Vicky.
You okay?
Umm...I... I'm just doing a bit of dog training...
I must have seemed like a nut.

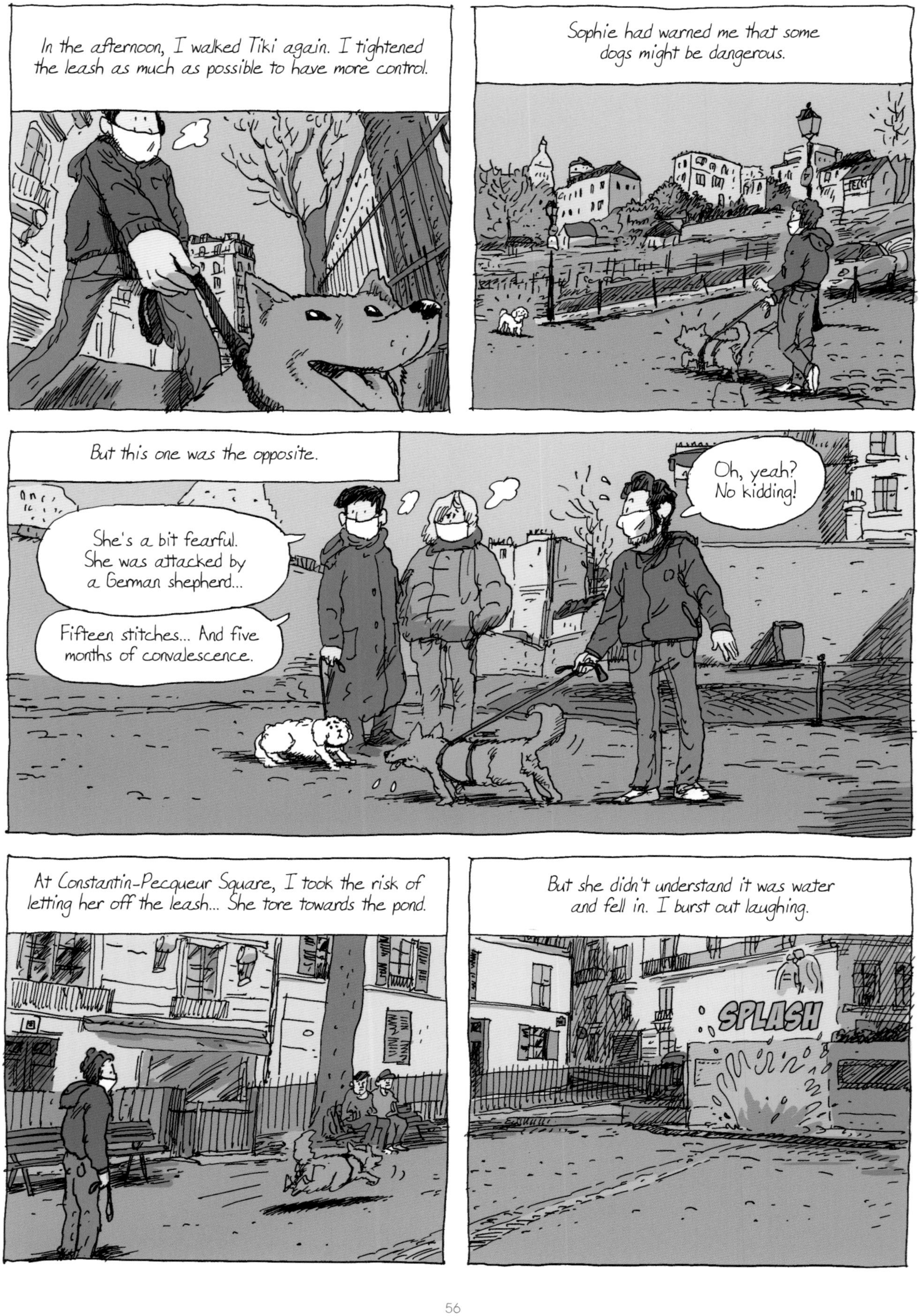
In the afternoon, I walked Tiki again. I tightened the leash as much as possible to have more control.
Sophie had warned me that some dogs might be dangerous.
But this one was the opposite.
She's a bit fearful. She was attacked by a German shepherd...
Fifteen stitches... And five months of convalescence.
Oh, yeah? No kidding!
At Constantin-Pecqueur Square, I took the risk of letting her off the leash... She tore towards the pond.
But she didn't understand it was water and fell in. I burst out laughing.
SPLASH

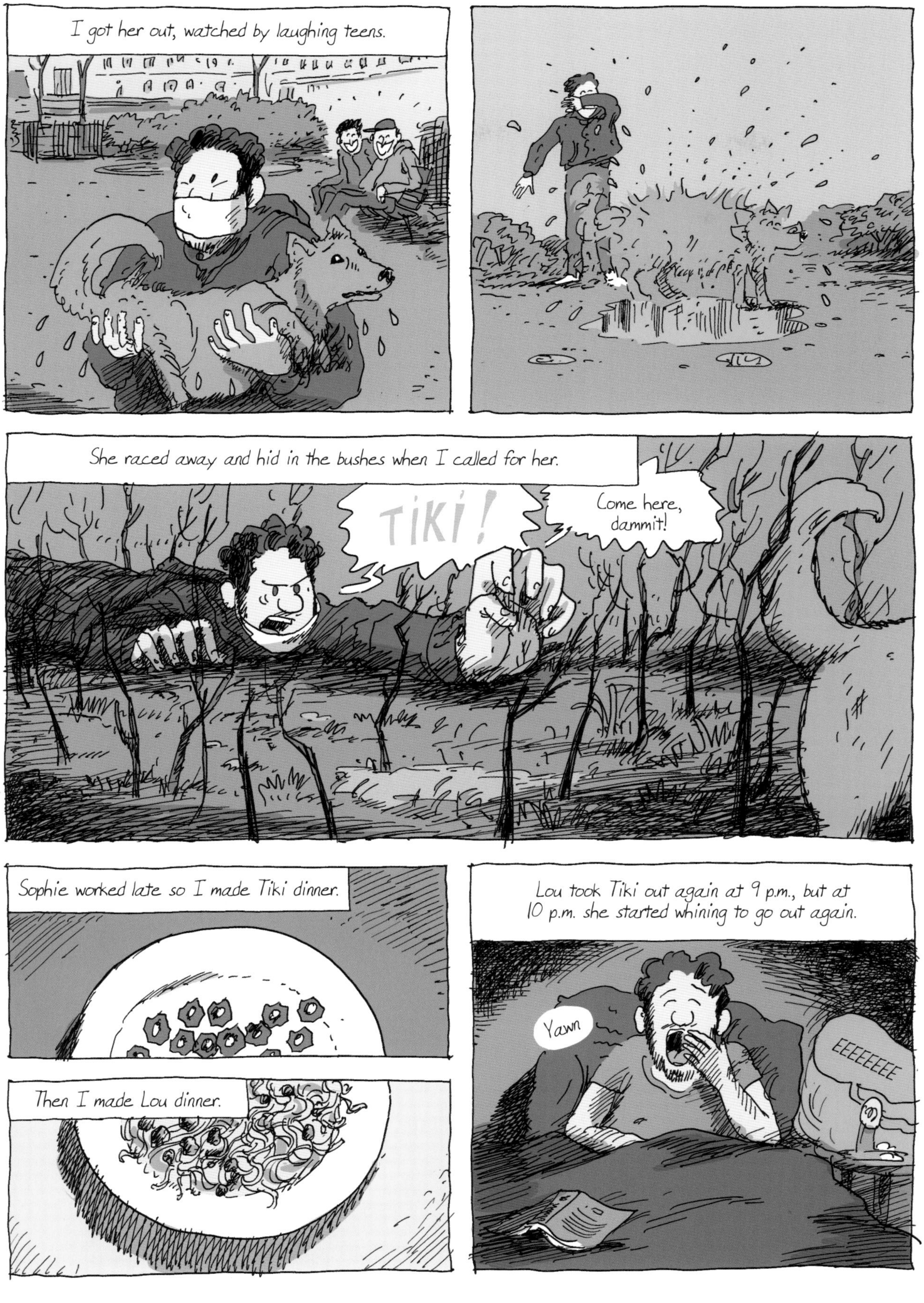
I got her out, watched by laughing teens.
She raced away and hid in the bushes when I called for her.
TIKI!
Come here, dammit!
Sophie worked late so I made Tiki dinner.
Then I made Lou dinner.
Lou took Tiki out again at 9 p.m., but at 10 p.m. she started whining to go out again.
Yawn
EEEEEEEE

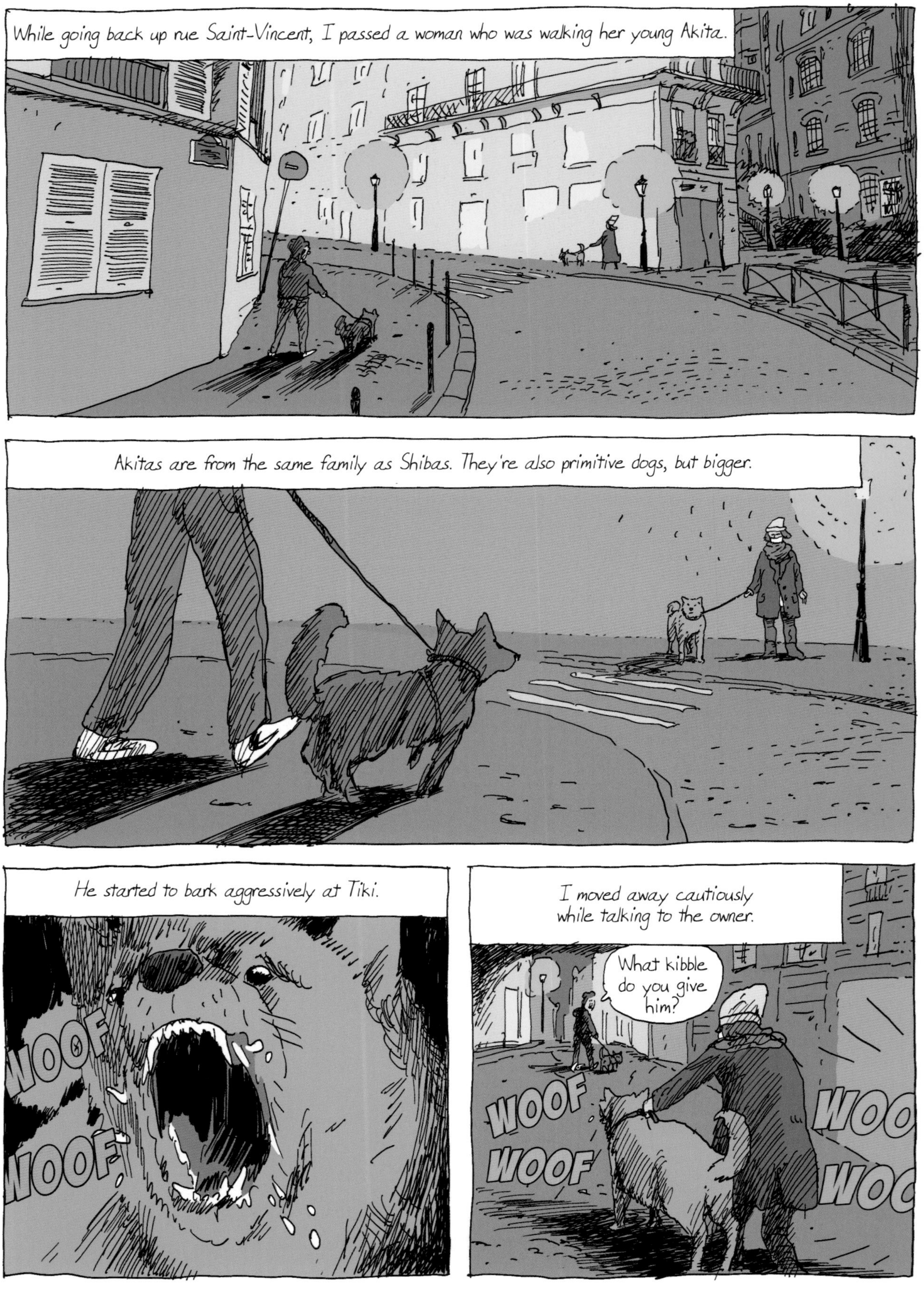
While going back up rue Saint-Vincent, I passed a woman who was walking her young Akita.
Akitas are from the same family as Shibas. They're also primitive dogs, but bigger.
He started to bark aggressively at Tiki.
WOOF
WOOF
I moved away cautiously while talking to the owner.
What kibble do you give him?
WOOF
WOOF
WOO
WOO

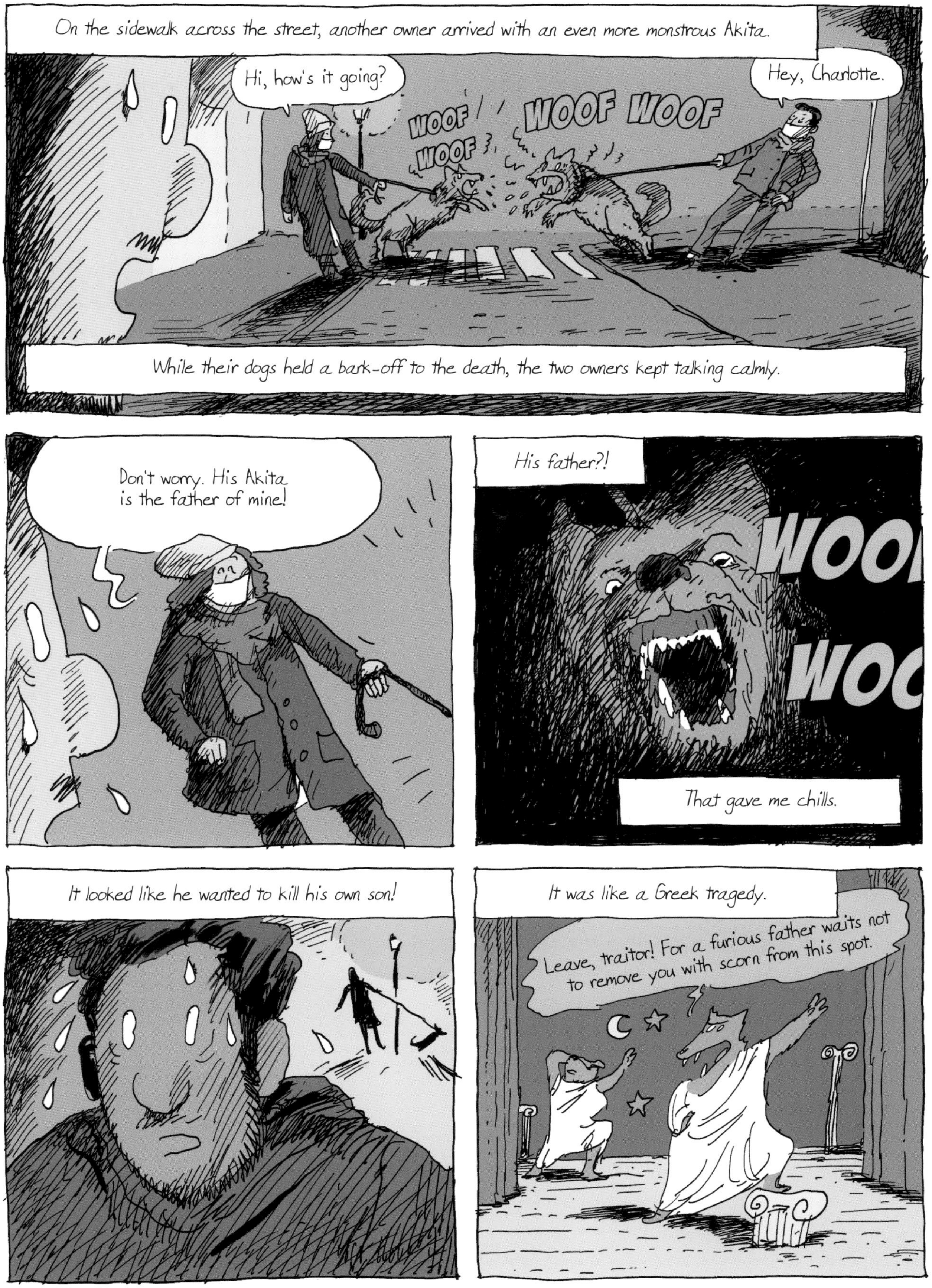
On the sidewalk across the street, another owner arrived with an even more monstrous Akita.
Hi, how's it going?
Hey, Charlotte.
WOOF
WOOF
WOOF WOOF
While their dogs held a bark-off to the death, the two owners kept talking calmly.
Don't worry. His Akita is the father of mine!
His father?!
That gave me chills.
It looked like he wanted to kill his own son!
It was like a Greek tragedy.
Leave, traitor! For a furious father waits not to remove you with scorn from this spot.

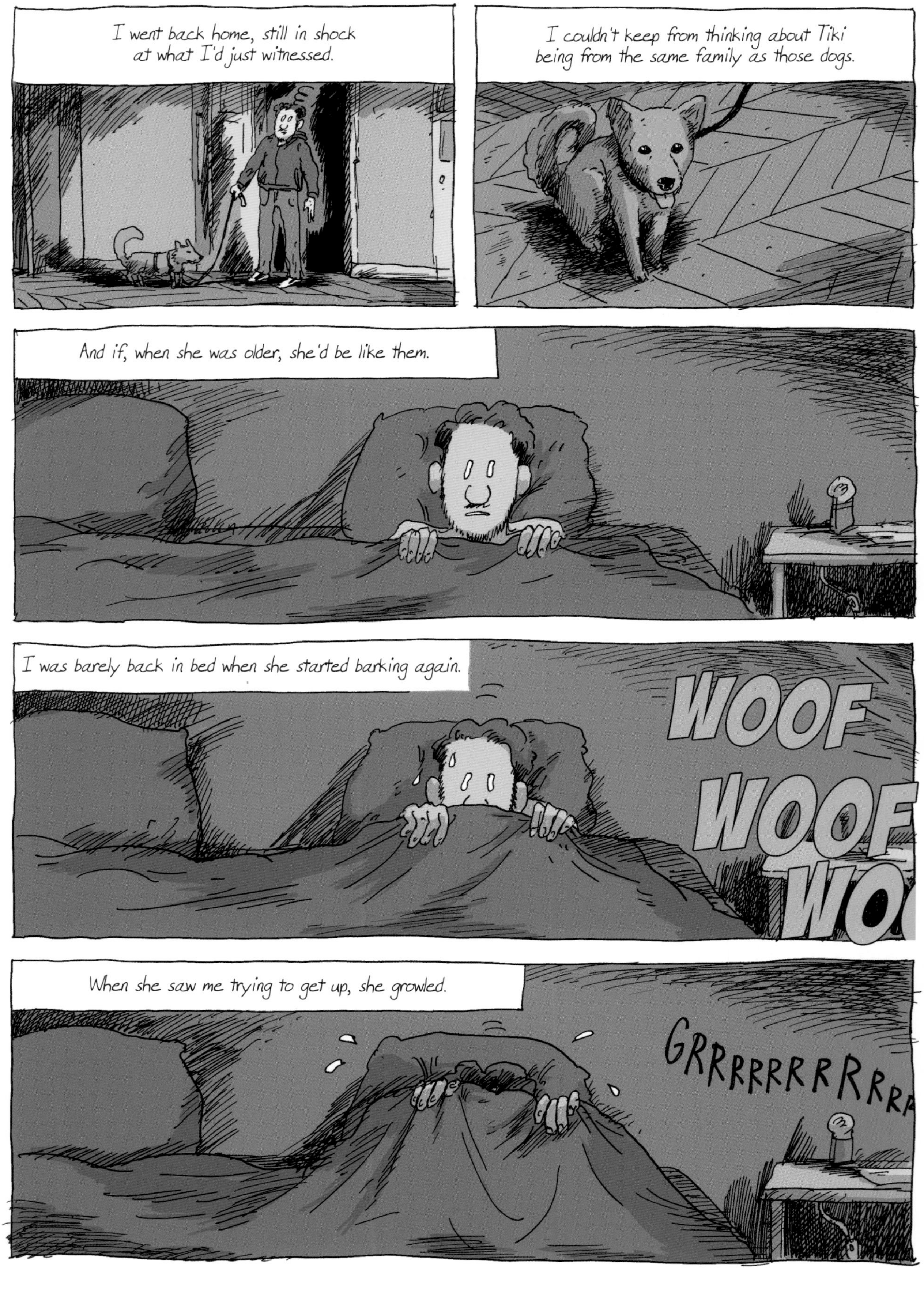
I went back home, still in shock at what I'd just witnessed.
I couldn't keep from thinking about Tiki being from the same family as those dogs.
And if, when she was older, she'd be like them.
I was barely back in bed when she started barking again.
WOOF
WOOF
WO
When she saw me trying to get up, she growled.
GRRRRRRRRRRR

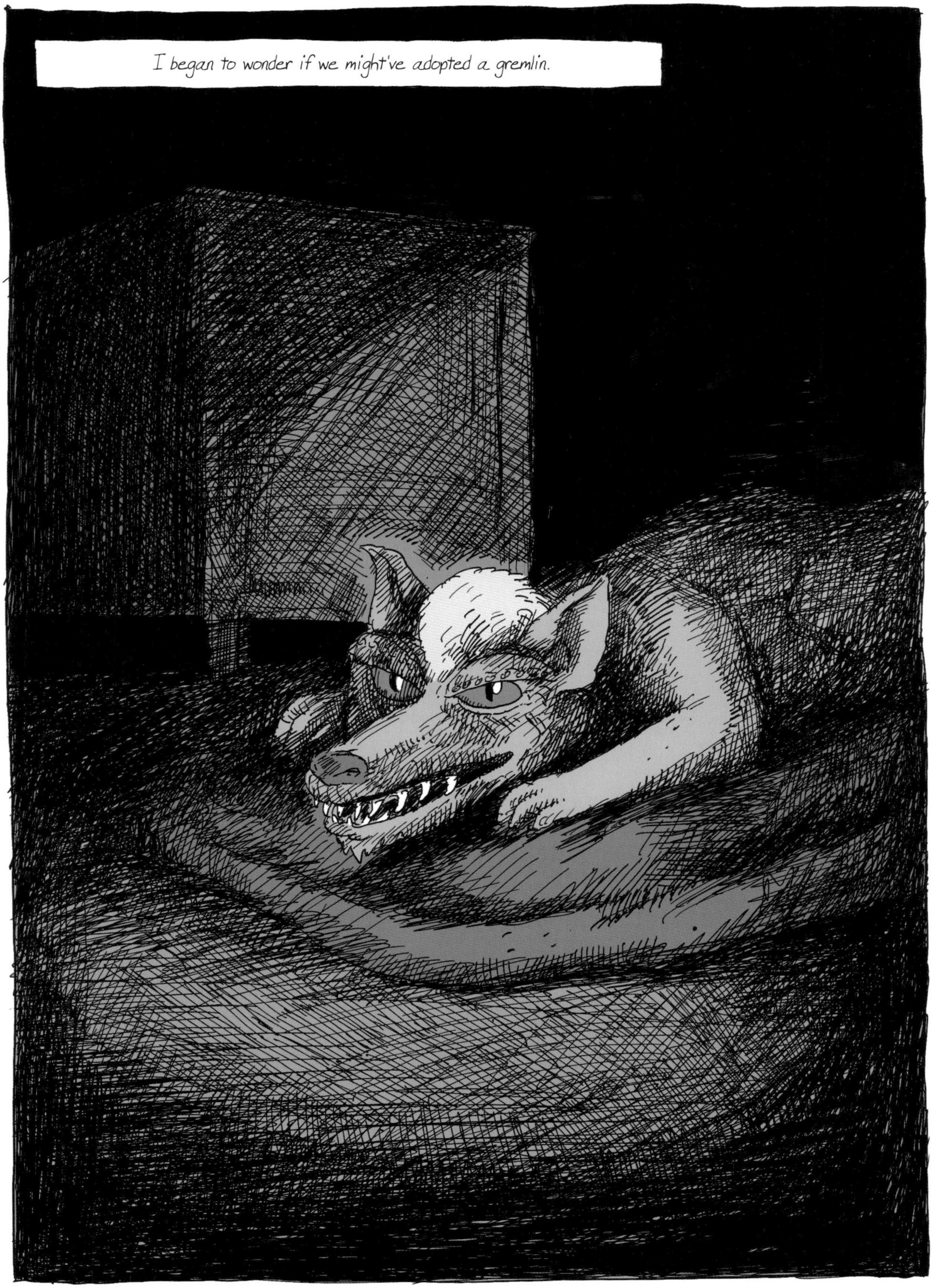
I began to wonder if we might've adopted a gremlin.

Chapter Four

The Dilemma

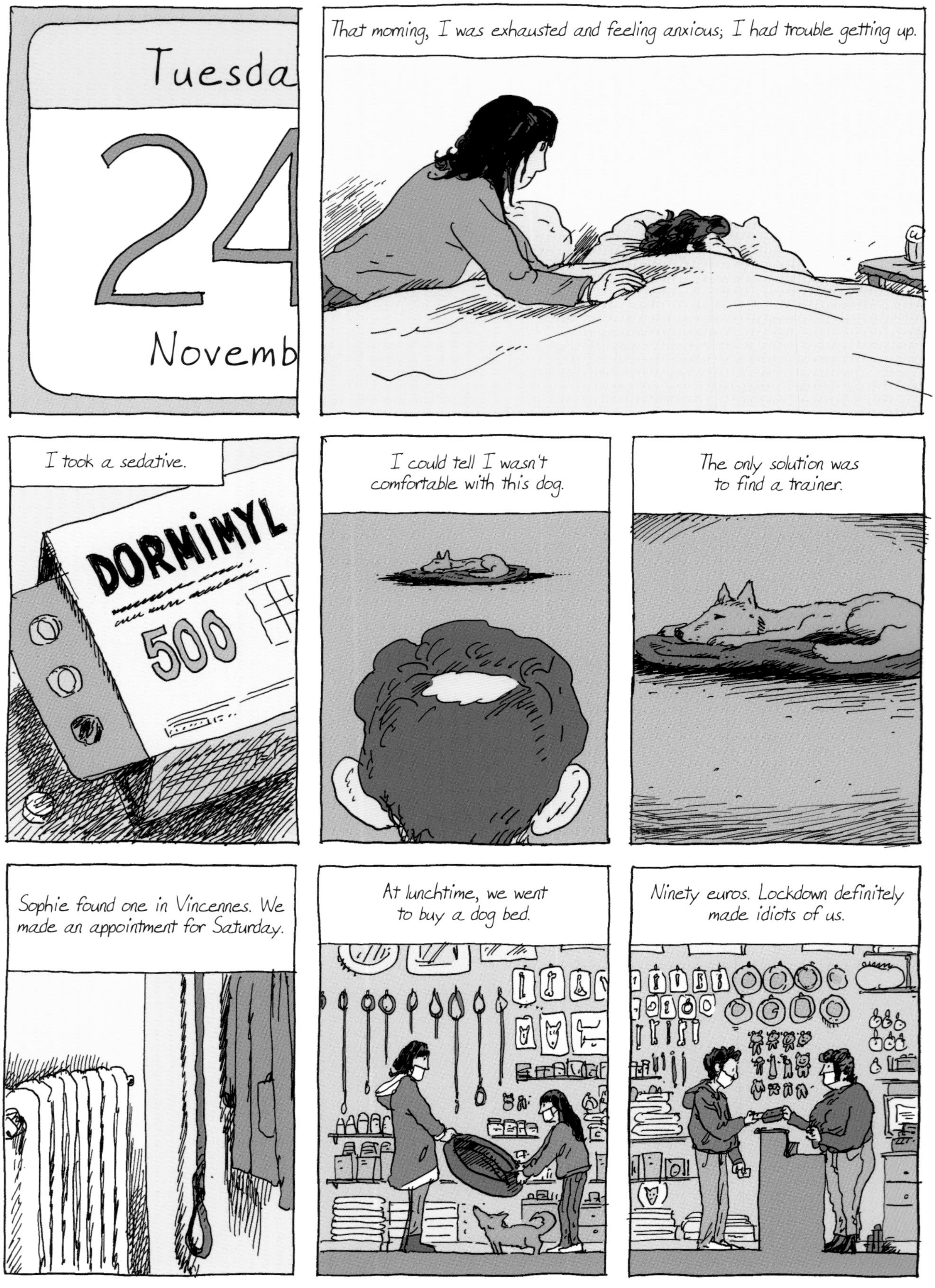
Tuesda
24
Novemb
That morning, I was exhausted and feeling anxious; I had trouble getting up.
I took a sedative.
DORMIMYL
500
I could tell I wasn't comfortable with this dog.
The only solution was to find a trainer.
Sophie found one in Vincennes. We made an appointment for Saturday.
At lunchtime, we went to buy a dog bed.
Ninety euros. Lockdown definitely made idiots of us.

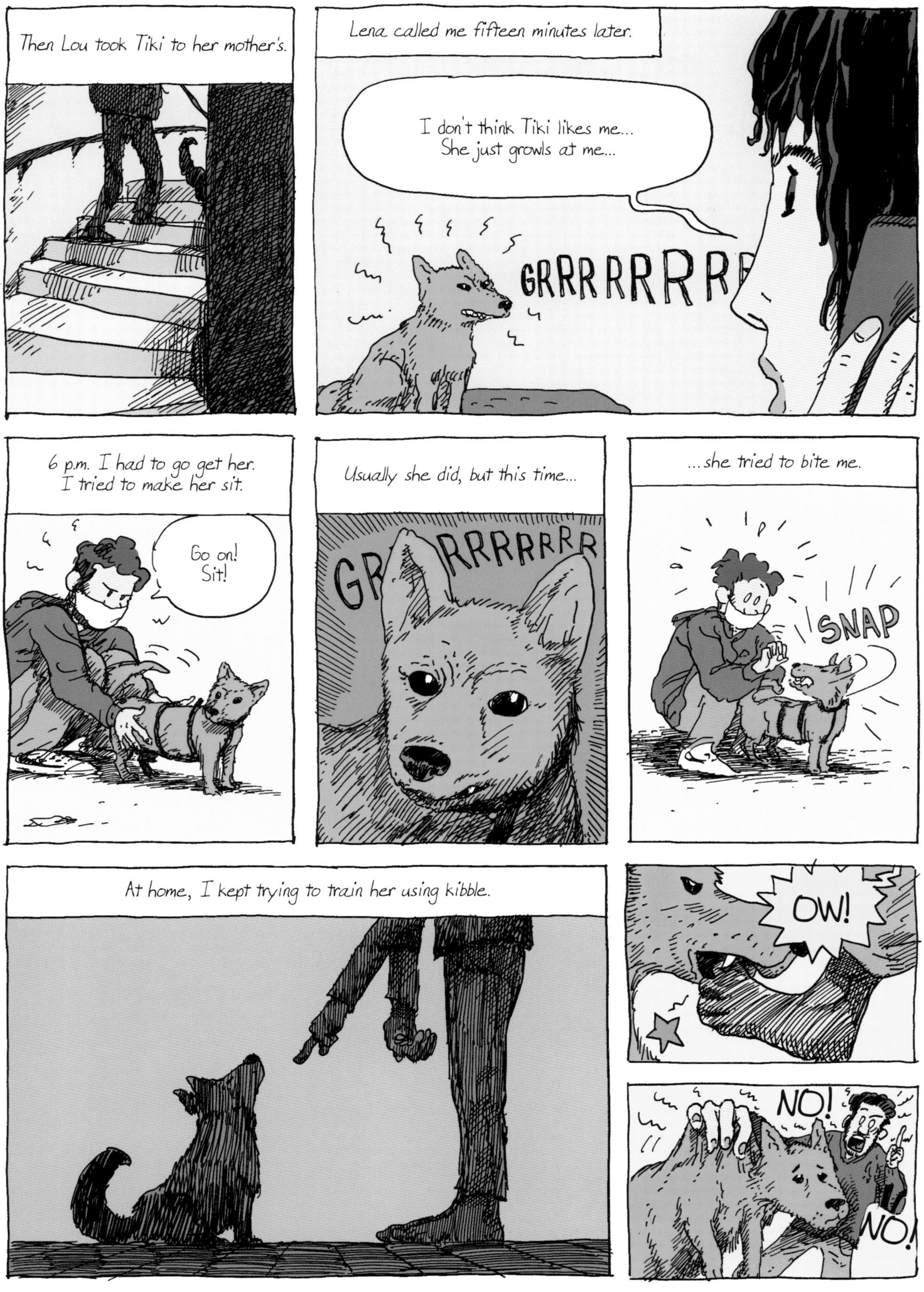

Then Lou took Tiki to her mother's.
Lena called me fifteen minutes later.
I don't think Tiki likes me... She just growls at me...
GRRRRRRR
6 p.m. I had to go get her. I tried to make her sit.
Go on! Sit!
Usually she did, but this time...
GRRRRRRRR
...she tried to bite me.
SNAP
At home, I kept trying to train her using kibble.
OW!
NO!
NO!

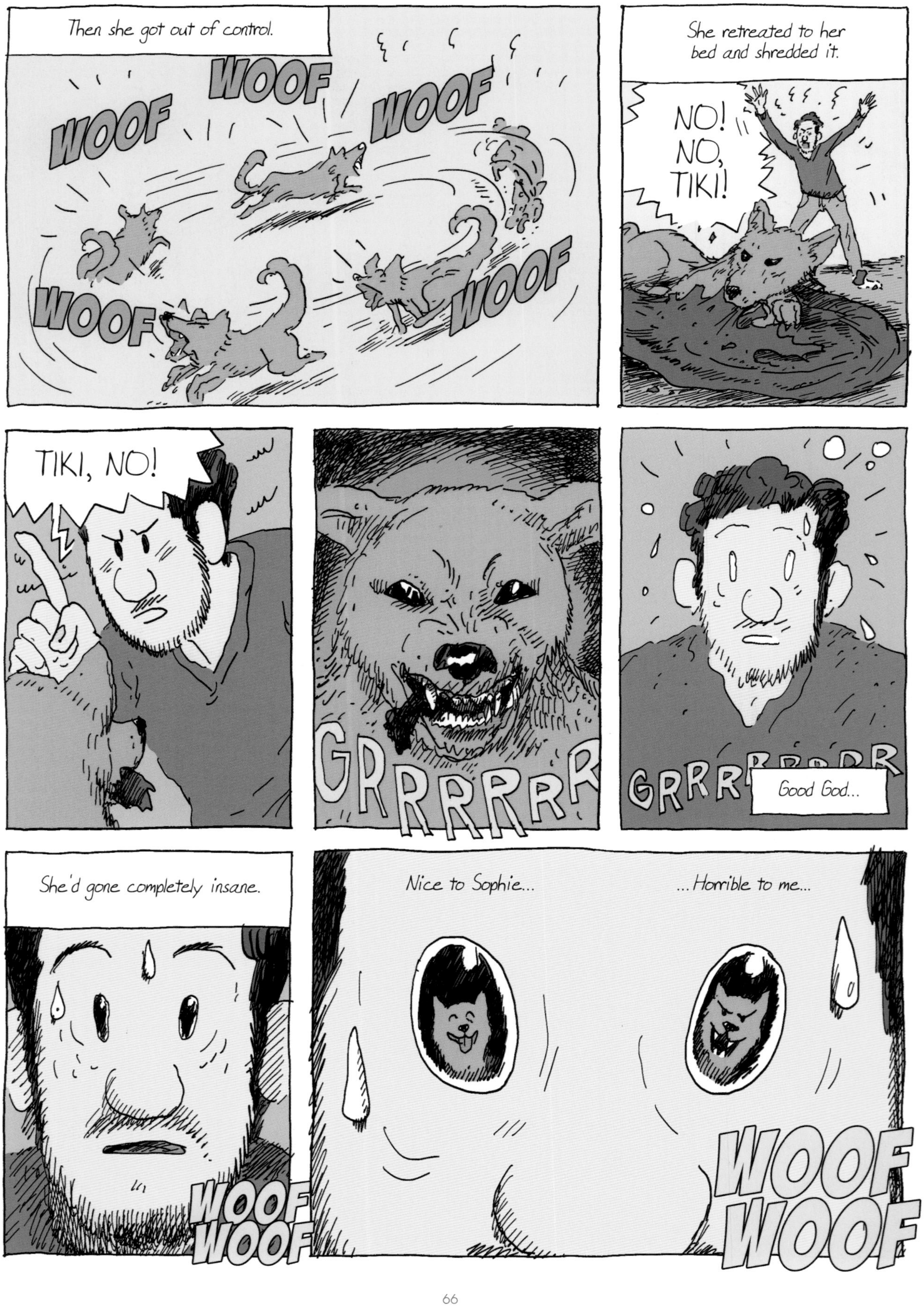
Then she got out of control.
WOOF
WOOF
WOOF
WOOF
WOOF
She retreated to her bed and shredded it.
NO! NO, TIKI!
TIKI, NO!
GRRRRRR
GRRRRRRR
Good God...
She'd gone completely insane.
WOOF WOOF
Nice to Sophie...
...Horrible to me...
WOOF WOOF

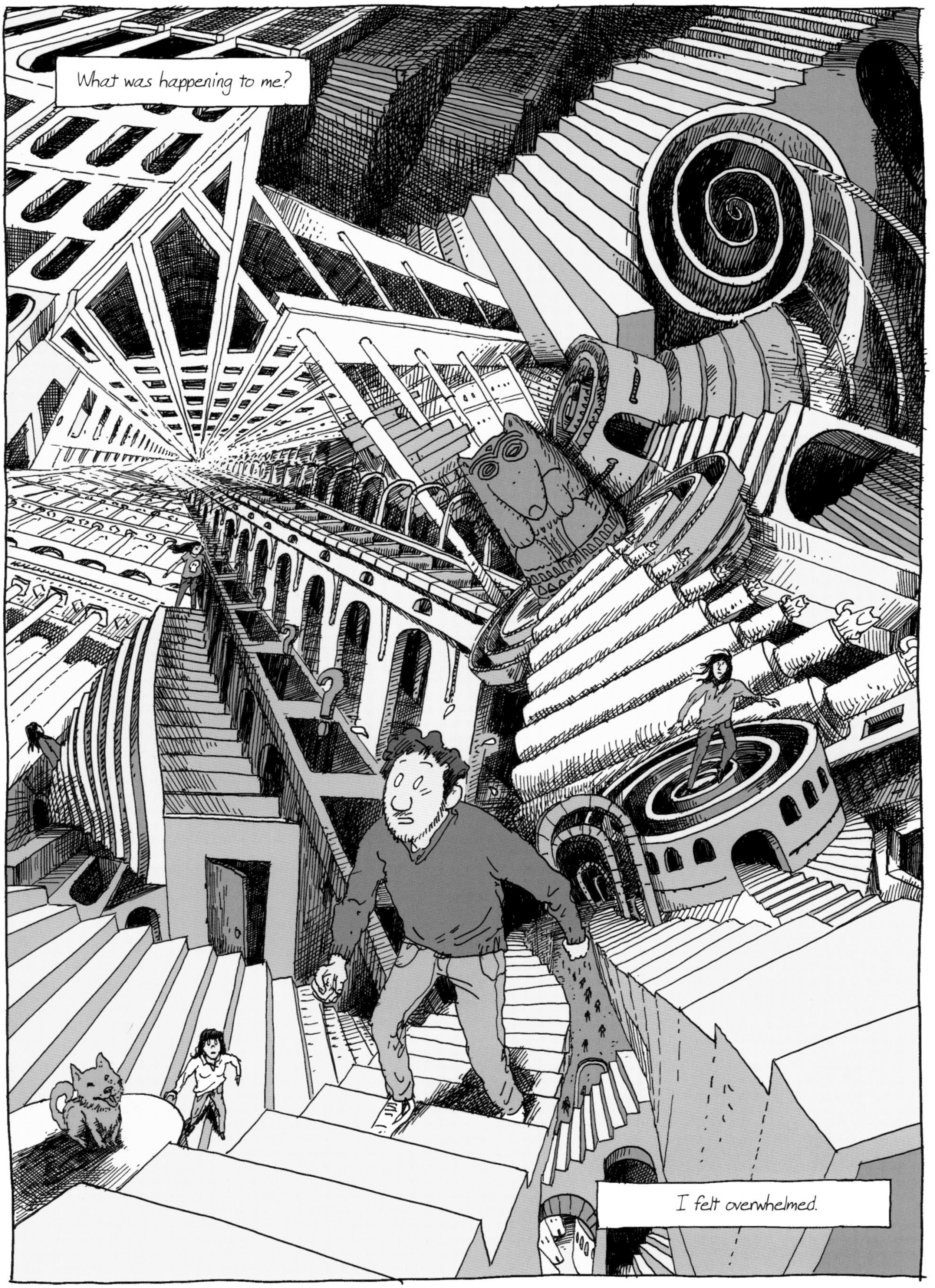
What was happening to me?
I felt overwhelmed.

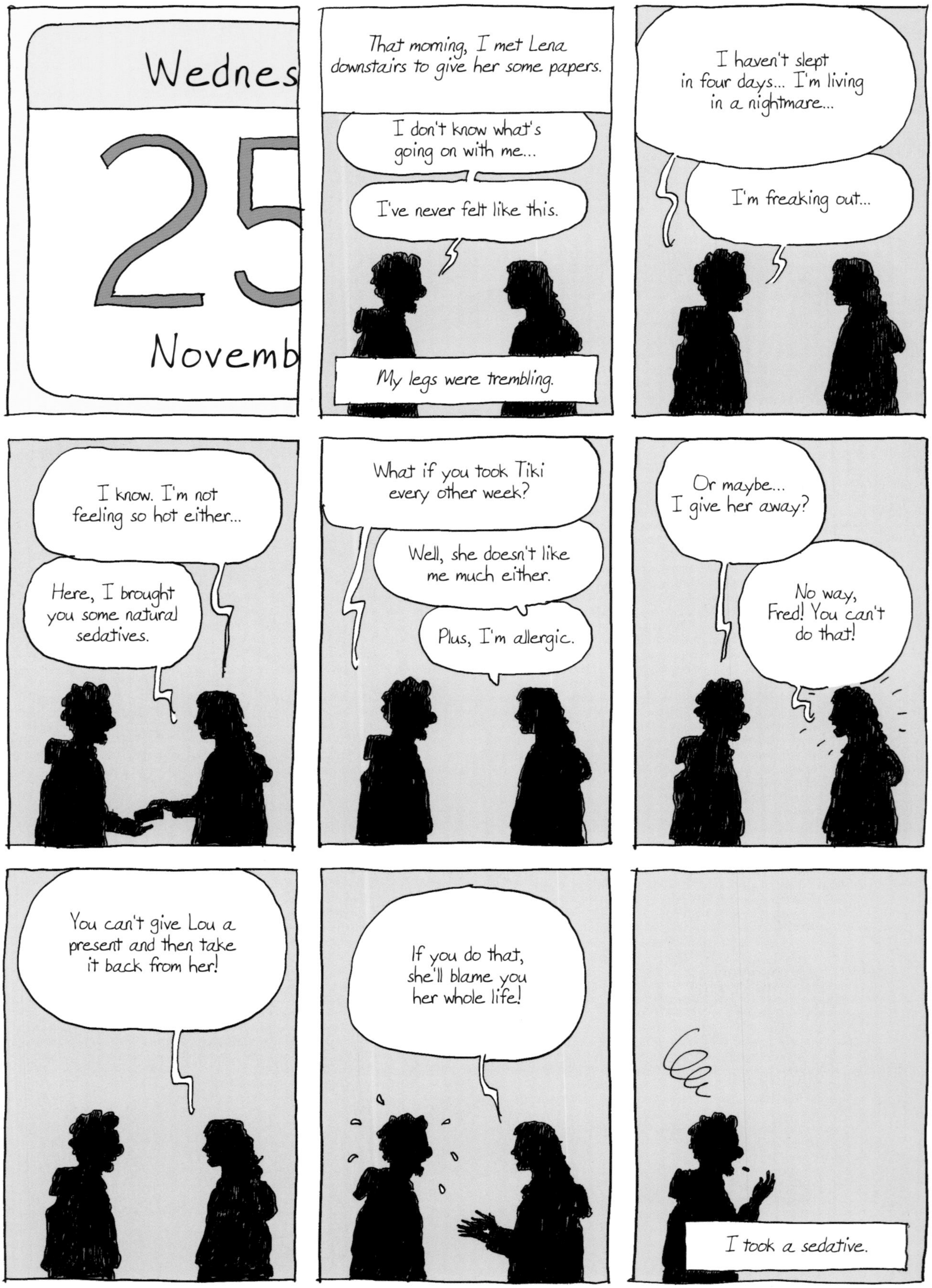

Wednes
25
Novemb
That morning, I met Lena downstairs to give her some papers.
I don't know what's going on with me...
I've never felt like this.
My legs were trembling.
I haven't slept in four days... I'm living in a nightmare...
I'm freaking out...
I know. I'm not feeling so hot either...
Here, I brought you some natural sedatives.
What if you took Tiki every other week?
Well, she doesn't like me much either.
Plus, I'm allergic.
Or maybe... I give her away?
No way, Fred! You can't do that!
You can't give Lou a present and then take it back from her!
If you do that, she'll blame you her whole life!
I took a sedative.

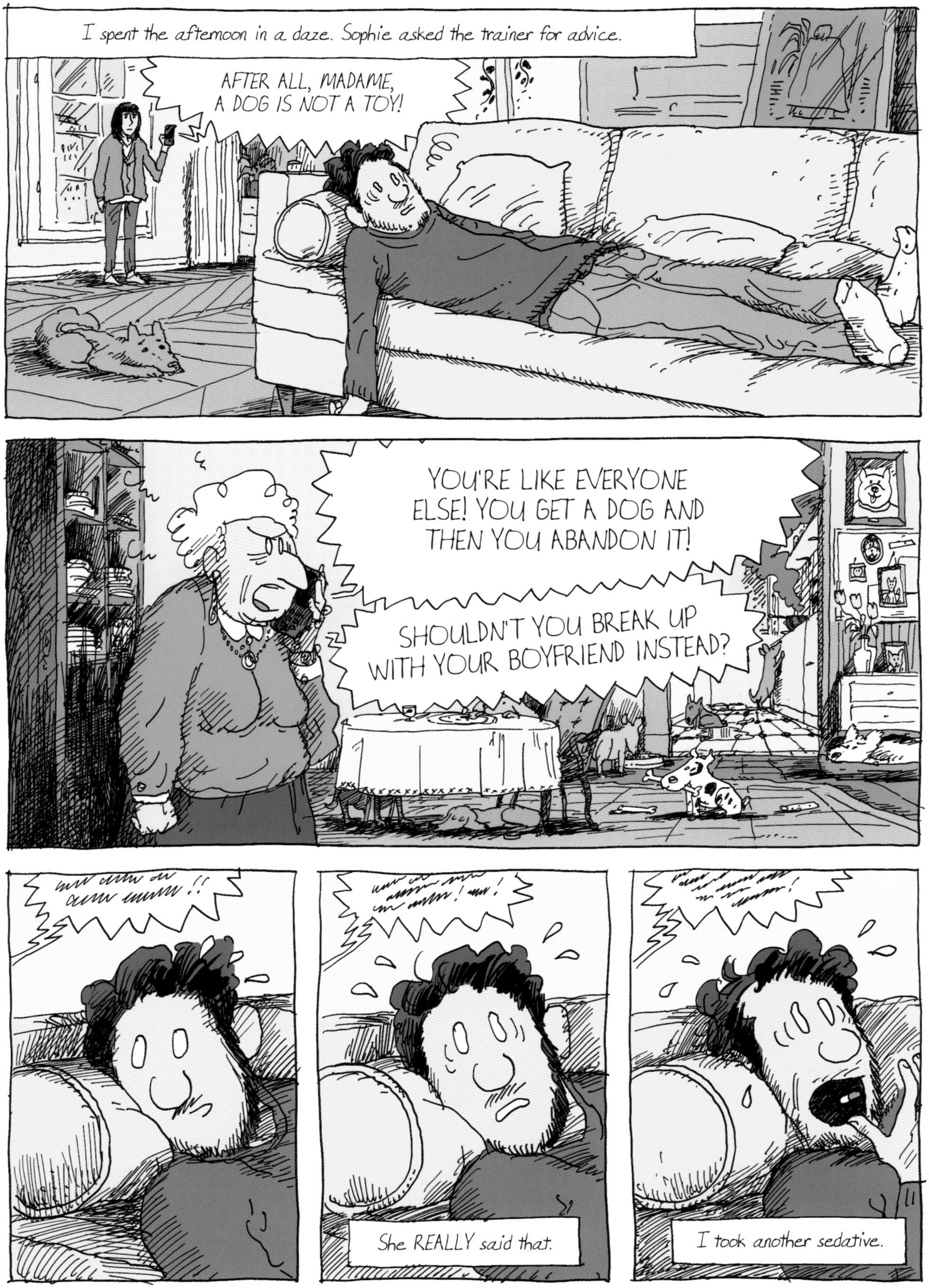
I spent the afternoon in a daze. Sophie asked the trainer for advice.
AFTER ALL, MADAME, A DOG IS NOT A TOY!
YOU'RE LIKE EVERYONE ELSE! YOU GET A DOG AND THEN YOU ABANDON IT!
SHOULDN'T YOU BREAK UP WITH YOUR BOYFRIEND INSTEAD?
She REALLY said that.
I took another sedative.

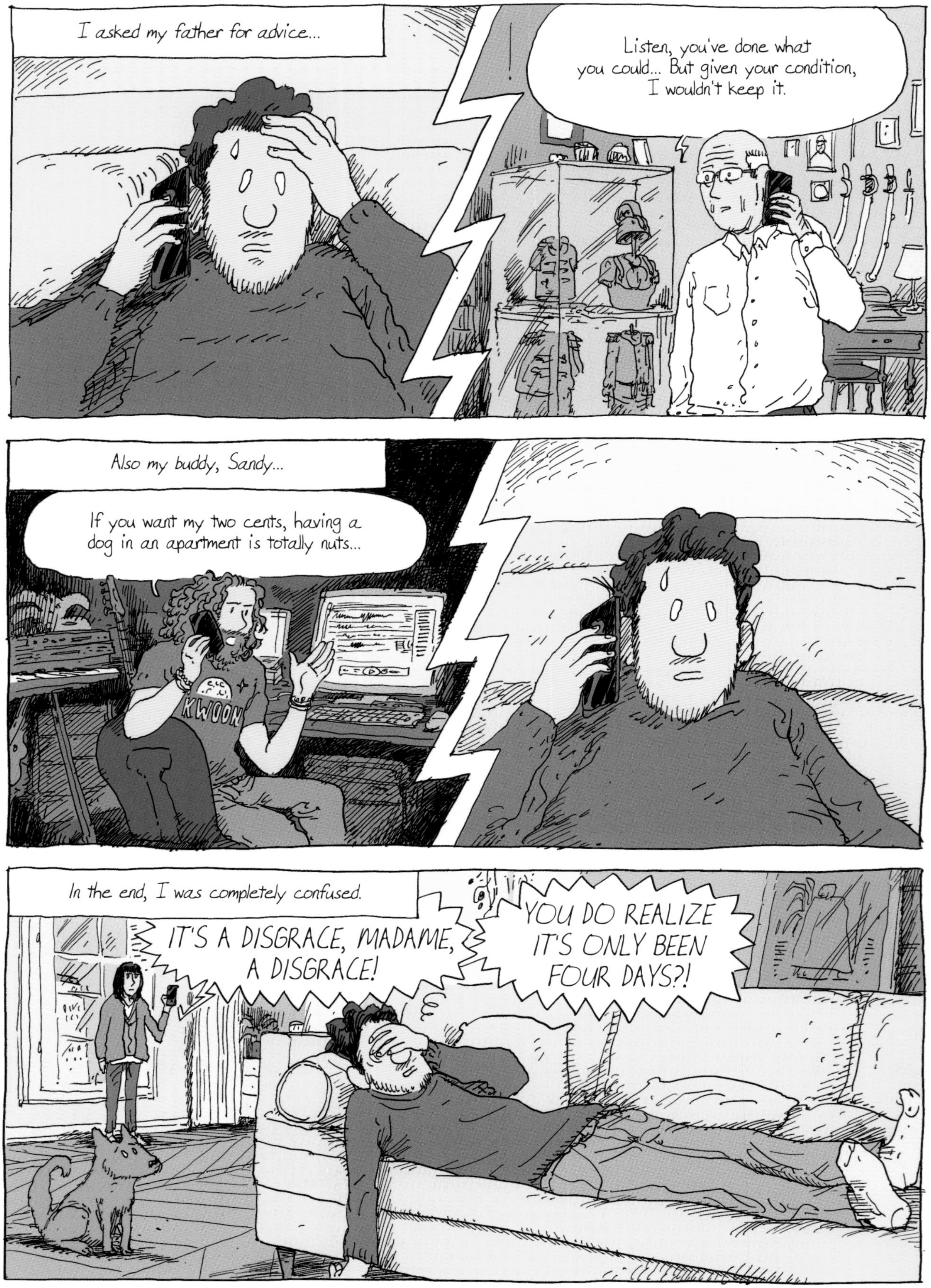
I asked my father for advice...
Listen, you've done what you could... But given your condition, I wouldn't keep it.
Also my buddy, Sandy...
If you want my two cents, having a dog in an apartment is totally nuts...
KWOON
In the end, I was completely confused.
IT'S A DISGRACE, MADAME, A DISGRACE!
YOU DO REALIZE IT'S ONLY BEEN FOUR DAYS?!

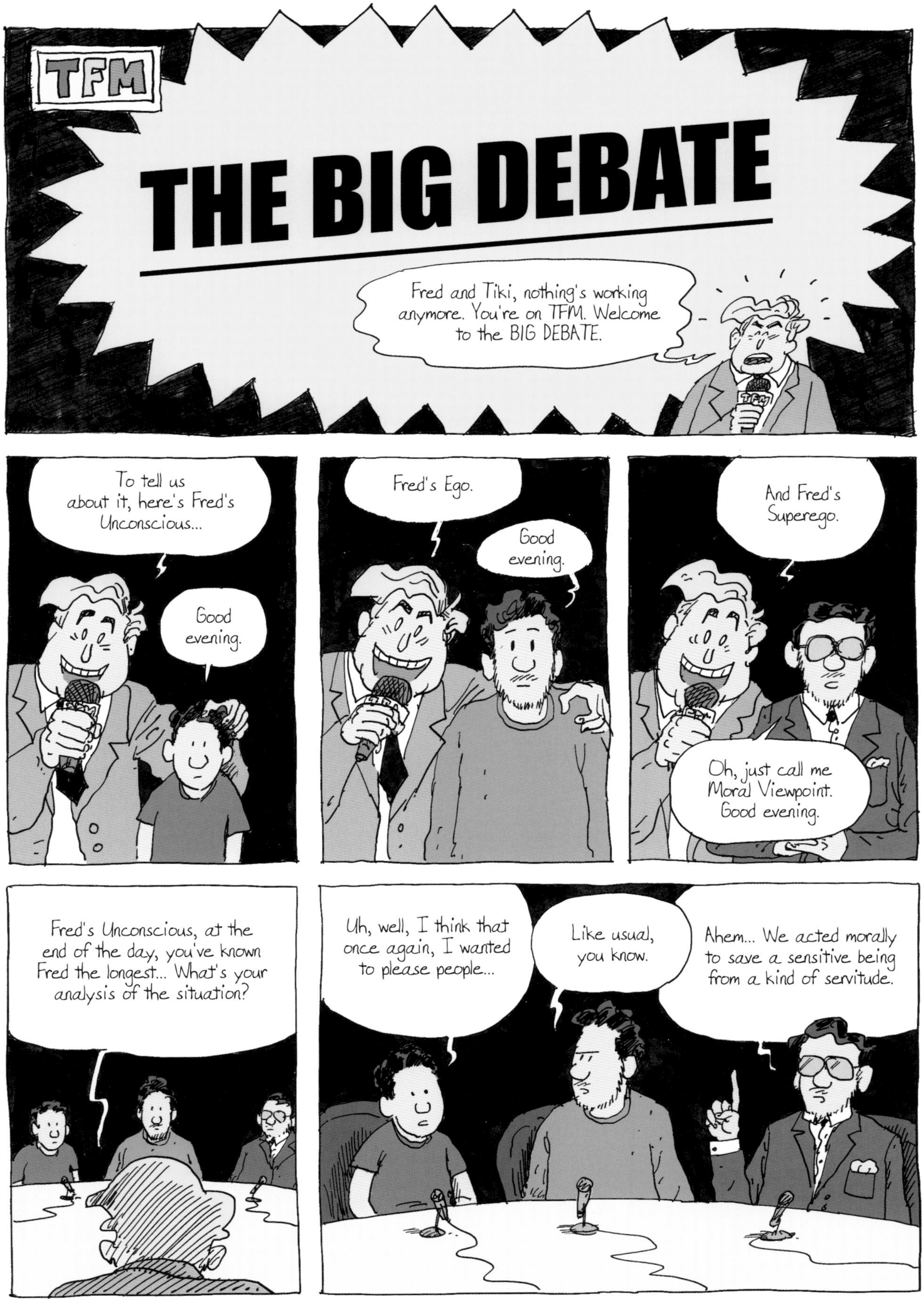
TFM
THE BIG DEBATE
Fred and Tiki, nothing's working anymore. You're on TFM. Welcome to the BIG DEBATE.
TFM
To tell us about it, here's Fred's Unconscious...
Good evening.
Fred's Ego.
Good evening.
And Fred's Superego.
Oh, just call me Moral Viewpoint. Good evening.
Fred's Unconscious, at the end of the day, you've known Fred the longest... What's your analysis of the situation?
Uh, well, I think that once again, I wanted to please people...
Like usual, you know.
Ahem... We acted morally to save a sensitive being from a kind of servitude.

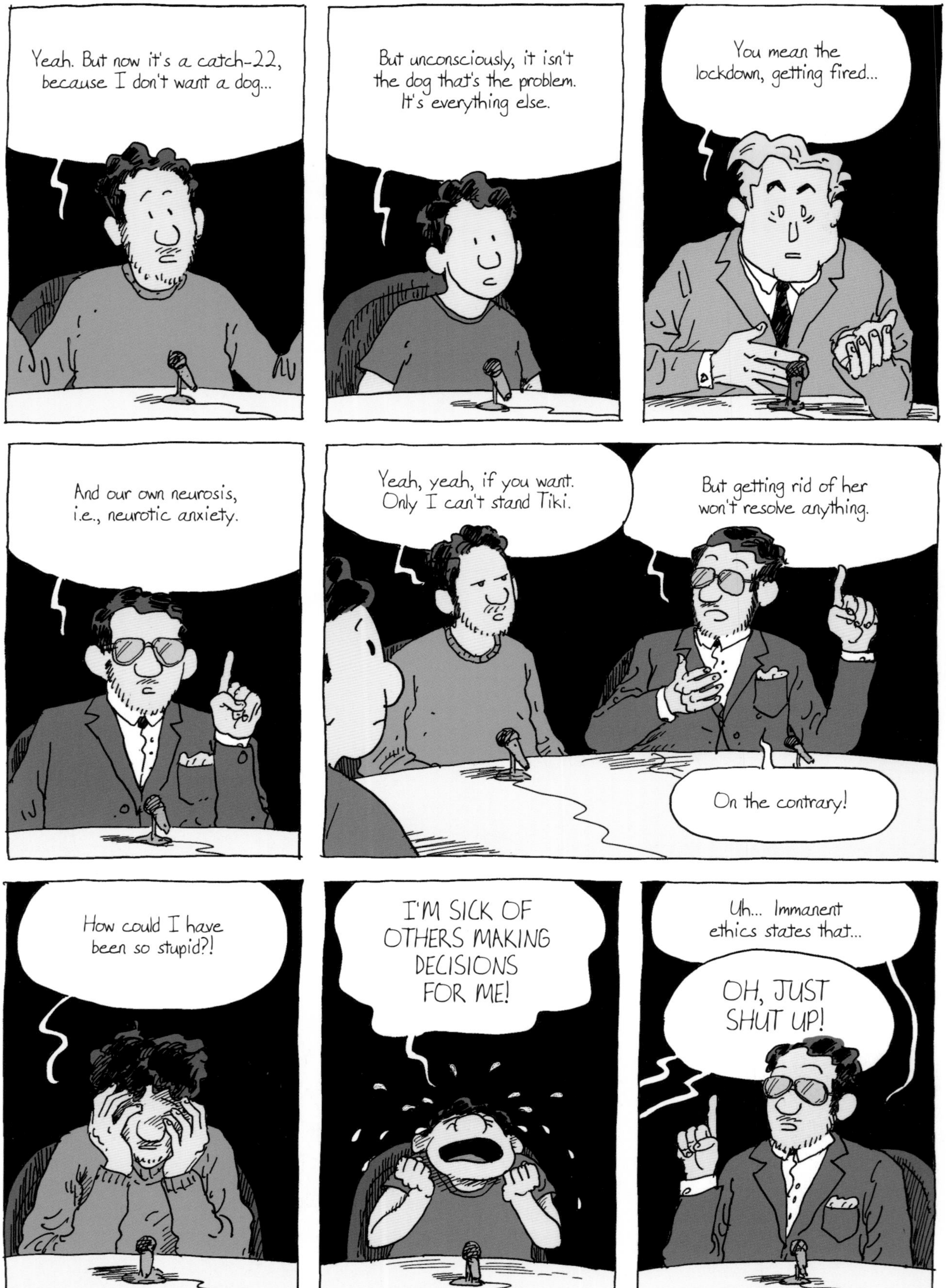
Yeah. But now it's a catch-22, because I don't want a dog...
But unconsciously, it isn't the dog that's the problem. It's everything else.
You mean the lockdown, getting fired...
And our own neurosis, i.e., neurotic anxiety.
Yeah, yeah, if you want. Only I can't stand Tiki.
But getting rid of her won't resolve anything.
On the contrary!
How could I have been so stupid?!
I'M SICK OF OTHERS MAKING DECISIONS FOR ME!
Uh... Immanent ethics states that...
OH, JUST SHUT UP!

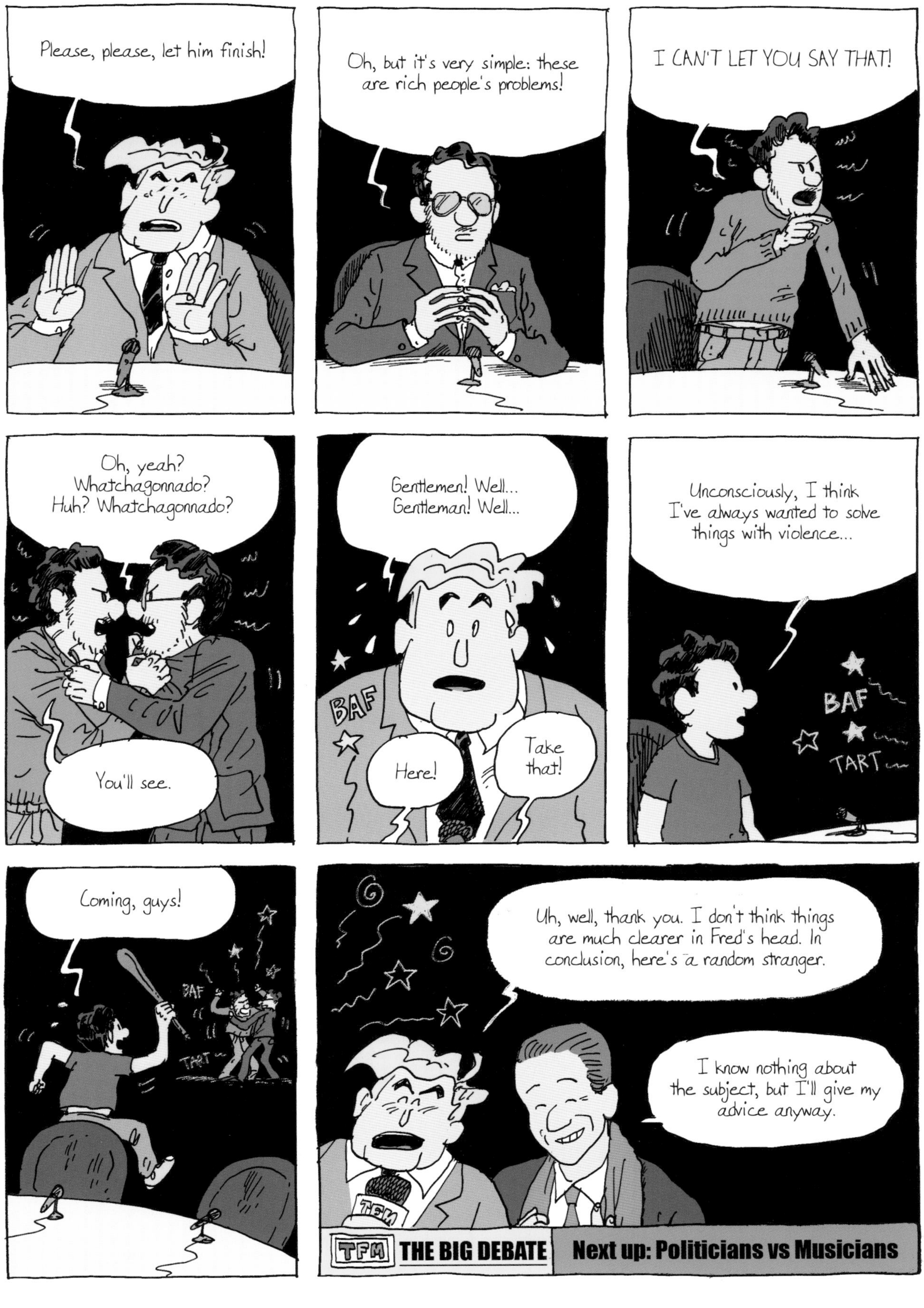

Please, please, let him finish!
Oh, but it's very simple: these are rich people's problems!
I CAN'T LET YOU SAY THAT!
Oh, yeah? Whatchagonnado? Huh? Whatchagonnado?
You'll see.
Gentlemen! Well... Gentleman! Well...
BAF
Here!
Take that!
Unconsciously, I think I've always wanted to solve things with violence...
BAF
TART
Coming, guys!
BAF
TART
Uh, well, thank you. I don't think things are much clearer in Fred's head. In conclusion, here's a random stranger.
I know nothing about the subject, but I'll give my advice anyway.
TFM
TFM THE BIG DEBATE
Next up: Politicians vs Musicians

Chapter Five

The Fall

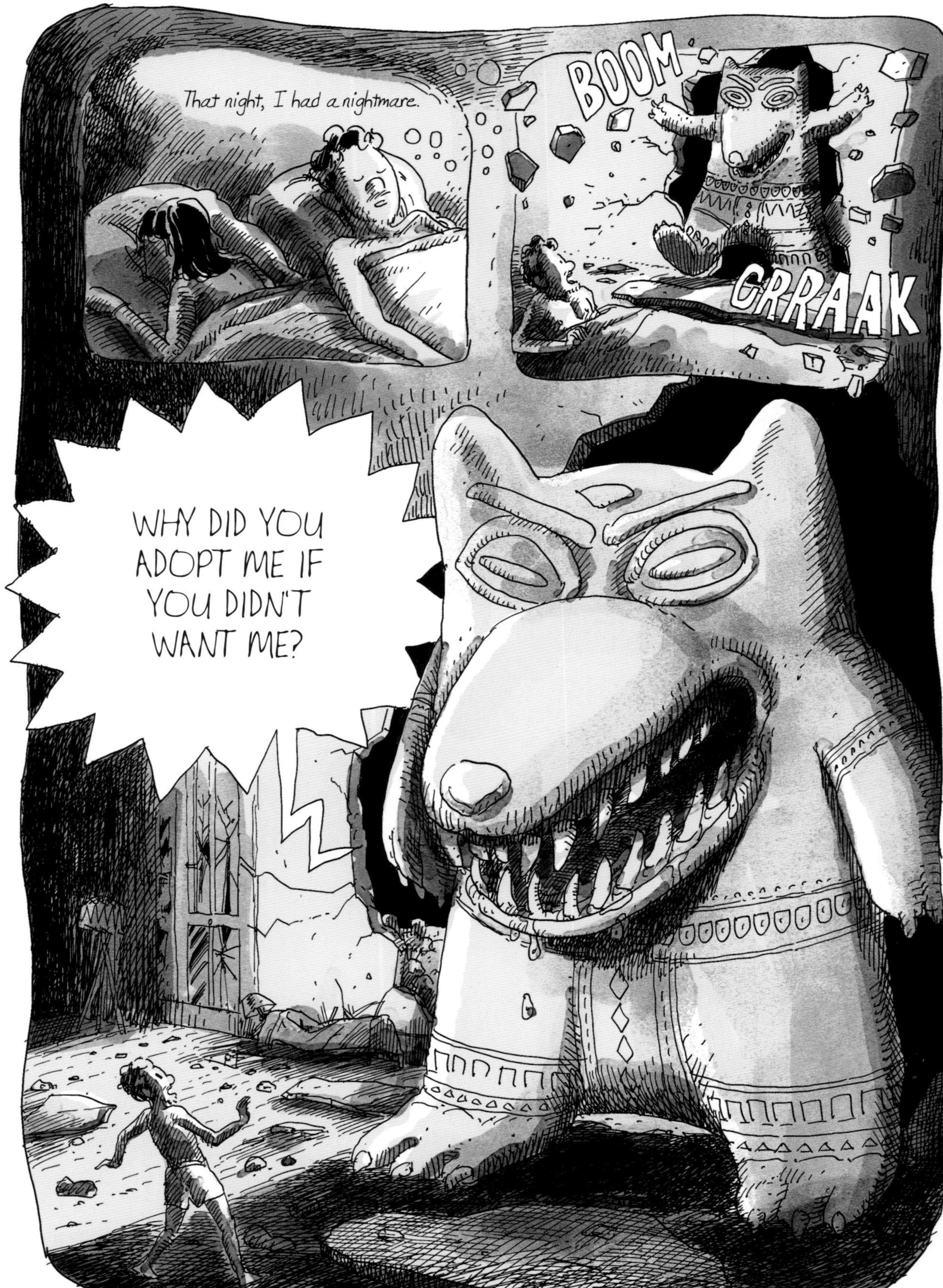
That night, I had a nightmare.
BOOM
GRRAAK
WHY DID YOU ADOPT ME IF YOU DIDN'T WANT ME?

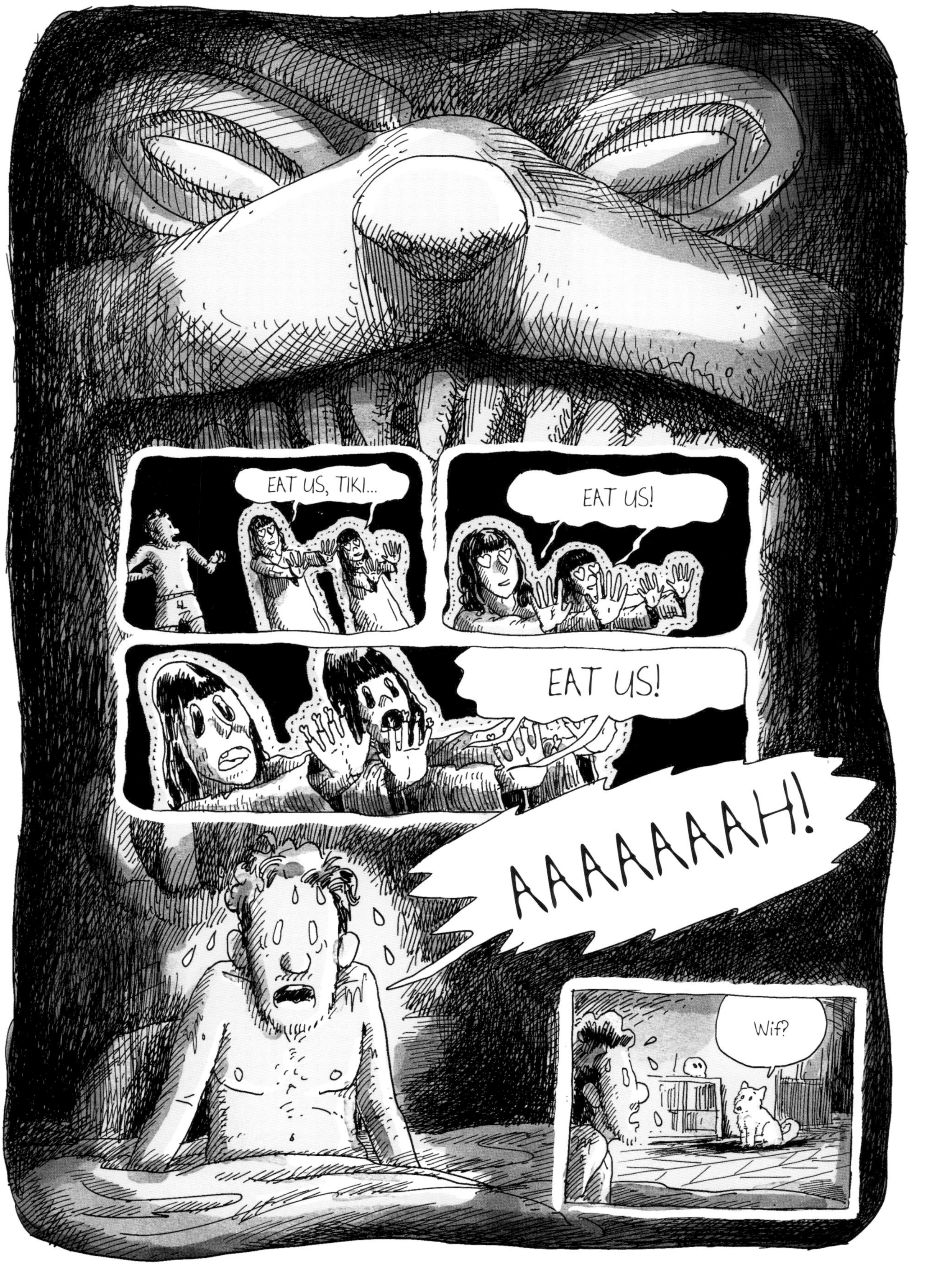
EAT US, TIKI...
EAT US!
EAT US!
AAAAAAAH!
Wif?

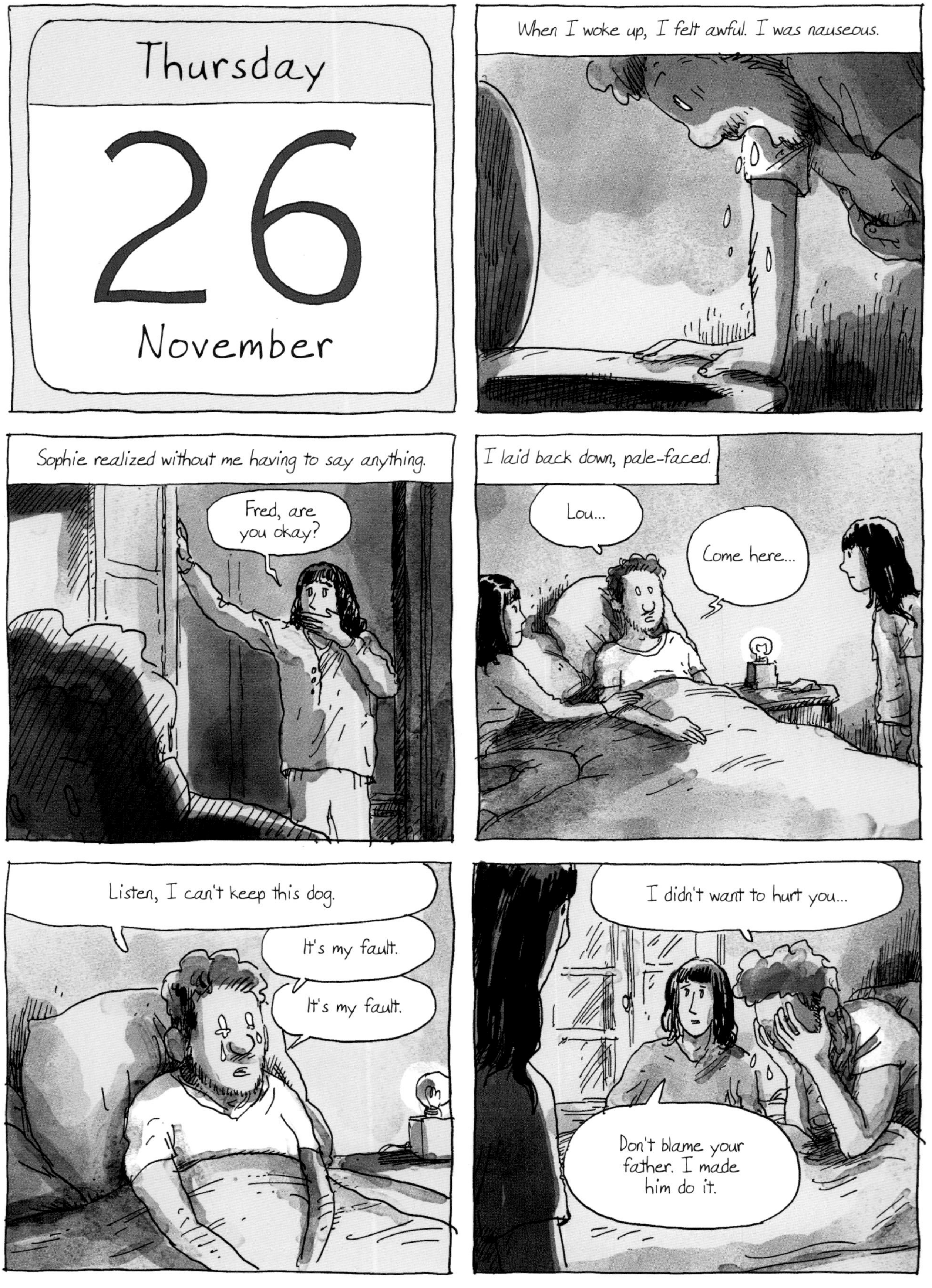
Thursday
26
November
When I woke up, I felt awful. I was nauseous.
Sophie realized without me having to say anything.
Fred, are you okay?
I laid back down, pale-faced.
Lou...
Come here...
Listen, I can't keep this dog.
It's my fault.
It's my fault.
I didn't want to hurt you...
Don't blame your father. I made him do it.

Lou was lost. She'd never seen me like that.

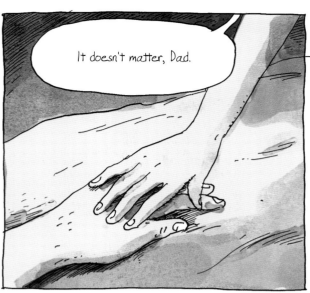

It doesn't matter, Dad.

But you know, my father can take her! He has a house with a garden.

We can go see her whenever we want!

Okay.

She left for school.

Woof?

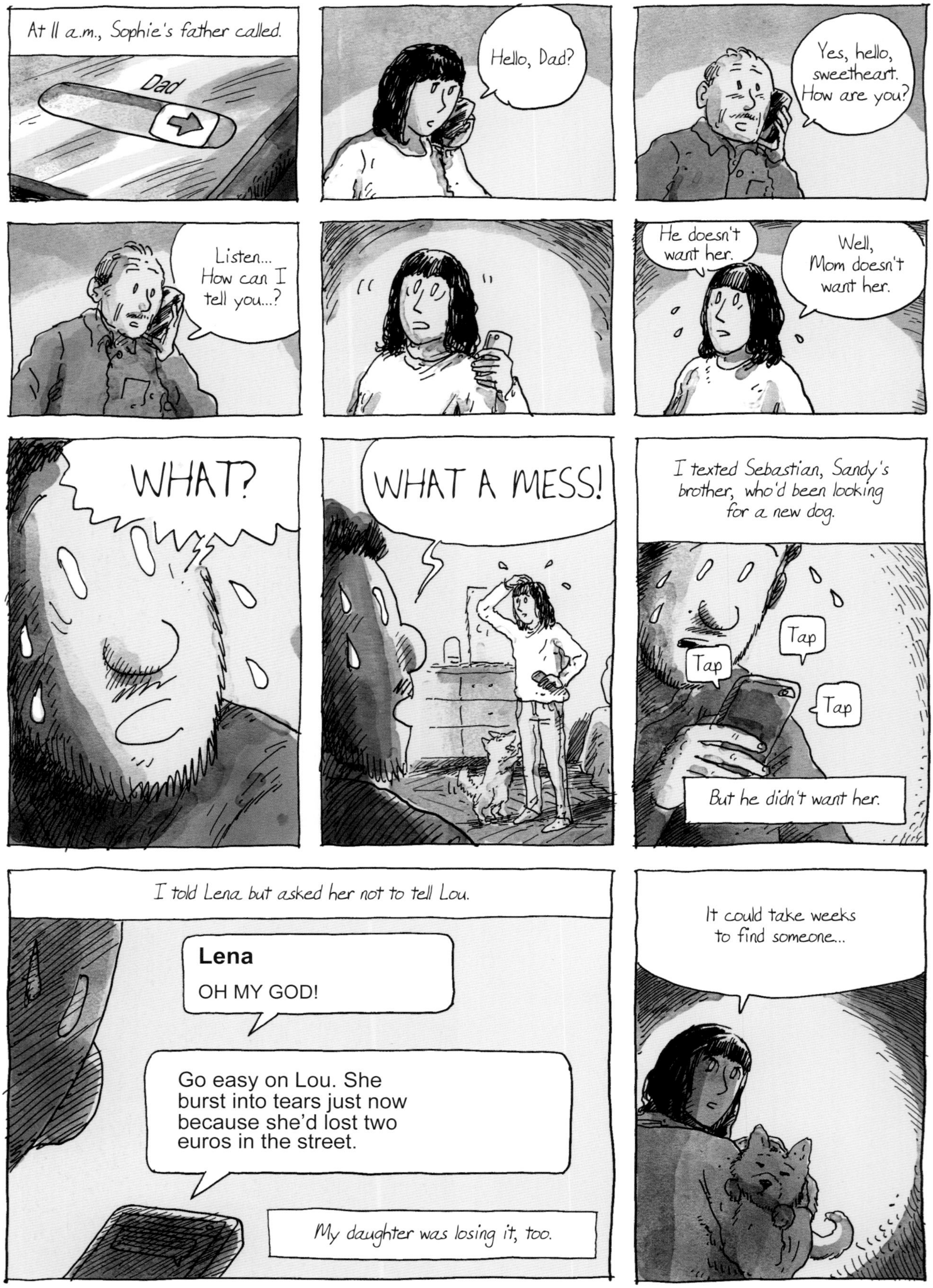

At 11 a.m., Sophie's father called.
Dad
Hello, Dad?
Yes, hello, sweetheart. How are you?
Listen... How can I tell you...?
He doesn't want her.
Well, Mom doesn't want her.
WHAT?
WHAT A MESS!
I texted Sebastian, Sandy's brother, who'd been looking for a new dog.
Tap
Tap
Tap
But he didn't want her.
I told Lena but asked her not to tell Lou.
Lena
OH MY GOD!
Go easy on Lou. She burst into tears just now because she'd lost two euros in the street.
My daughter was losing it, too.
It could take weeks to find someone...

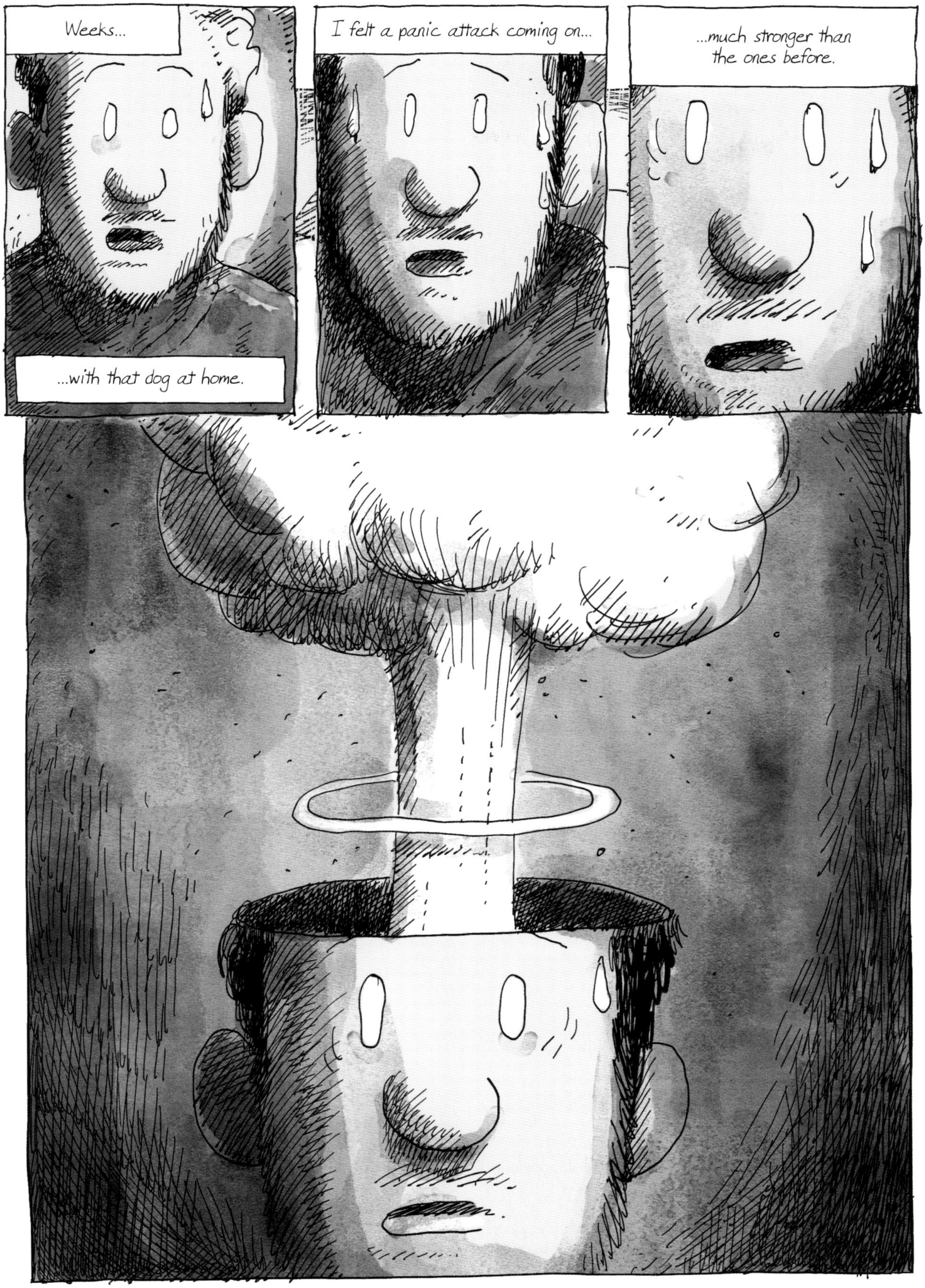
Weeks...
...with that dog at home.
I felt a panic attack coming on...
...much stronger than the ones before.

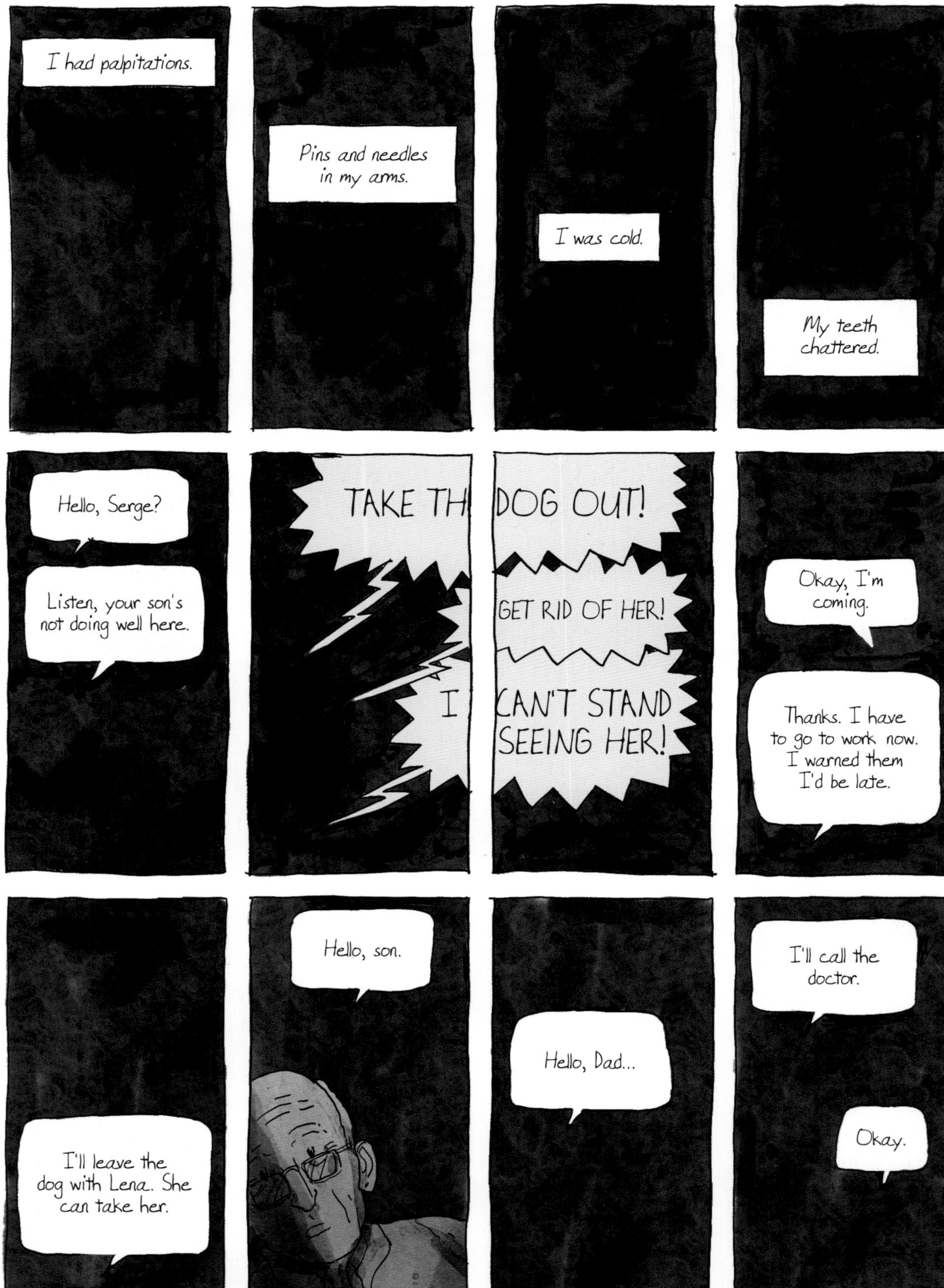
I had palpitations.
Pins and needles in my arms.
I was cold.
My teeth chattered.
Hello, Serge?
Listen, your son's not doing well here.
TAKE THE DOG OUT!
GET RID OF HER!
I CAN'T STAND SEEING HER!
Okay, I'm coming.
Thanks. I have to go to work now. I warned them I'd be late.
I'll leave the dog with Lena. She can take her.
Hello, son.
Hello, Dad...
I'll call the doctor.
Okay.

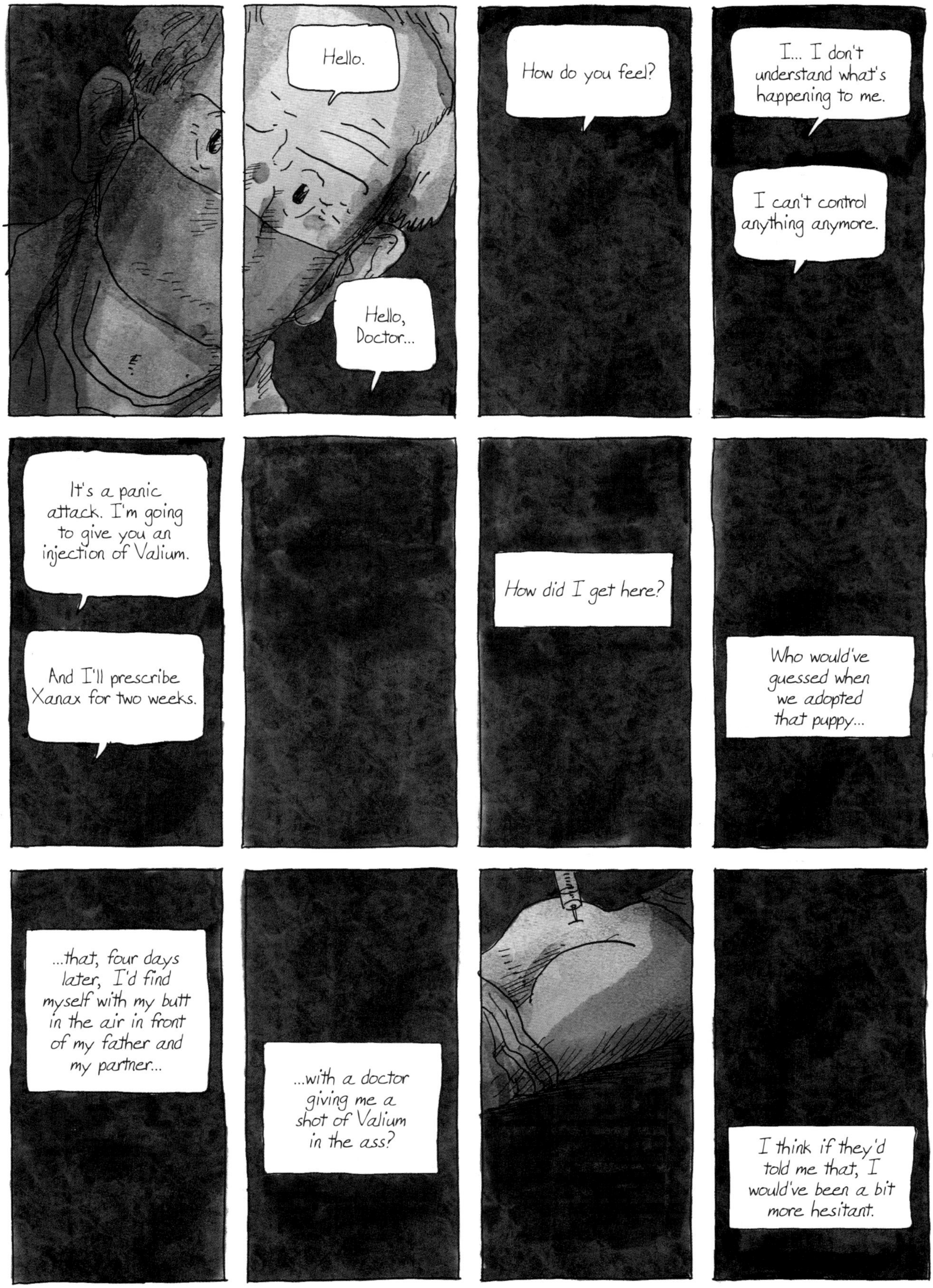

Hello.
Hello, Doctor...
How do you feel?
I... I don't understand what's happening to me.
I can't control anything anymore.
It's a panic attack. I'm going to give you an injection of Valium.
And I'll prescribe Xanax for two weeks.
How did I get here?
Who would've guessed when we adopted that puppy...
...that, four days later, I'd find myself with my butt in the air in front of my father and my partner...
...with a doctor giving me a shot of Valium in the ass?
I think if they'd told me that, I would've been a bit more hesitant.

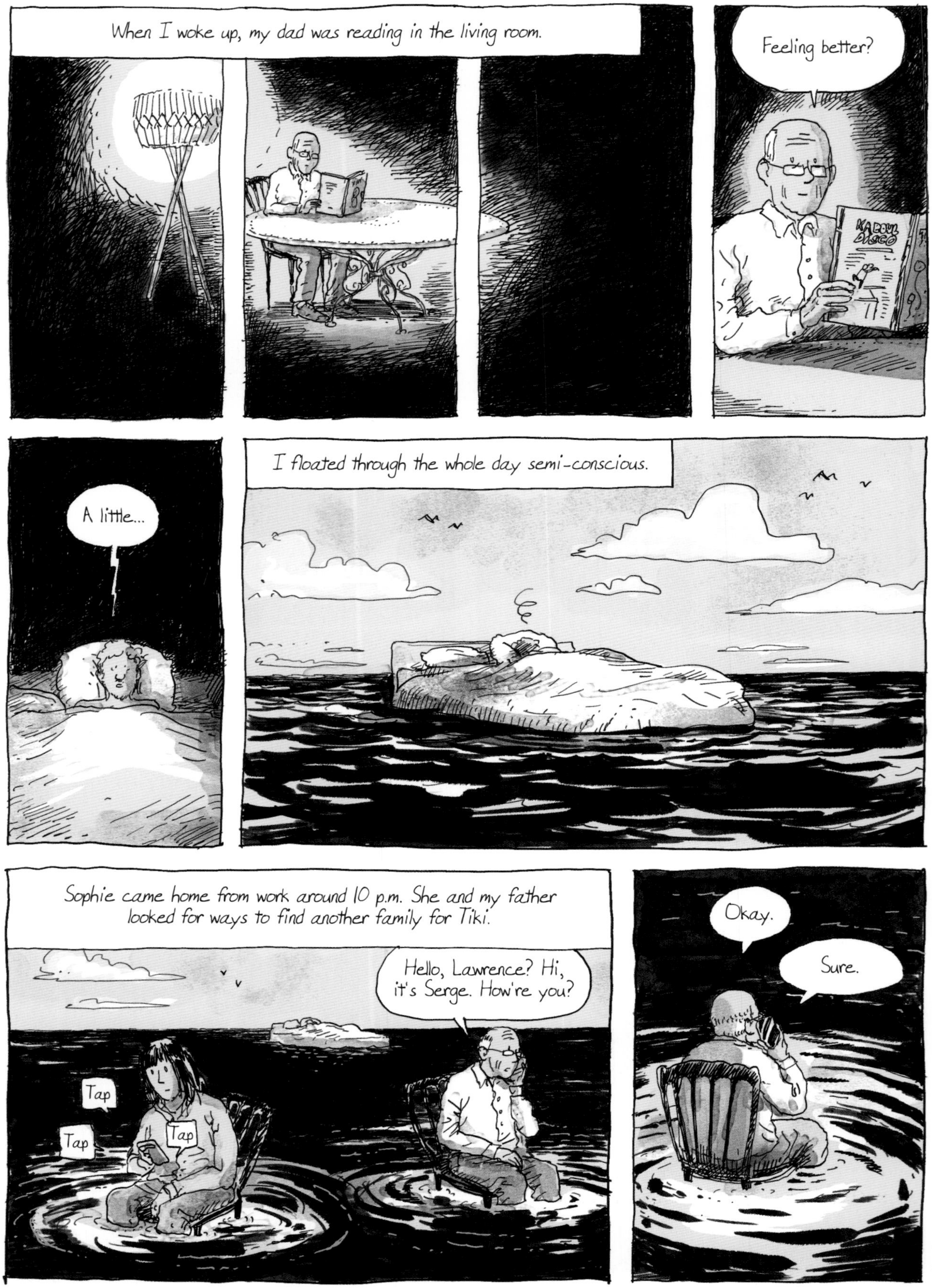
When I woke up, my dad was reading in the living room.
Feeling better?
KABOUL DISCO
A little...
I floated through the whole day semi-conscious.
Sophie came home from work around 10 p.m. She and my father looked for ways to find another family for Tiki.
Tap
Tap
Tap
Hello, Lawrence? Hi, it's Serge. How're you?
Okay.
Sure.

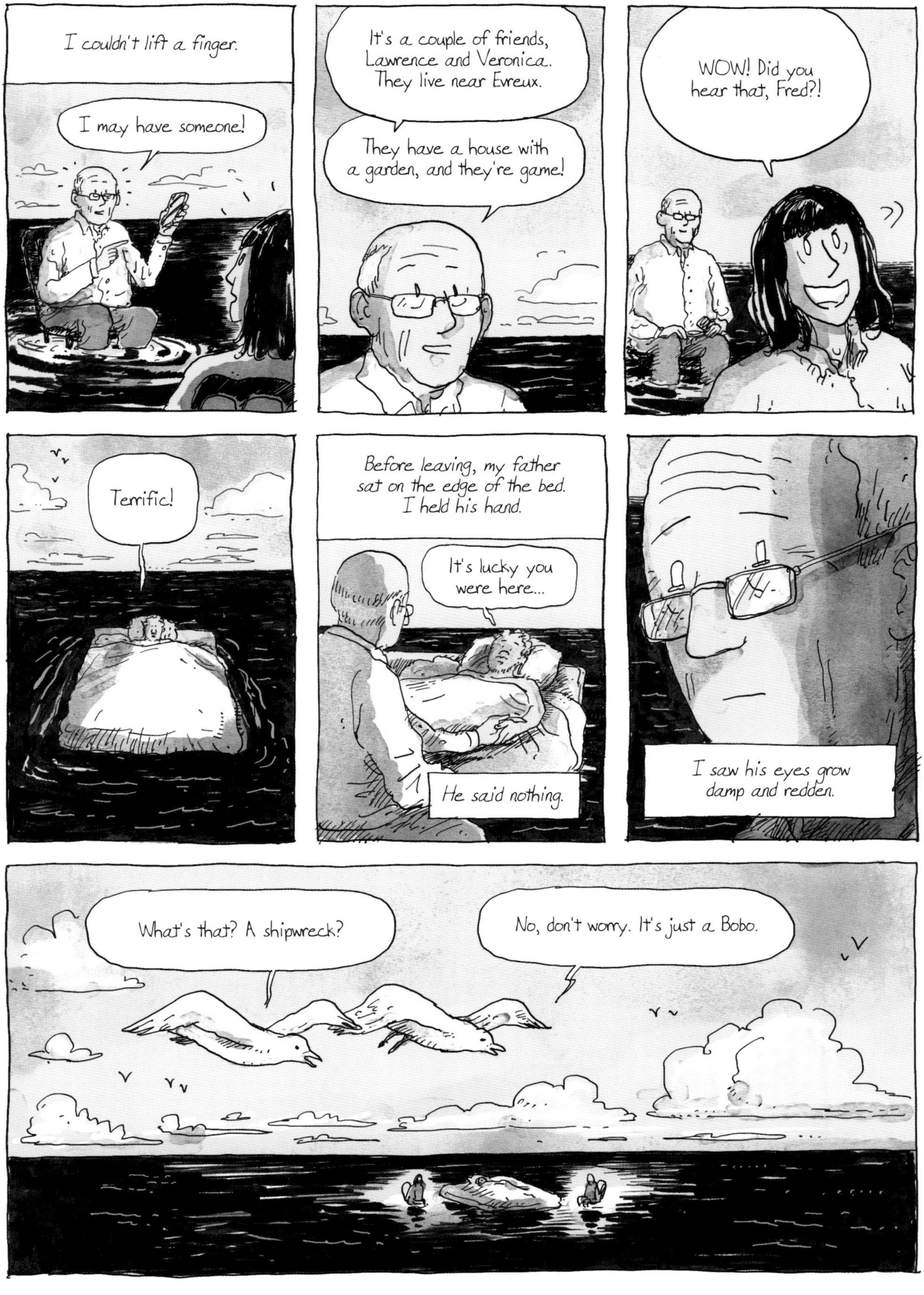
I couldn't lift a finger.
I may have someone!
It's a couple of friends, Lawrence and Veronica. They live near Evreux.
They have a house with a garden, and they're game!
WOW! Did you hear that, Fred?!
Terrific!
Before leaving, my father sat on the edge of the bed. I held his hand.
It's lucky you were here...
He said nothing.
I saw his eyes grow damp and redden.
What's that? A shipwreck?
No, don't worry. It's just a Bobo.

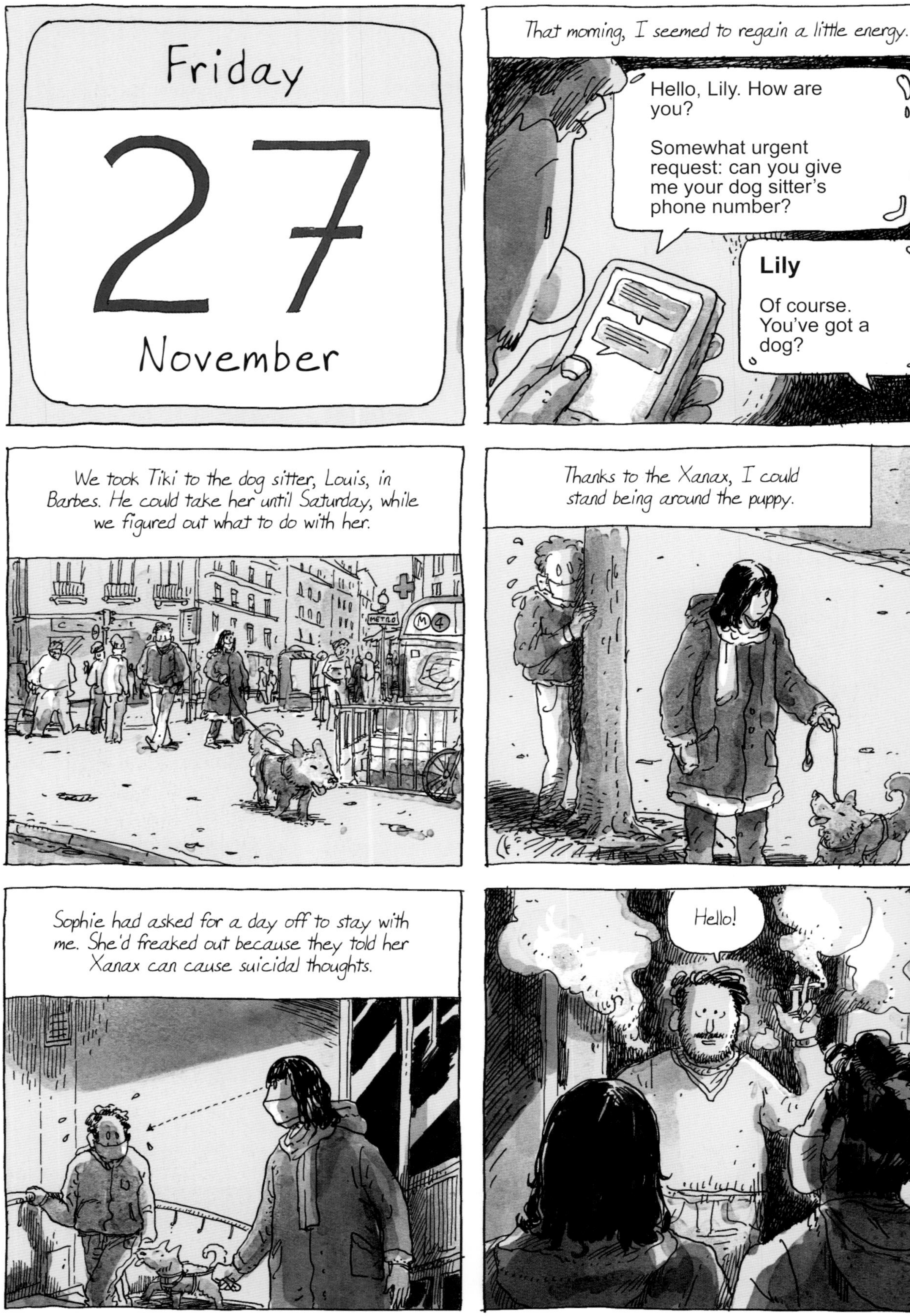
Friday
27
November
That morning, I seemed to regain a little energy.
Hello, Lily. How are you?
Somewhat urgent request: can you give me your dog sitter's phone number?
Lily
Of course. You've got a dog?
We took Tiki to the dog sitter, Louis, in Barbes. He could take her until Saturday, while we figured out what to do with her.
METRO
Thanks to the Xanax, I could stand being around the puppy.
Sophie had asked for a day off to stay with me. She'd freaked out because they told her Xanax can cause suicidal thoughts.
Hello!

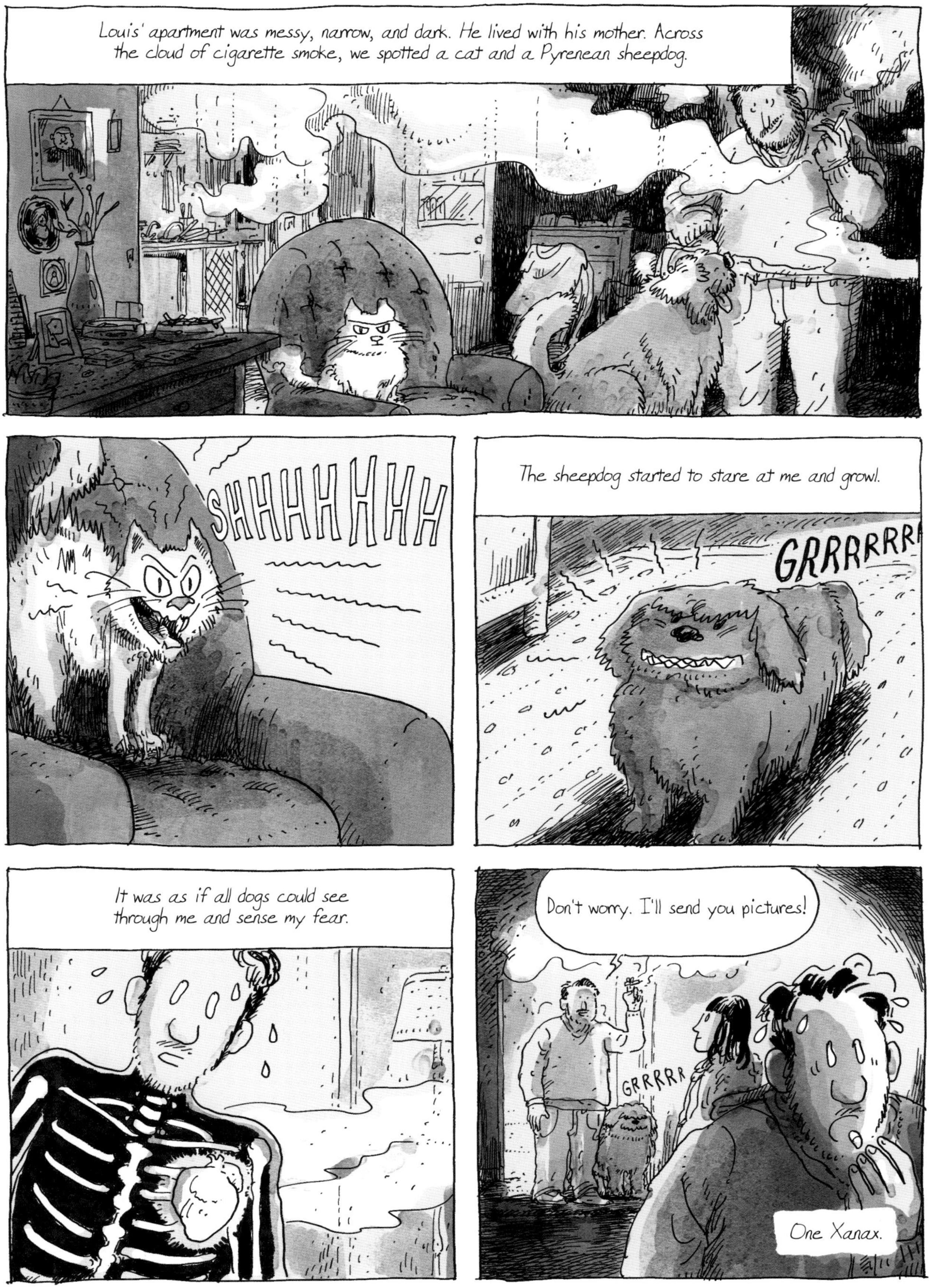
Louis' apartment was messy, narrow, and dark. He lived with his mother. Across the cloud of cigarette smoke, we spotted a cat and a Pyrenean sheepdog.
SHHHHHHH
The sheepdog started to stare at me and growl.
GRRRRRR
It was as if all dogs could see through me and sense my fear.
Don't worry. I'll send you pictures!
GRRRRR
One Xanax.

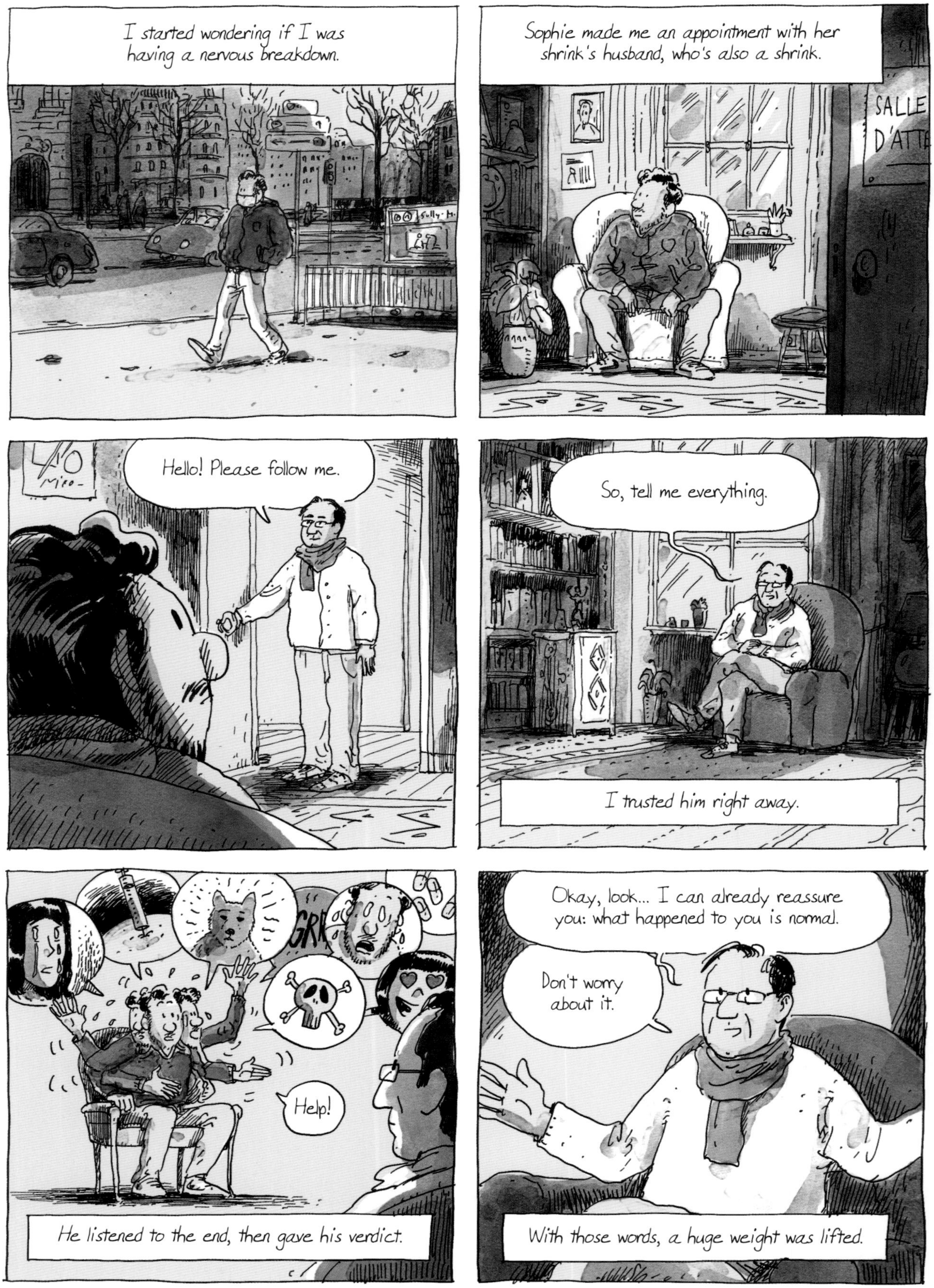

I started wondering if I was having a nervous breakdown.
Sophie made me an appointment with her shrink's husband, who's also a shrink.
SALLE D'ATT
Hello! Please follow me.
So, tell me everything.
I trusted him right away.
Help!
He listened to the end, then gave his verdict.
Okay, look... I can already reassure you: what happened to you is normal.
Don't worry about it.
With those words, a huge weight was lifted.

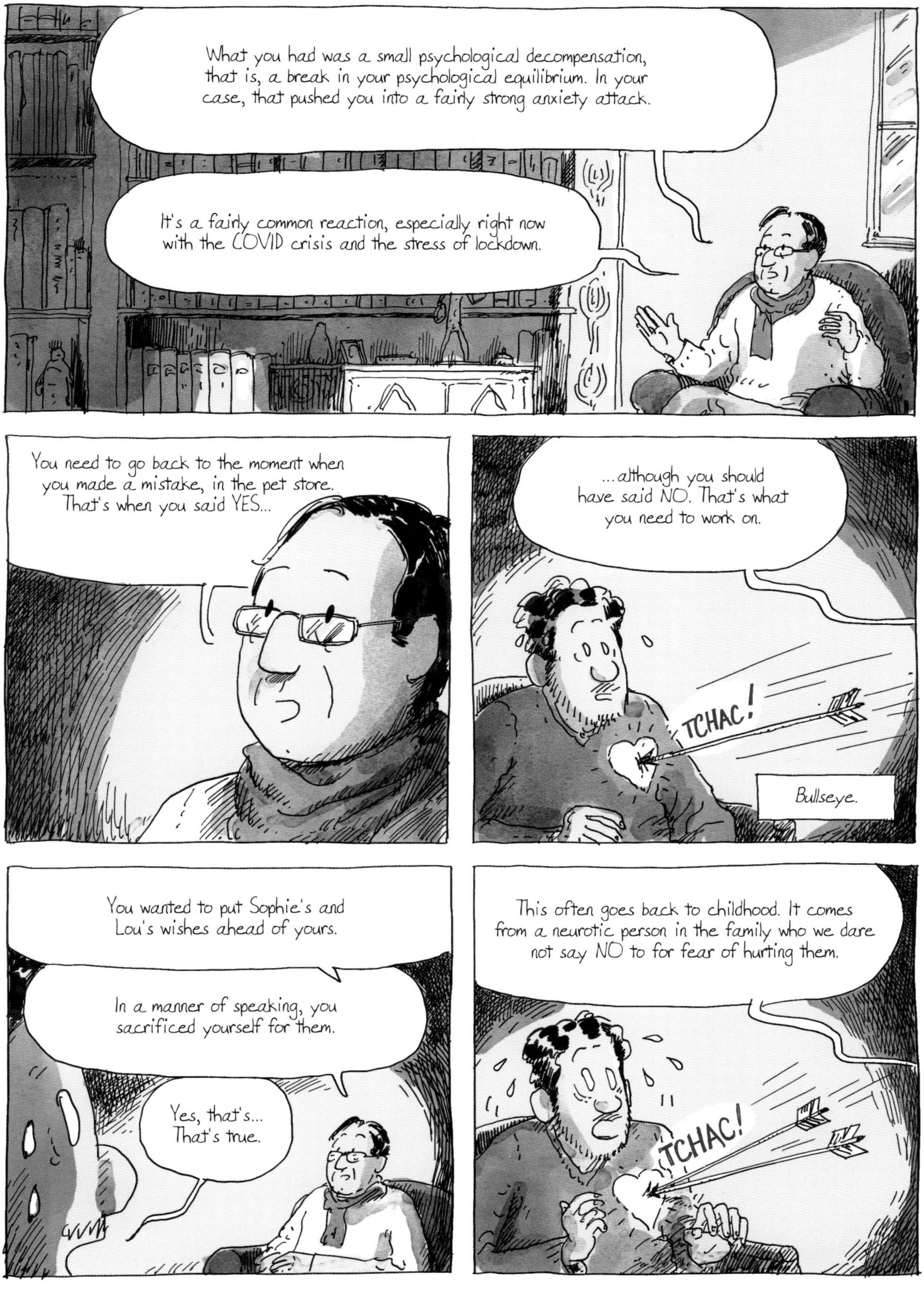
What you had was a small psychological decompensation, that is, a break in your psychological equilibrium. In your case, that pushed you into a fairly strong anxiety attack.
It's a fairly common reaction, especially right now with the COVID crisis and the stress of lockdown.
You need to go back to the moment when you made a mistake, in the pet store. That's when you said YES...
...although you should have said NO. That's what you need to work on.
TCHAC!
Bullseye.
You wanted to put Sophie's and Lou's wishes ahead of yours.
In a manner of speaking, you sacrificed yourself for them.
Yes, that's... That's true.
This often goes back to childhood. It comes from a neurotic person in the family who we dare not say NO to for fear of hurting them.
TCHAC!

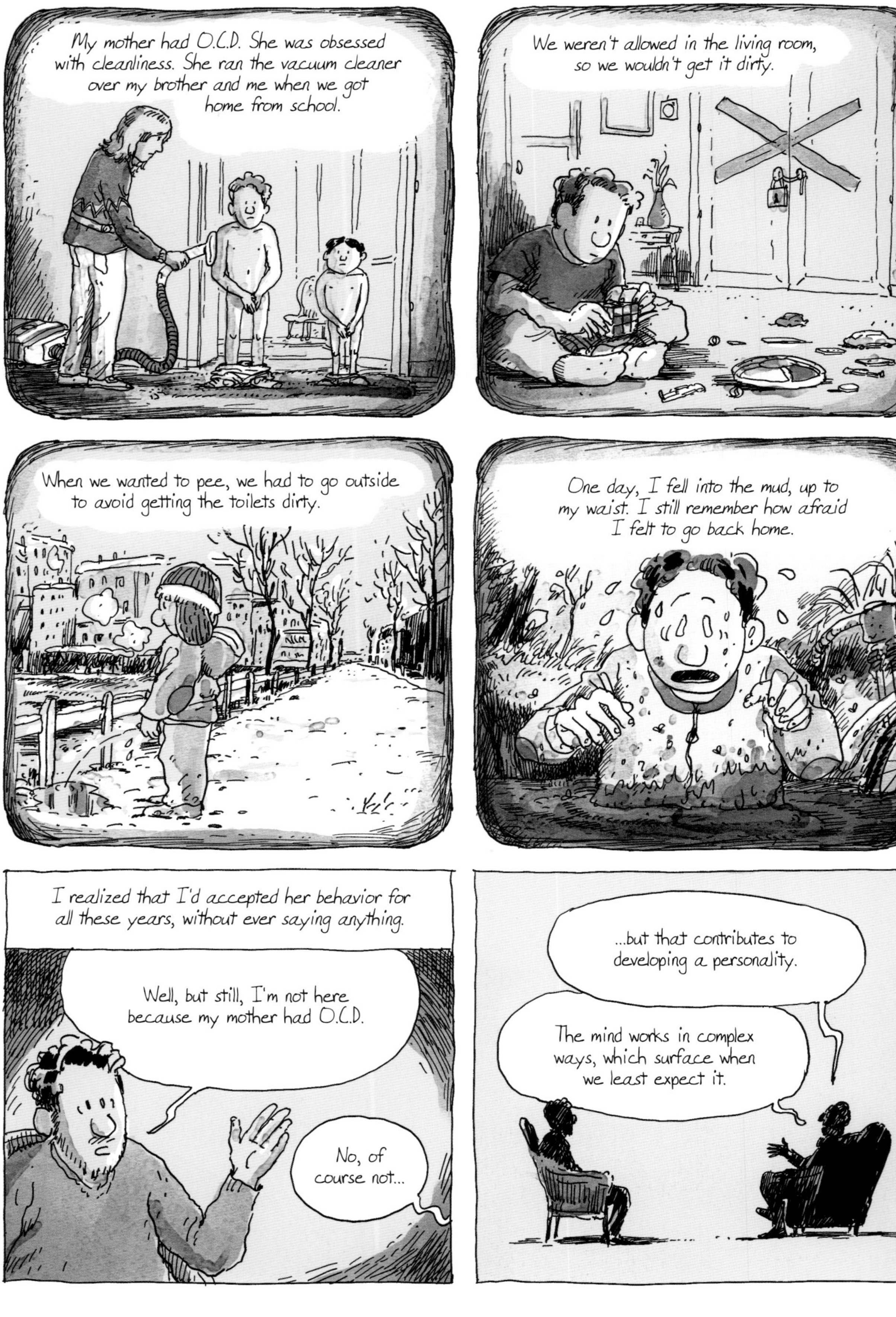
My mother had O.C.D. She was obsessed with cleanliness. She ran the vacuum cleaner over my brother and me when we got home from school.
We weren't allowed in the living room, so we wouldn't get it dirty.
When we wanted to pee, we had to go outside to avoid getting the toilets dirty.
One day, I fell into the mud, up to my waist. I still remember how afraid I felt to go back home.
I realized that I'd accepted her behavior for all these years, without ever saying anything.
Well, but still, I'm not here because my mother had O.C.D.
No, of course not...
...but that contributes to developing a personality.
The mind works in complex ways, which surface when we least expect it.

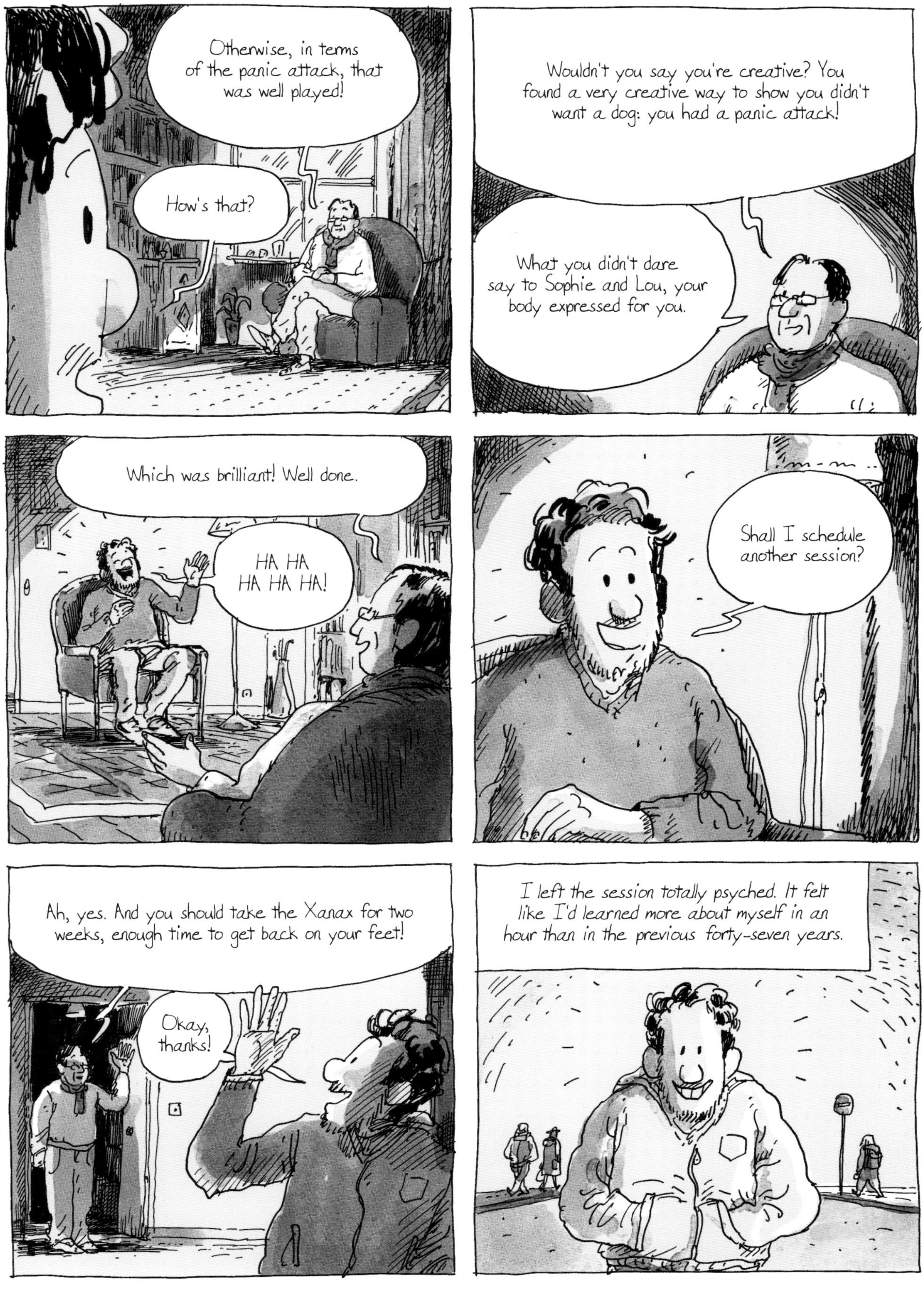
Otherwise, in terms of the panic attack, that was well played!
How's that?
Wouldn't you say you're creative? You found a very creative way to show you didn't want a dog: you had a panic attack!
What you didn't dare say to Sophie and Lou, your body expressed for you.
Which was brilliant! Well done.
HA HA HA HA HA!
Shall I schedule another session?
Ah, yes. And you should take the Xanax for two weeks, enough time to get back on your feet!
Okay, thanks!
I left the session totally psyched. It felt like I'd learned more about myself in an hour than in the previous forty-seven years.

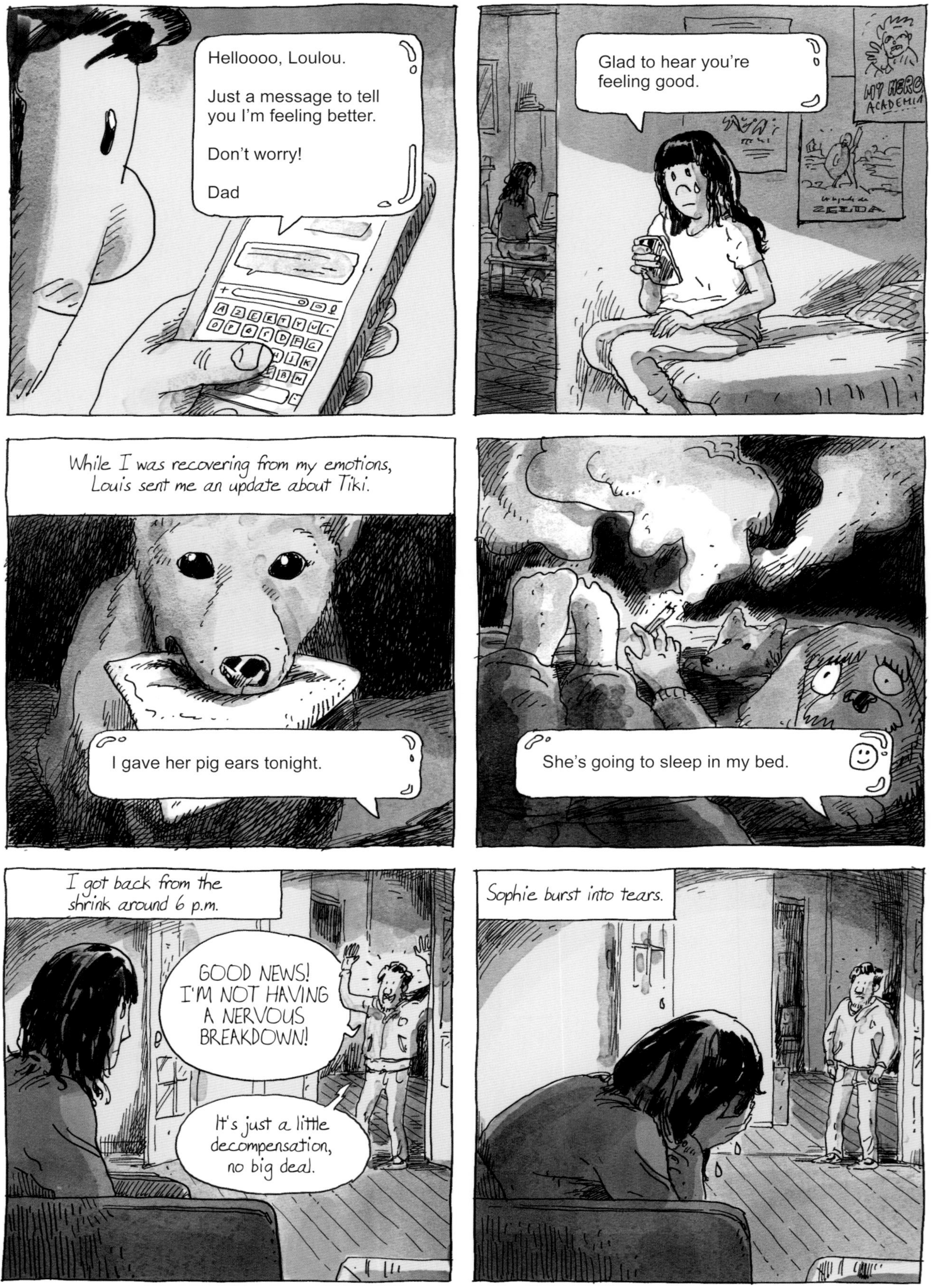
Helloooo, Loulou.
Just a message to tell you I'm feeling better.
Don't worry!
Dad
MY HERO ACADEMIA
ZELDA
Glad to hear you're feeling good.
While I was recovering from my emotions, Louis sent me an update about Tiki.
I gave her pig ears tonight.
She's going to sleep in my bed.
I got back from the shrink around 6 p.m.
GOOD NEWS! I'M NOT HAVING A NERVOUS BREAKDOWN!
It's just a little decompensation, no big deal.
Sophie burst into tears.

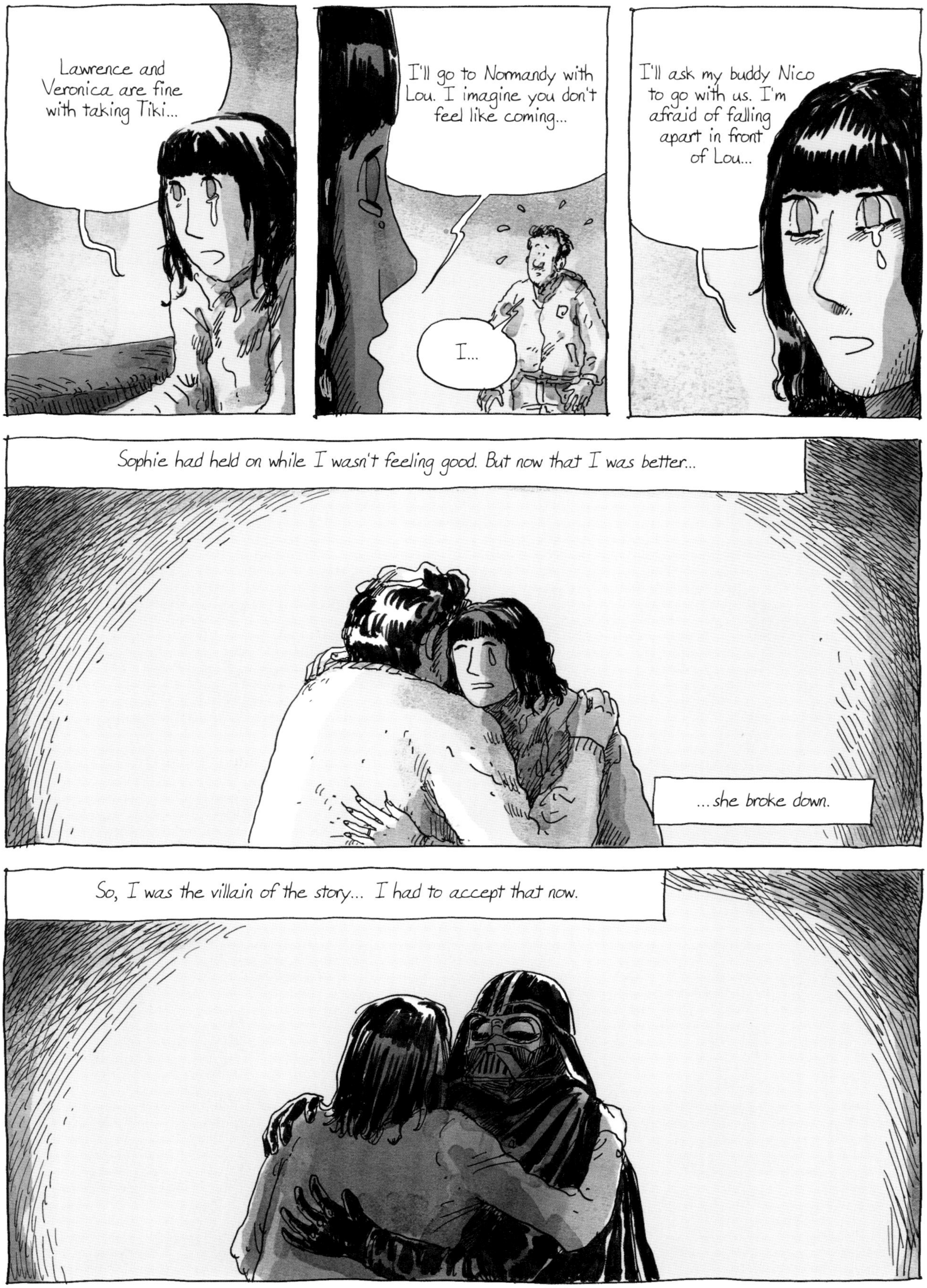

Lawrence and Veronica are fine with taking Tiki...
I'll go to Normandy with Lou. I imagine you don't feel like coming...
I...
I'll ask my buddy Nico to go with us. I'm afraid of falling apart in front of Lou...
Sophie had held on while I wasn't feeling good. But now that I was better...
...she broke down.
So, I was the villain of the story... I had to accept that now.

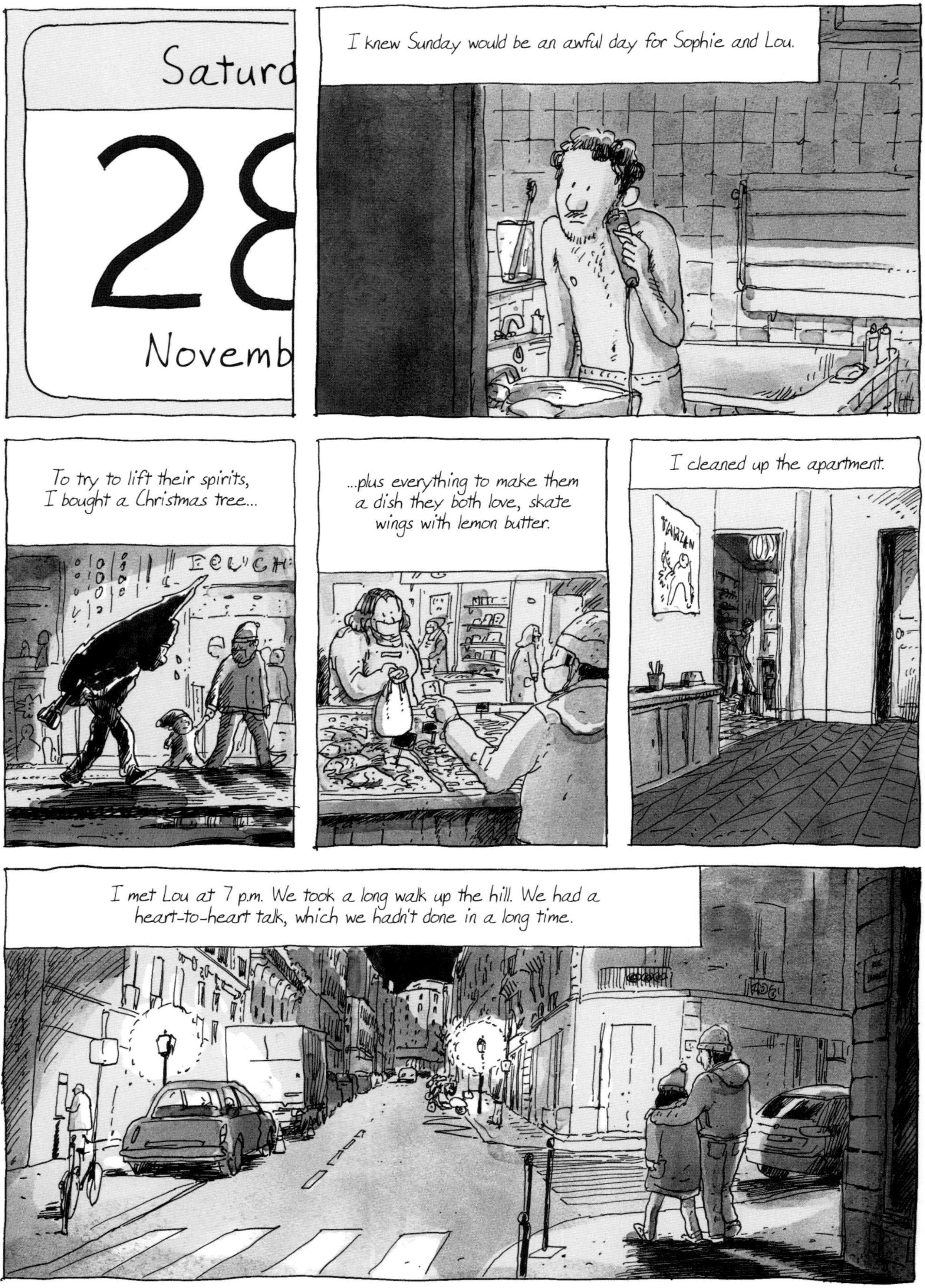
Saturd
28
Novemb
I knew Sunday would be an awful day for Sophie and Lou.
To try to lift their spirits, I bought a Christmas tree...
...plus everything to make them a dish they both love, skate wings with lemon butter.
I cleaned up the apartment.
TARZAN
I met Lou at 7 p.m. We took a long walk up the hill. We had a heart-to-heart talk, which we hadn't done in a long time.

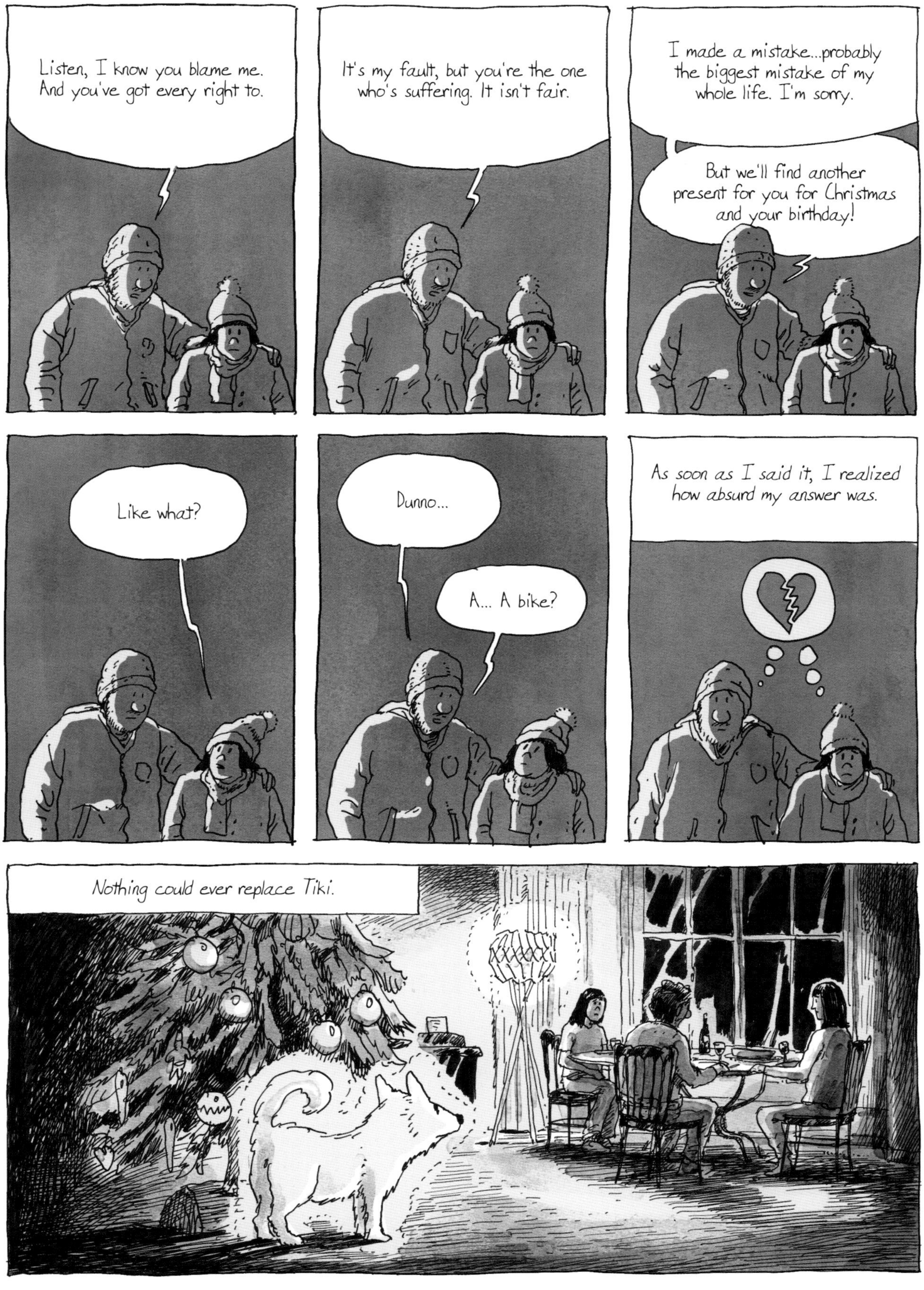
Listen, I know you blame me. And you've got every right to.
It's my fault, but you're the one who's suffering. It isn't fair.
I made a mistake...probably the biggest mistake of my whole life. I'm sorry.
But we'll find another present for you for Christmas and your birthday!
Like what?
Dunno...
A... A bike?
As soon as I said it, I realized how absurd my answer was.
Nothing could ever replace Tiki.

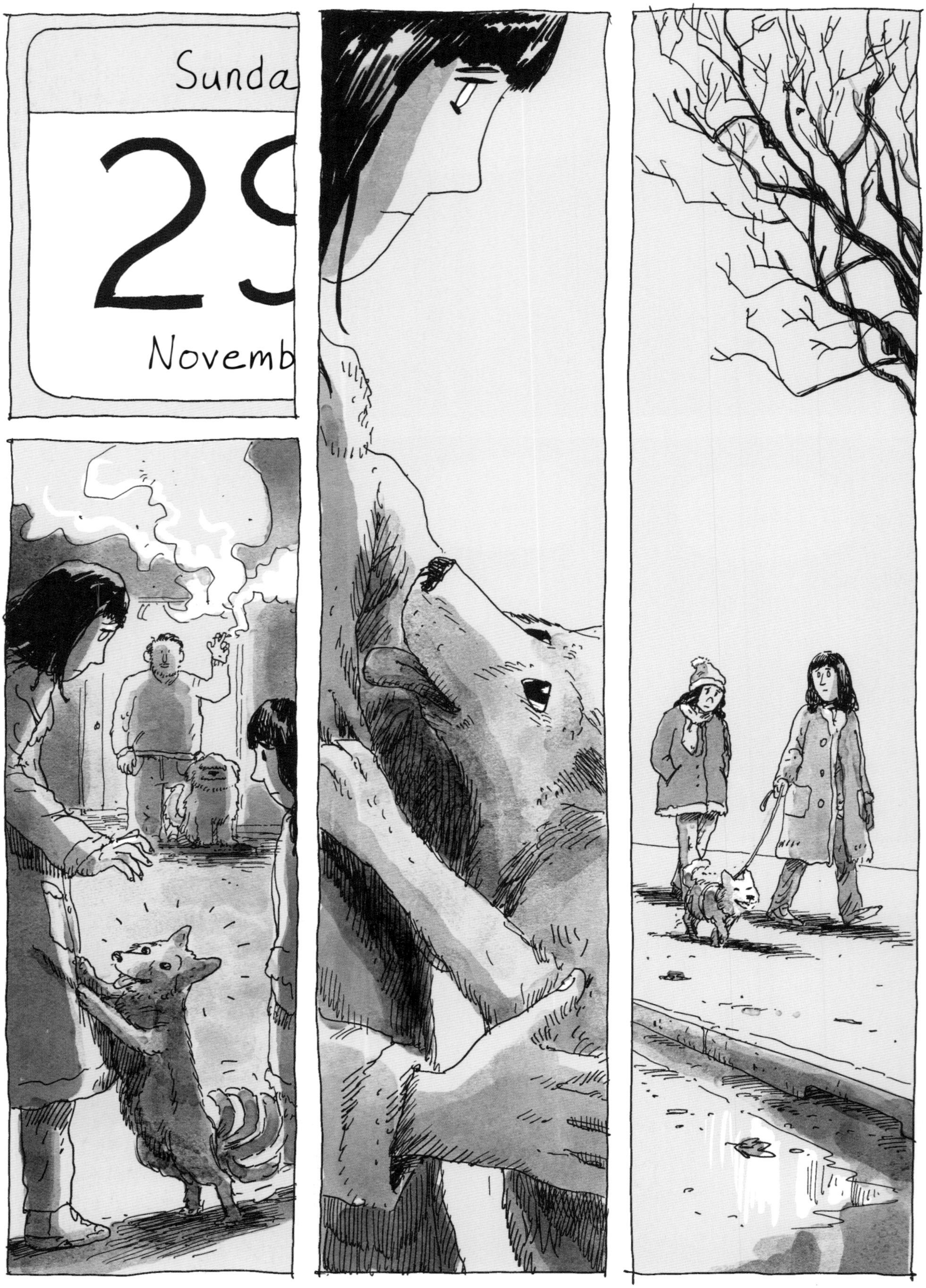
Sunda
29
Novemb

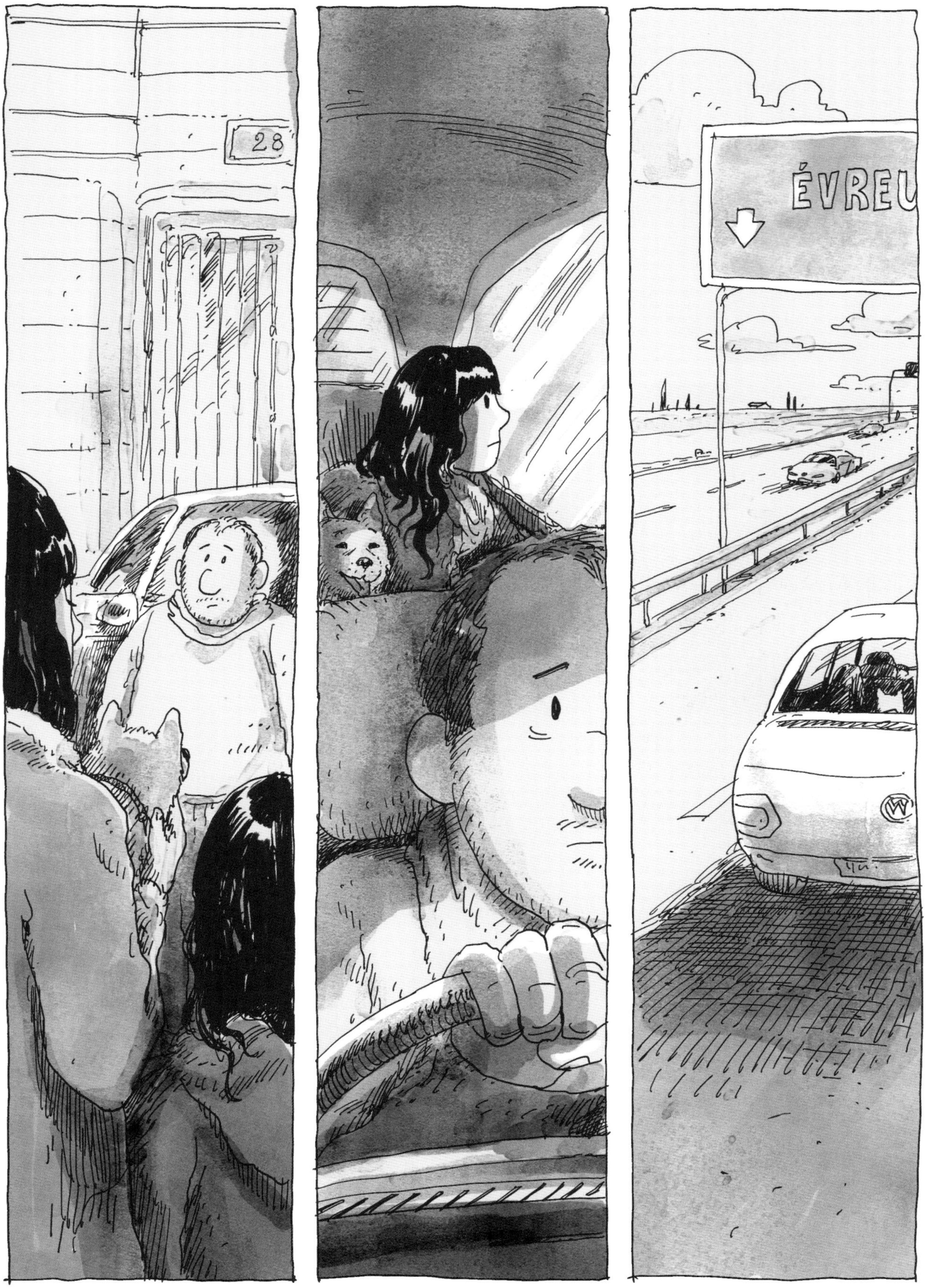
28
ÉVREU

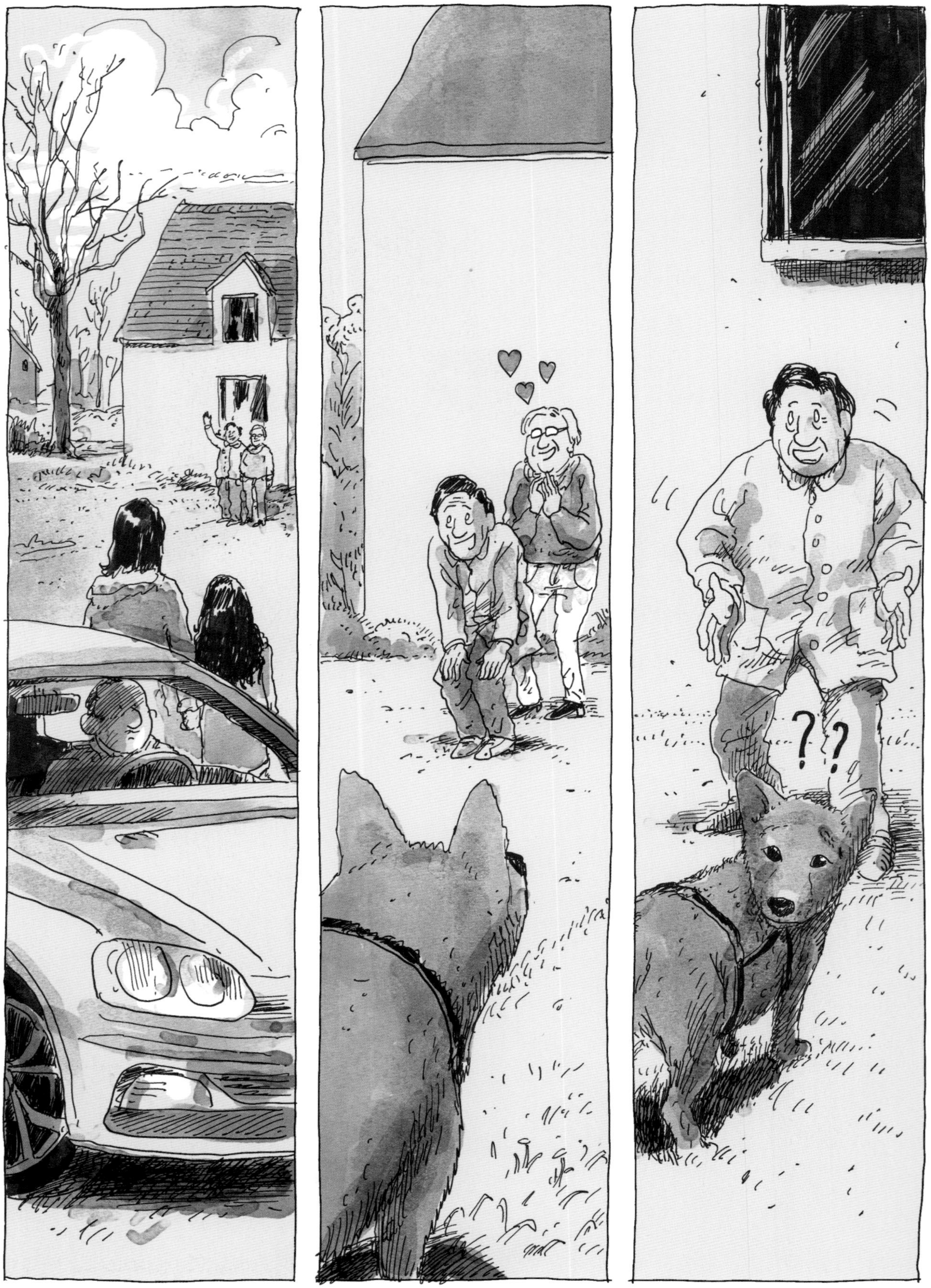
??

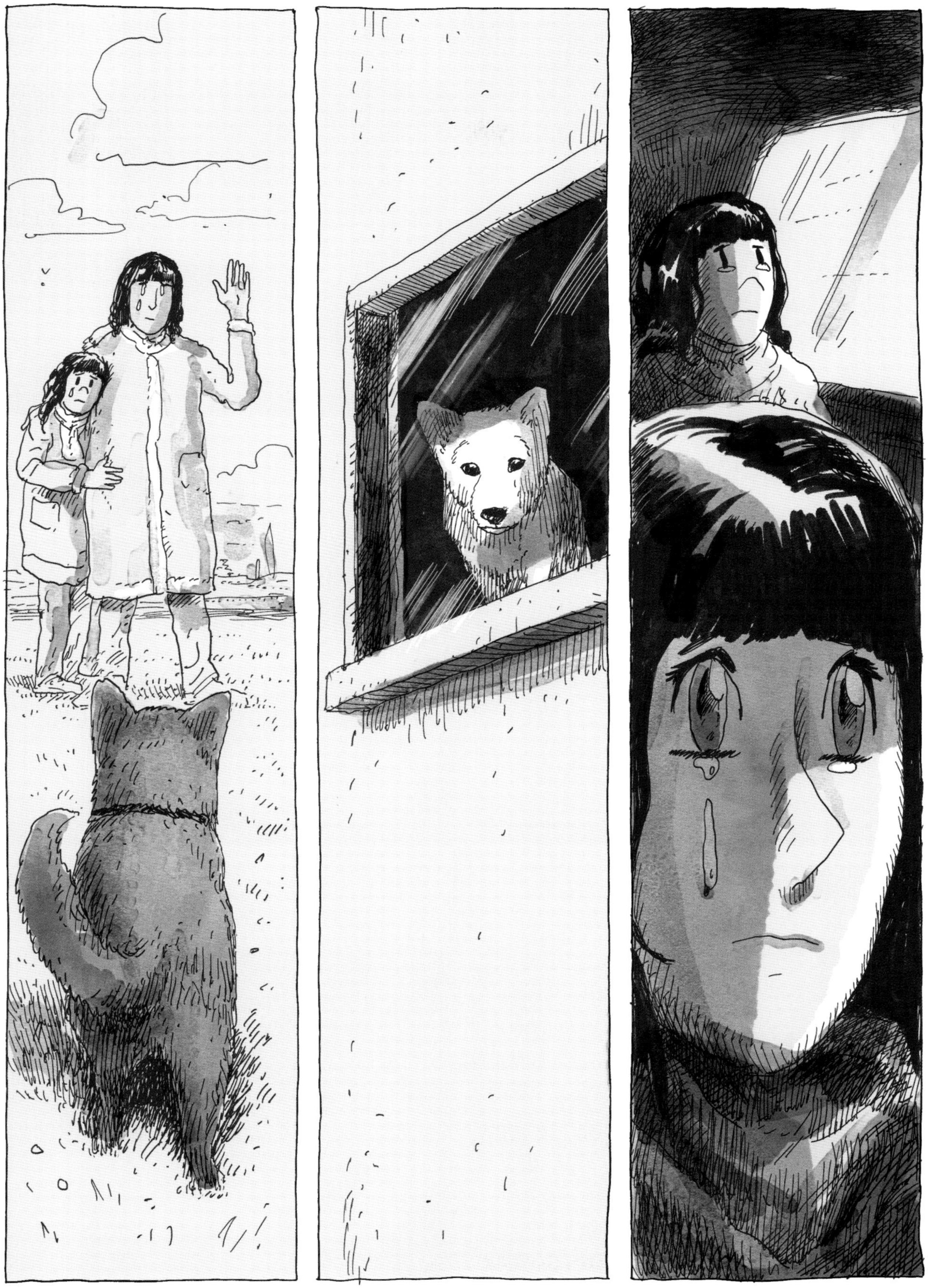

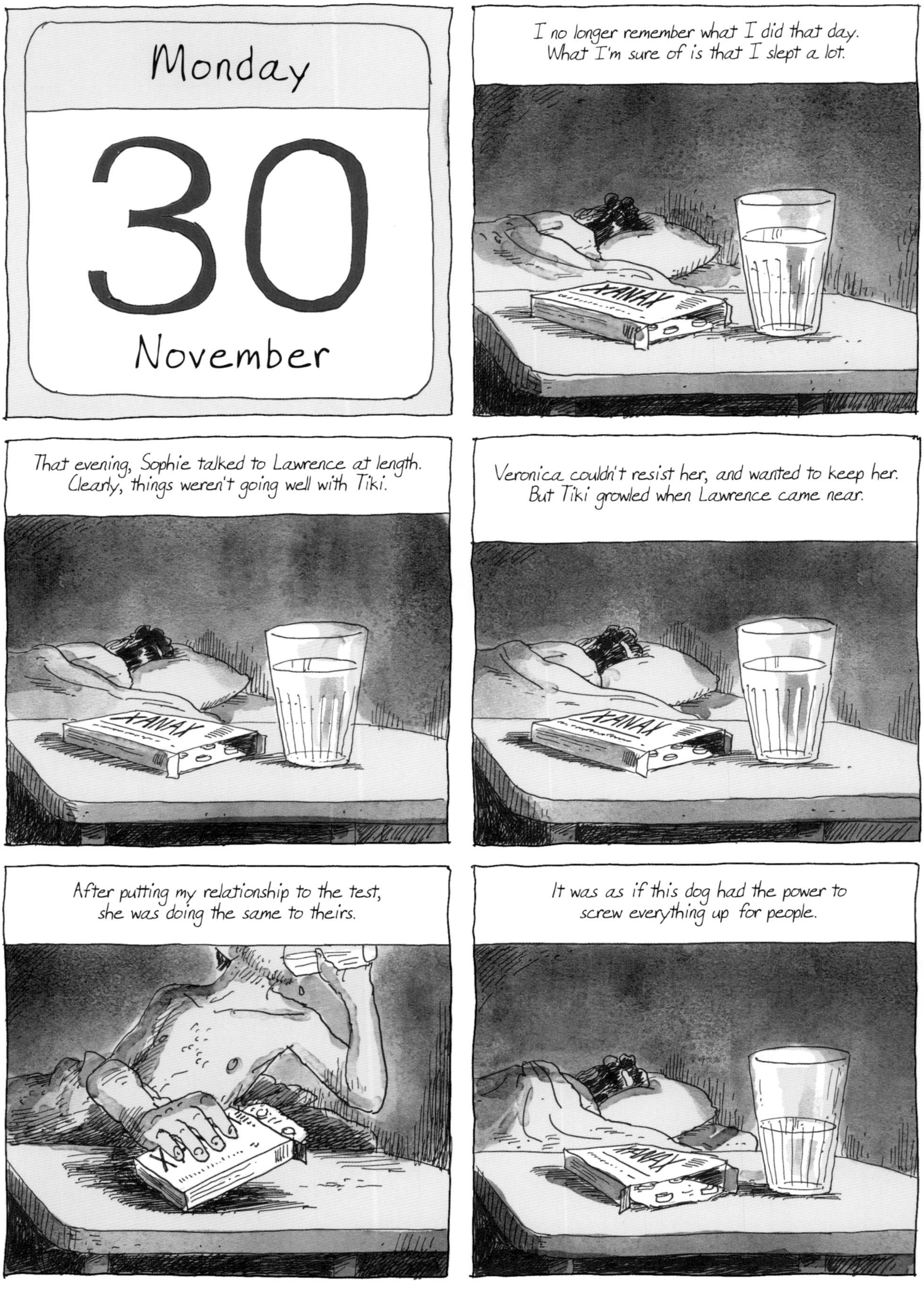

Monday
30
November
I no longer remember what I did that day. What I'm sure of is that I slept a lot.
XANAX
That evening, Sophie talked to Lawrence at length. Clearly, things weren't going well with Tiki.
XANAX
Veronica couldn't resist her, and wanted to keep her. But Tiki growled when Lawrence came near.
XANAX
After putting my relationship to the test, she was doing the same to theirs.
It was as if this dog had the power to screw everything up for people.
XANAX

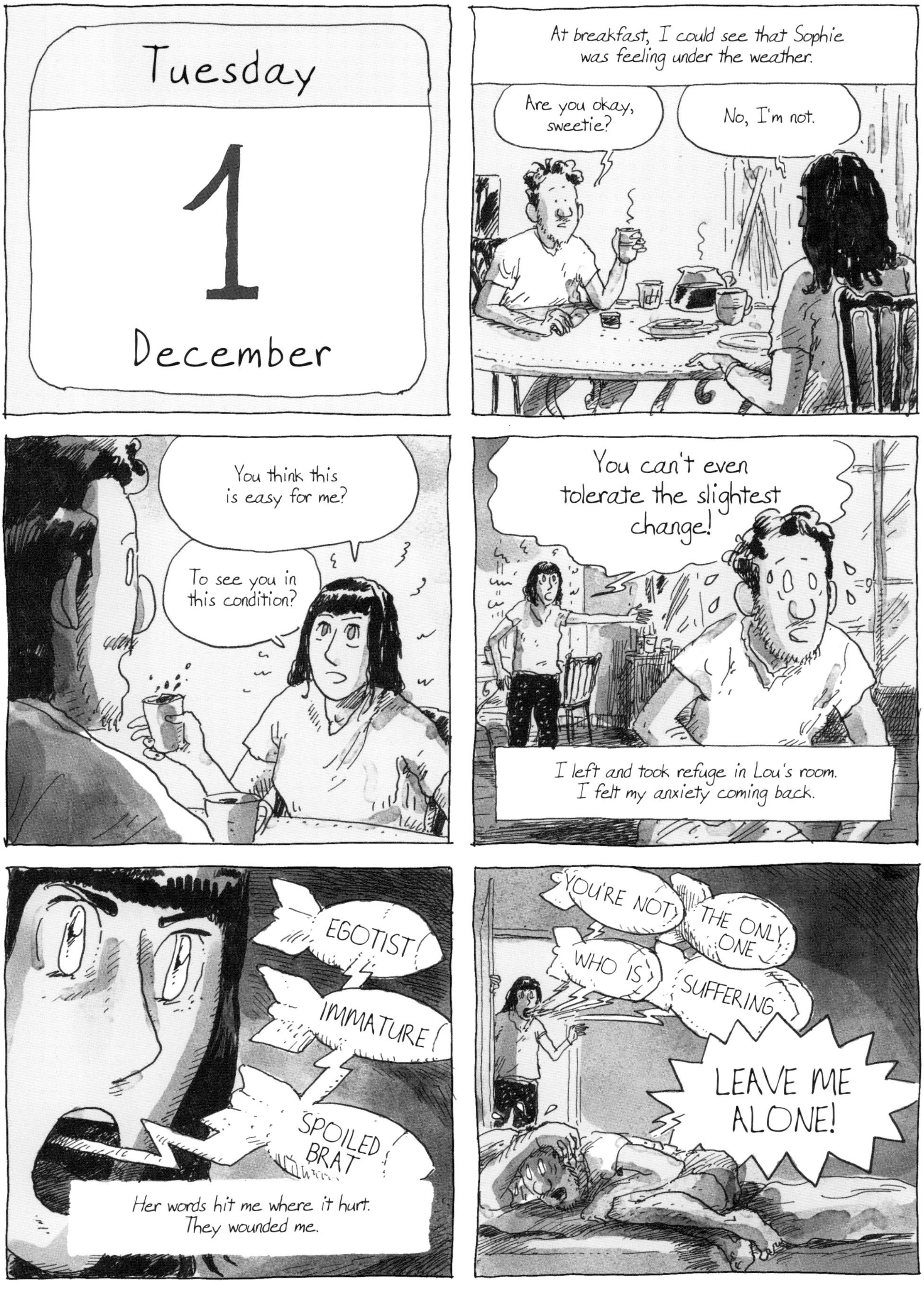
Tuesday
1
December
At breakfast, I could see that Sophie was feeling under the weather.
Are you okay, sweetie?
No, I'm not.
You think this is easy for me?
To see you in this condition?
You can't even tolerate the slightest change!
I left and took refuge in Lou's room. I felt my anxiety coming back.
EGOTIST
IMMATURE
SPOILED BRAT
Her words hit me where it hurt. They wounded me.
YOU'RE NOT THE ONLY ONE WHO IS SUFFERING
LEAVE ME ALONE!

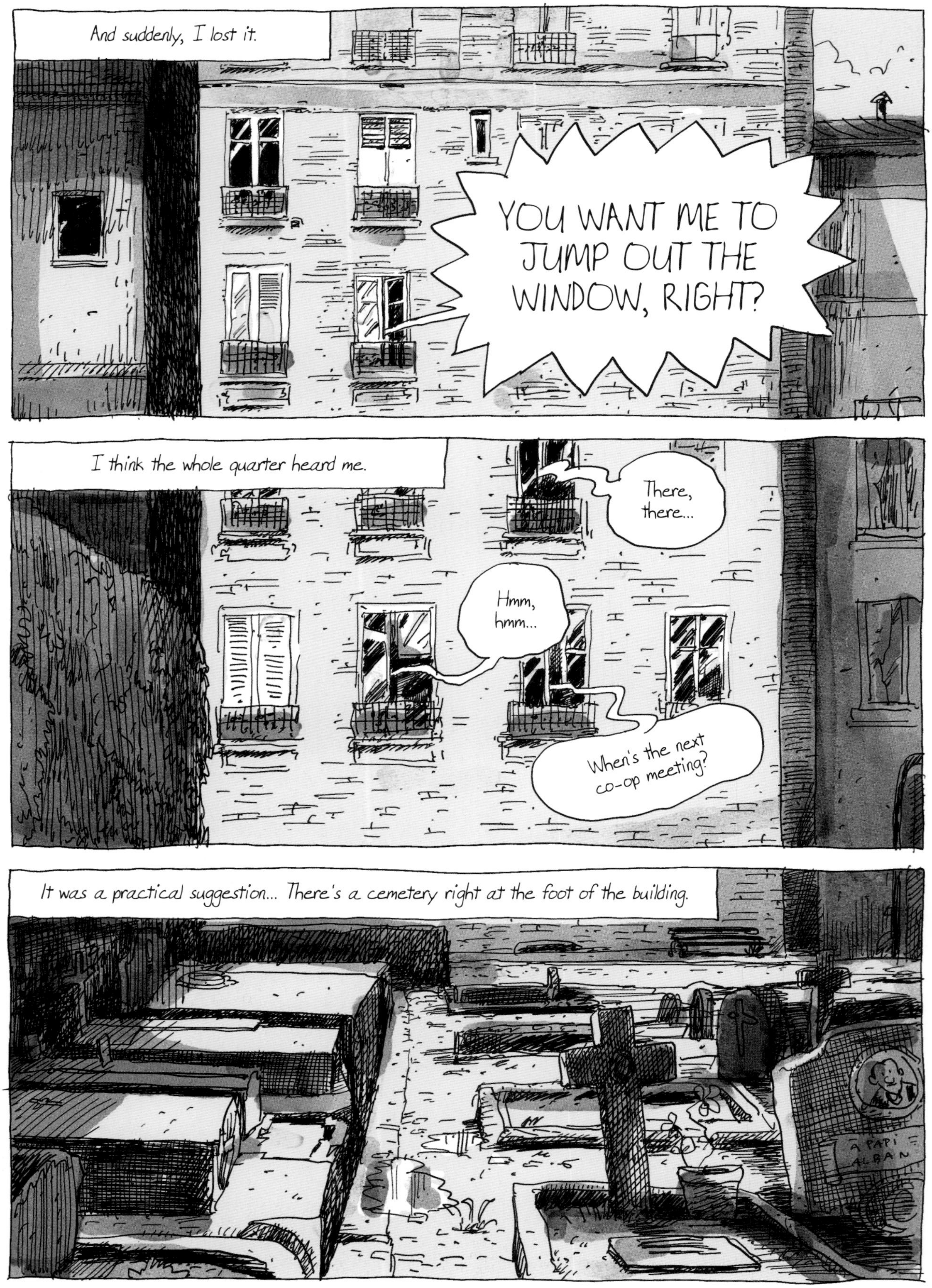
And suddenly, I lost it.
YOU WANT ME TO JUMP OUT THE WINDOW, RIGHT?
I think the whole quarter heard me.
There, there...
Hmm, hmm...
When's the next co-op meeting?
It was a practical suggestion... There's a cemetery right at the foot of the building.
A PAPI ALBAN

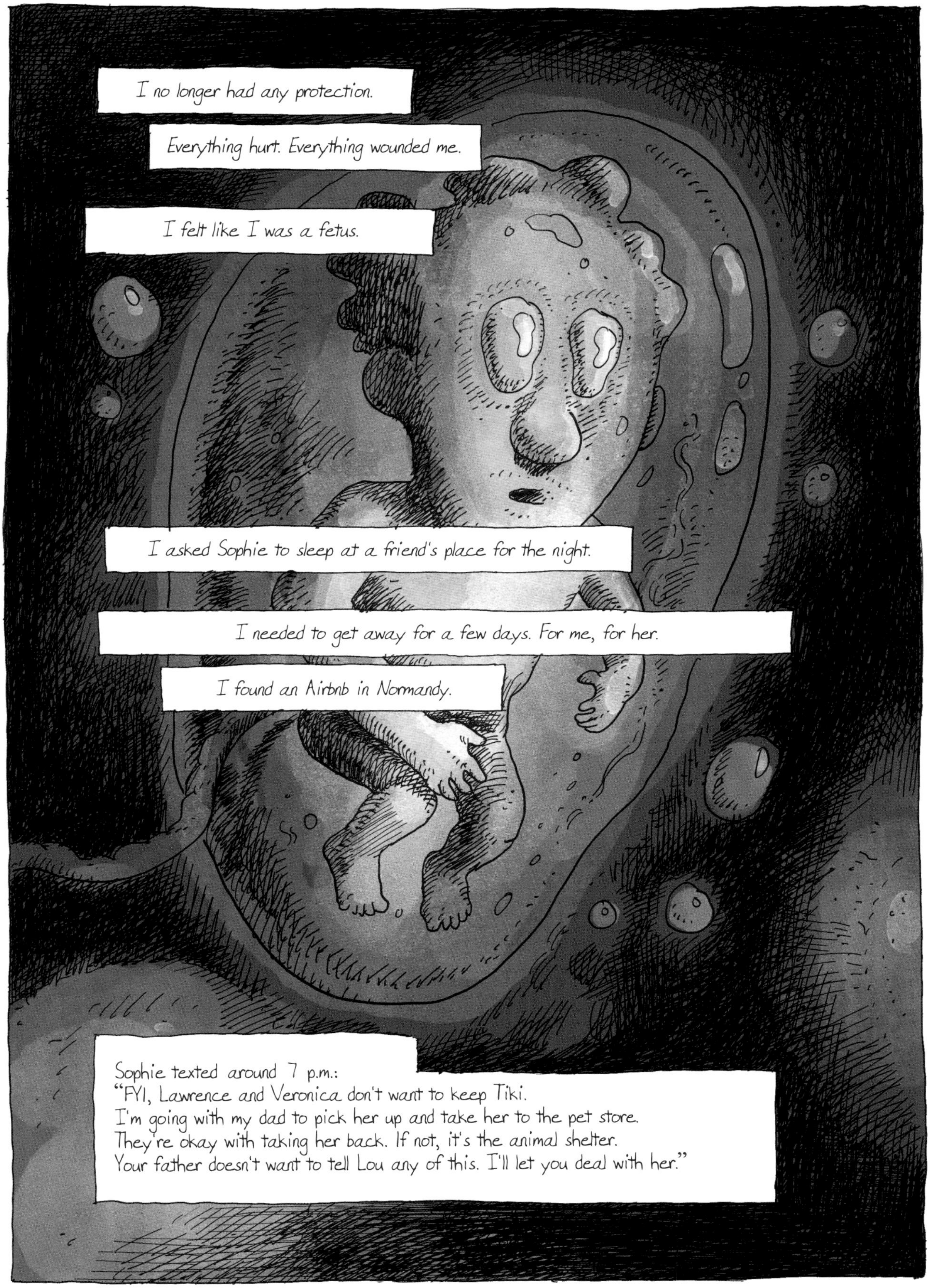
I no longer had any protection.
Everything hurt. Everything wounded me.
I felt like I was a fetus.
I asked Sophie to sleep at a friend's place for the night.
I needed to get away for a few days. For me, for her.
I found an Airbnb in Normandy.
Sophie texted around 7 p.m.: "FYI, Lawrence and Veronica don't want to keep Tiki. I'm going with my dad to pick her up and take her to the pet store. They're okay with taking her back. If not, it's the animal shelter. Your father doesn't want to tell Lou any of this. I'll let you deal with her."

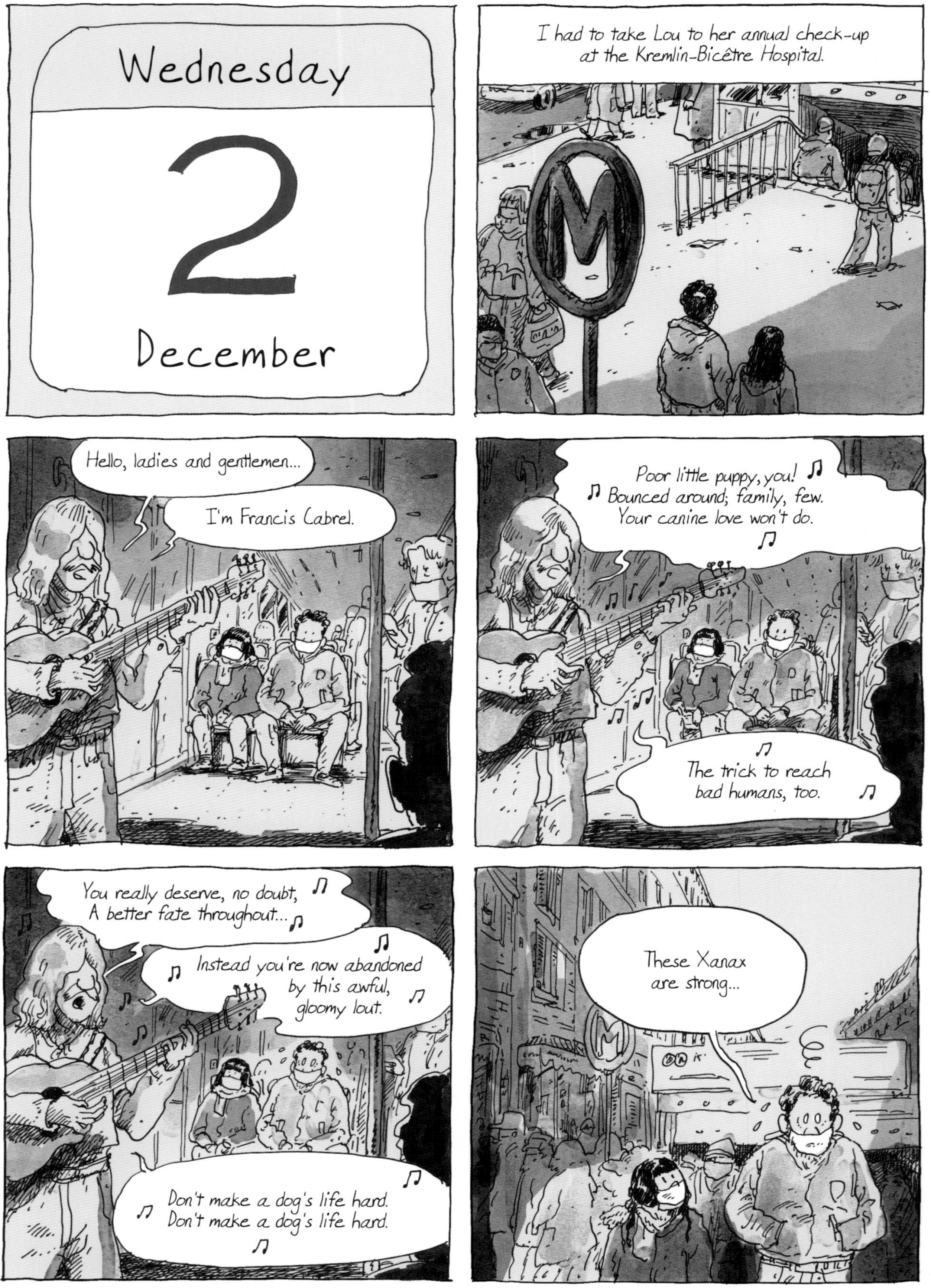
Wednesday
2
December
I had to take Lou to her annual check-up at the Kremlin-Bicêtre Hospital.
Hello, ladies and gentlemen...
I'm Francis Cabrel.
Poor little puppy, you! Bounced around; family, few. Your canine love won't do.
The trick to reach bad humans, too.
You really deserve, no doubt, A better fate throughout...
Instead you're now abandoned by this awful, gloomy lout.
Don't make a dog's life hard. Don't make a dog's life hard.
These Xanax are strong...

ADMISSIONS
Sophie
New message
I'll never forgive myself for having added insult to injury. I hurt you when you were down. You're my love, my soulmate, my double...
I'm done, Dad.
Come on, let's go home.

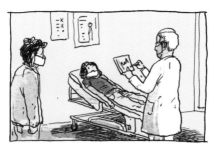

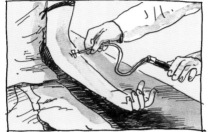

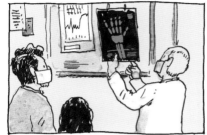

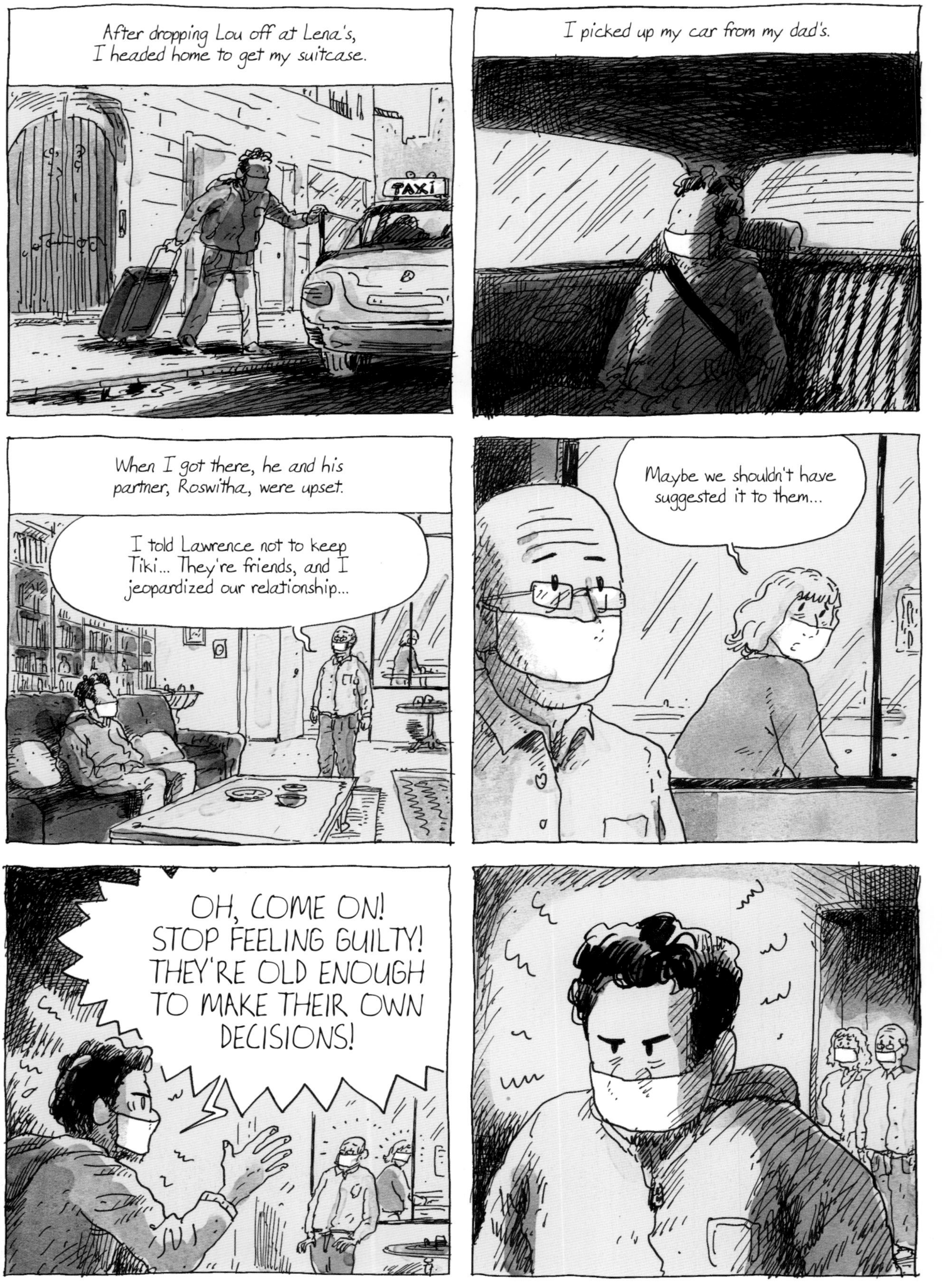
After dropping Lou off at Lena's, I headed home to get my suitcase.
TAXI
I picked up my car from my dad's.
When I got there, he and his partner, Roswitha, were upset.
I told Lawrence not to keep Tiki... They're friends, and I jeopardized our relationship...
Maybe we shouldn't have suggested it to them...
OH, COME ON! STOP FEELING GUILTY! THEY'RE OLD ENOUGH TO MAKE THEIR OWN DECISIONS!

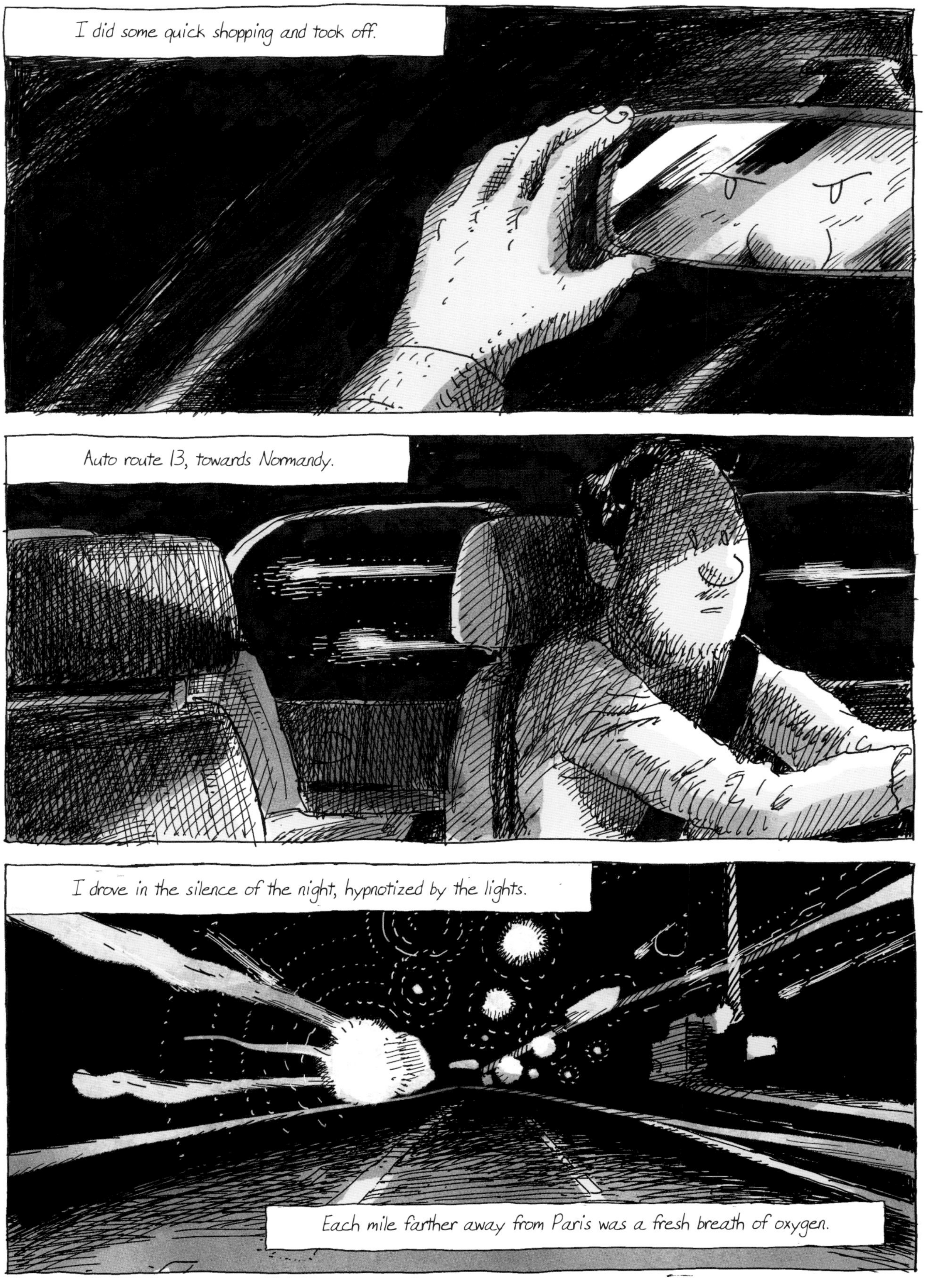
I did some quick shopping and took off.
Auto route 13, towards Normandy.
I drove in the silence of the night, hypnotized by the lights.
Each mile farther away from Paris was a fresh breath of oxygen.

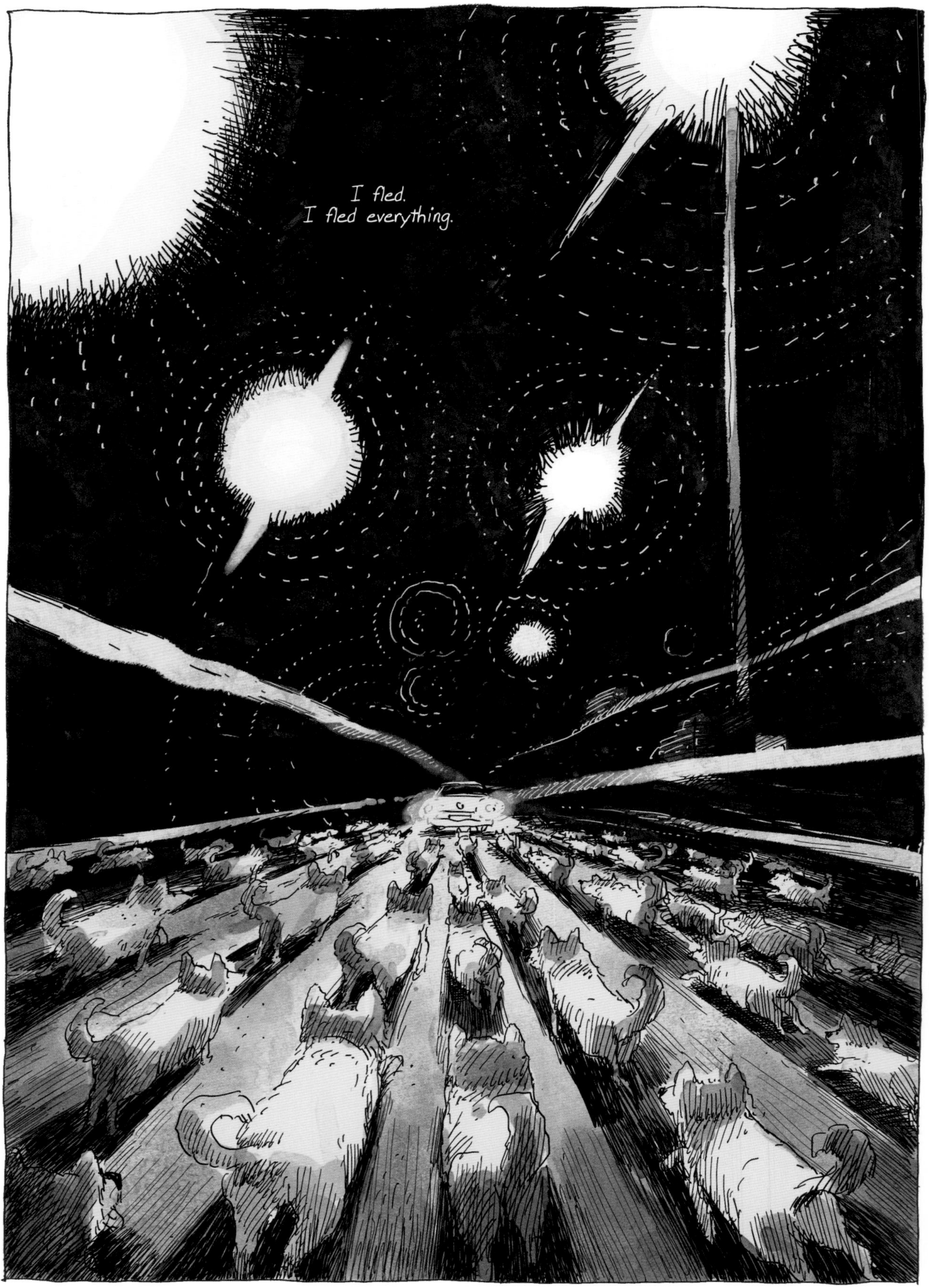
I fled.
I fled everything.

Chapter Six

Breathing

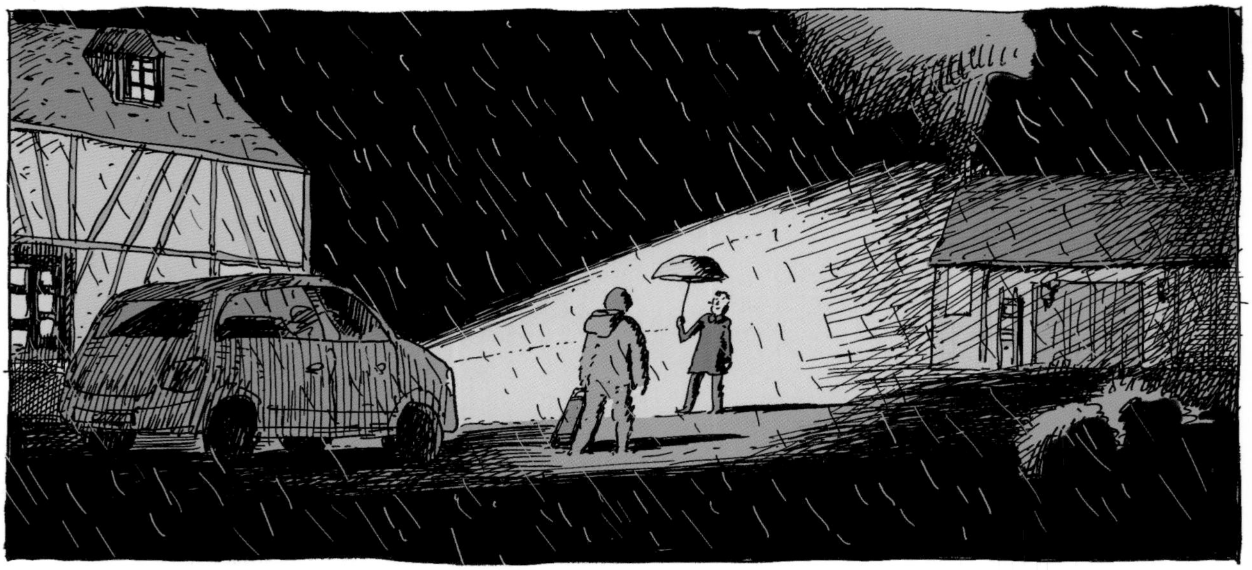

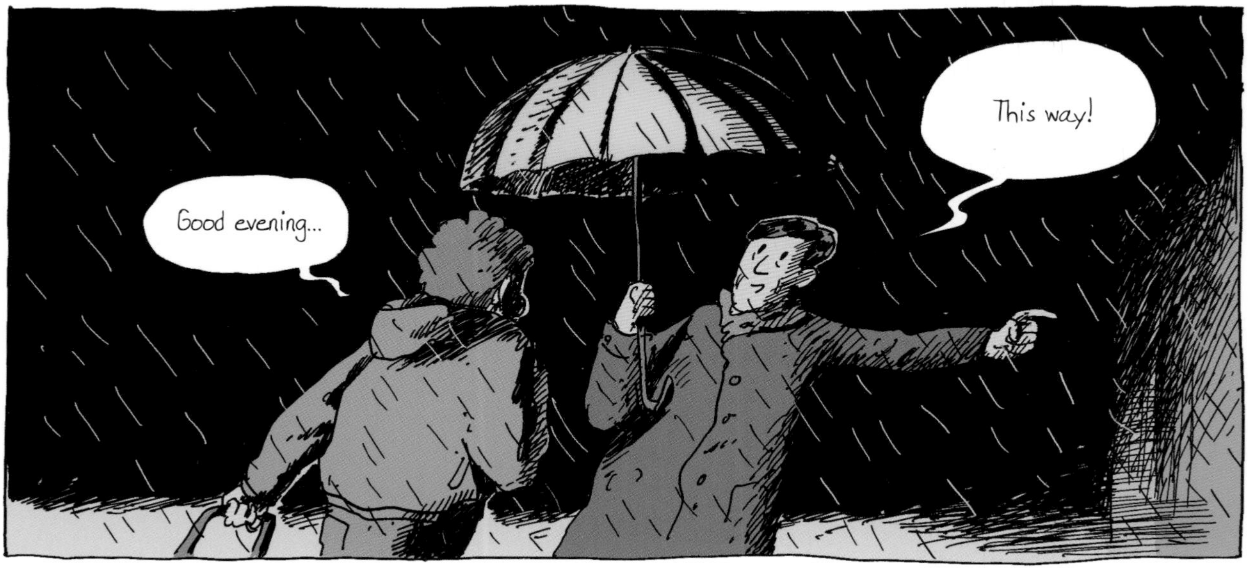
Good evening...
This way!

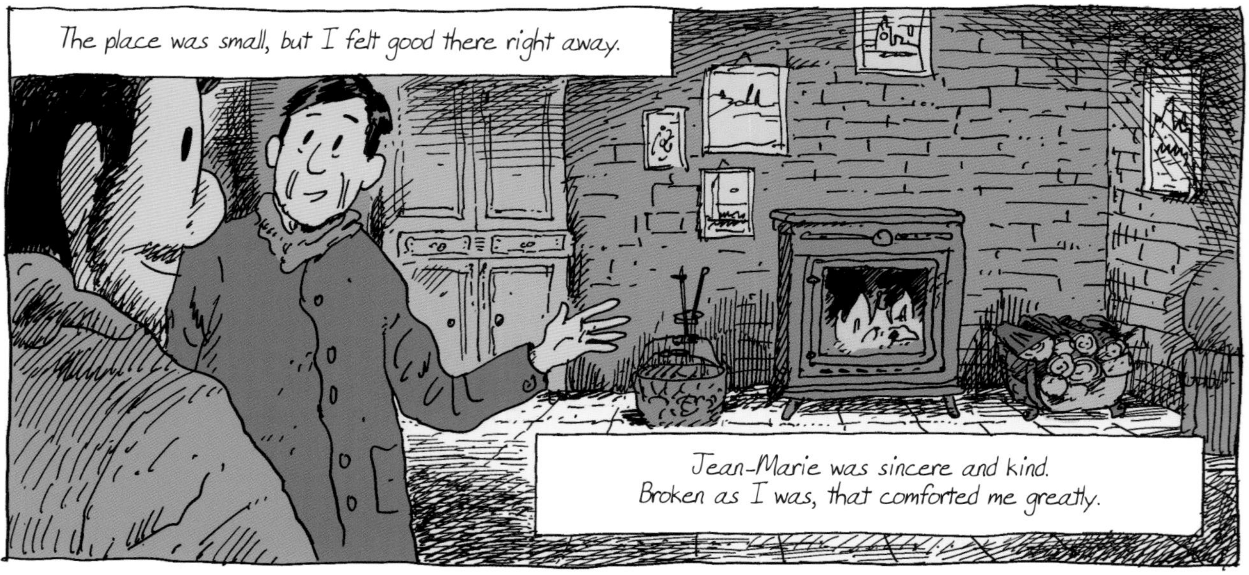
The place was small, but I felt good there right away.
Jean-Marie was sincere and kind.
Broken as I was, that comforted me greatly.

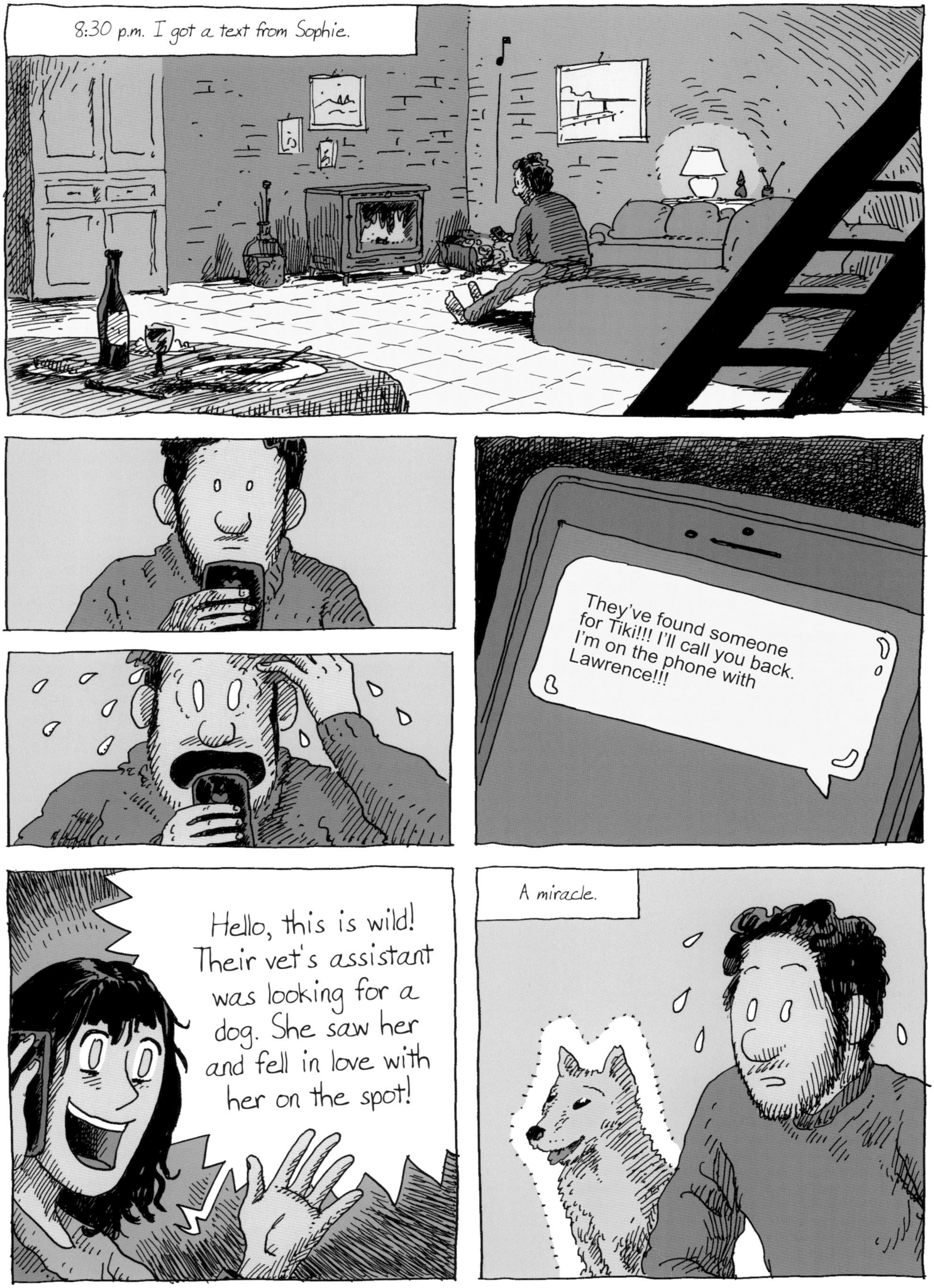
8:30 p.m. I got a text from Sophie.
They've found someone for Tiki!!! I'll call you back. I'm on the phone with Lawrence!!!
Hello, this is wild! Their vet's assistant was looking for a dog. She saw her and fell in love with her on the spot!
A miracle.

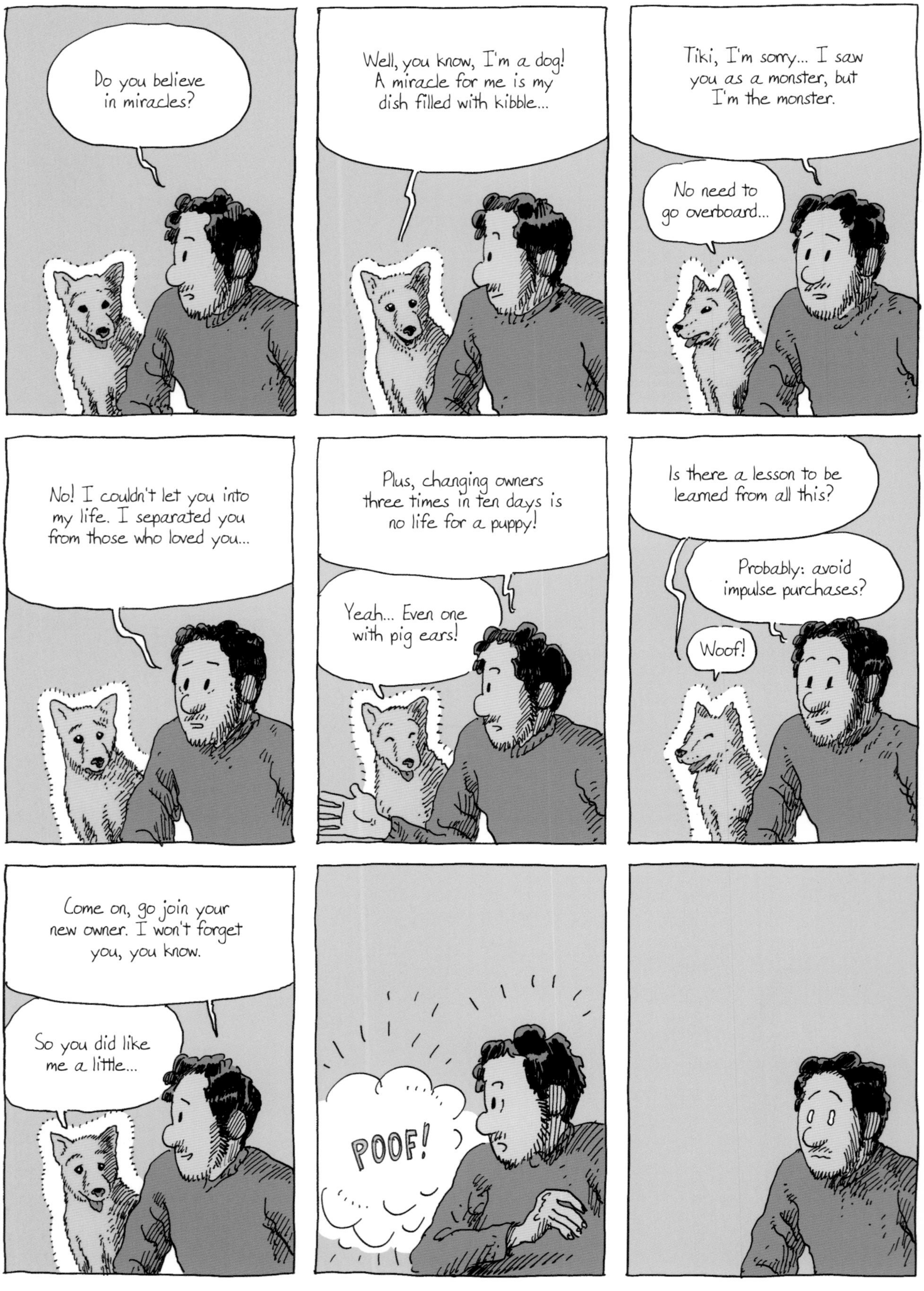
Do you believe in miracles?
Well, you know, I'm a dog! A miracle for me is my dish filled with kibble...
Tiki, I'm sorry... I saw you as a monster, but I'm the monster.
No need to go overboard...
No! I couldn't let you into my life. I separated you from those who loved you...
Plus, changing owners three times in ten days is no life for a puppy!
Yeah... Even one with pig ears!
Is there a lesson to be learned from all this?
Probably: avoid impulse purchases?
Woof!
Come on, go join your new owner. I won't forget you, you know.
So you did like me a little...
POOF!

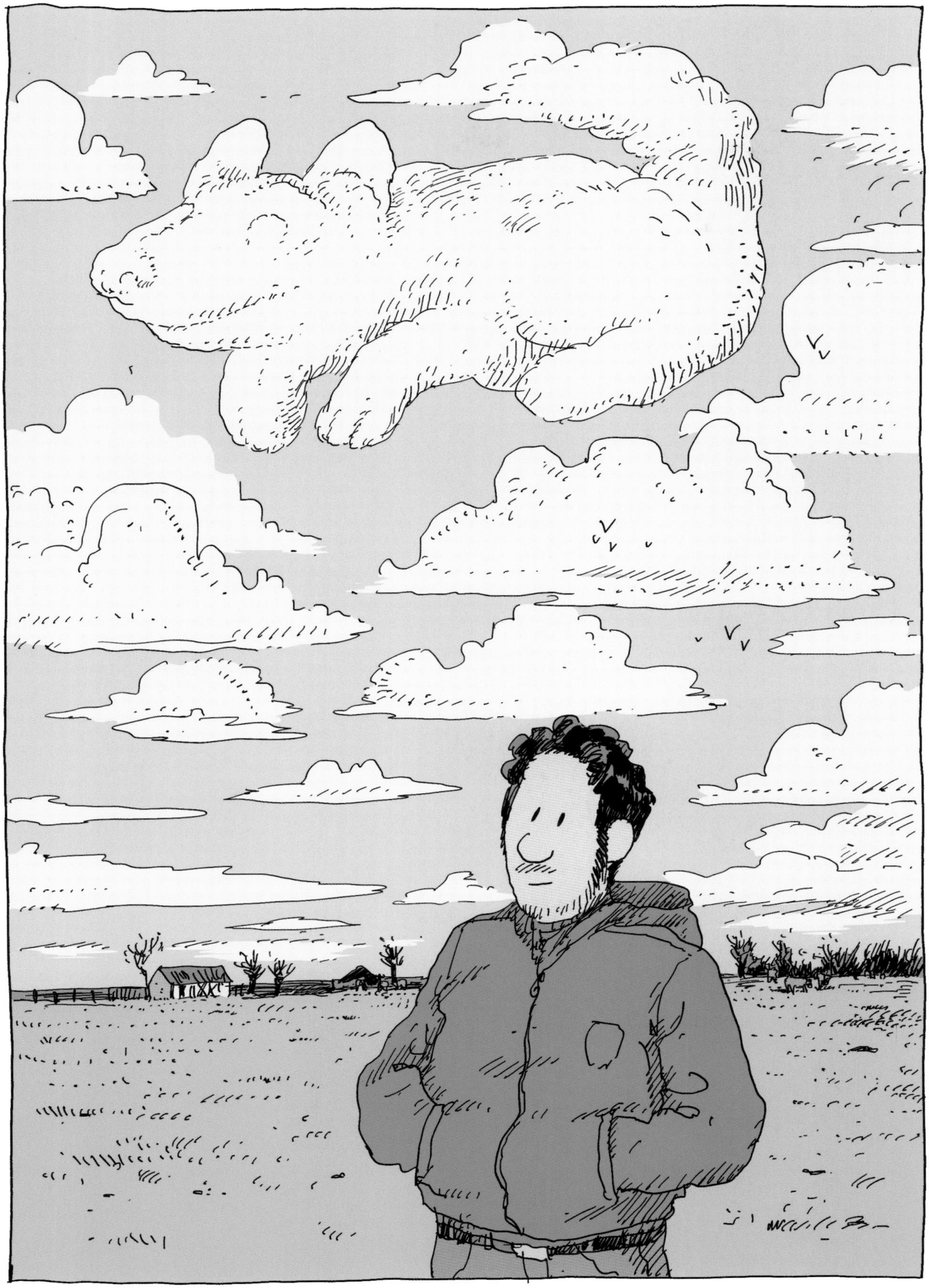

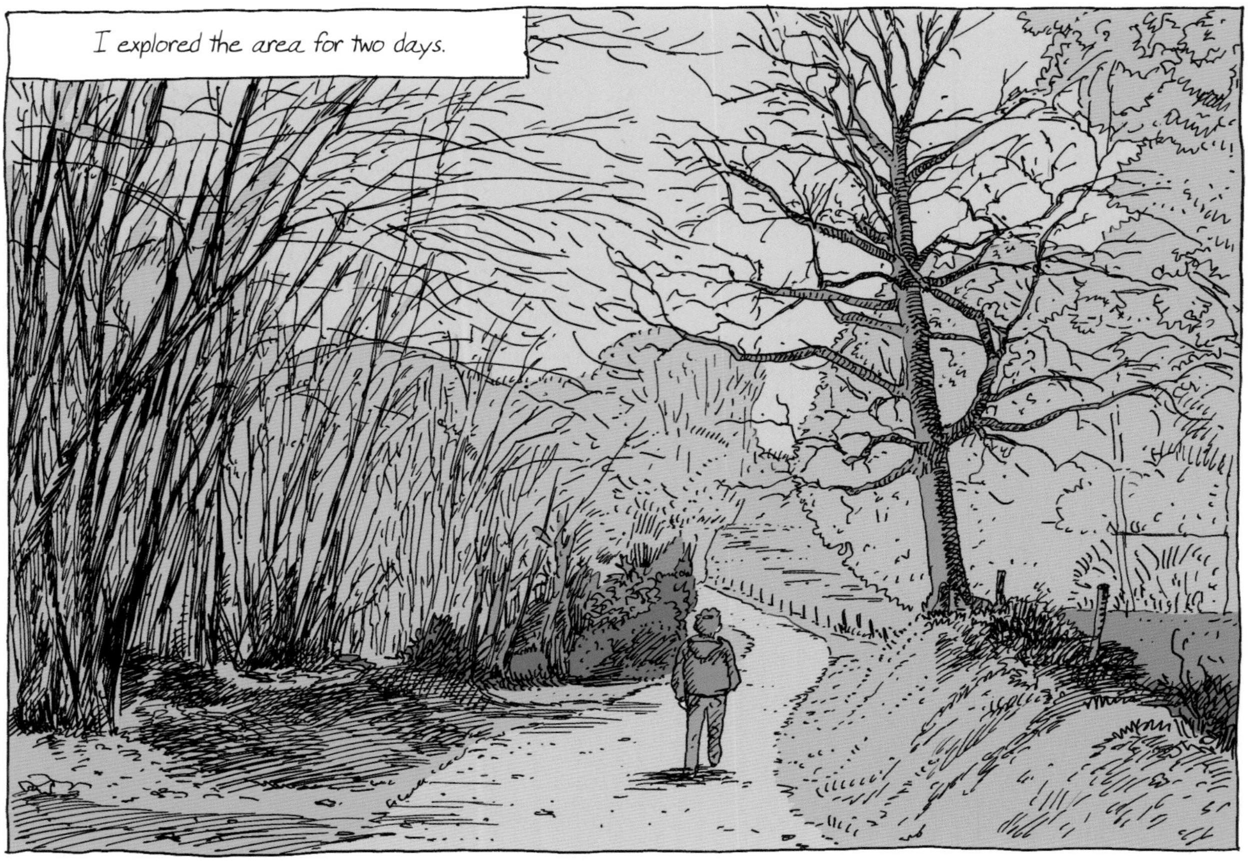
I explored the area for two days.

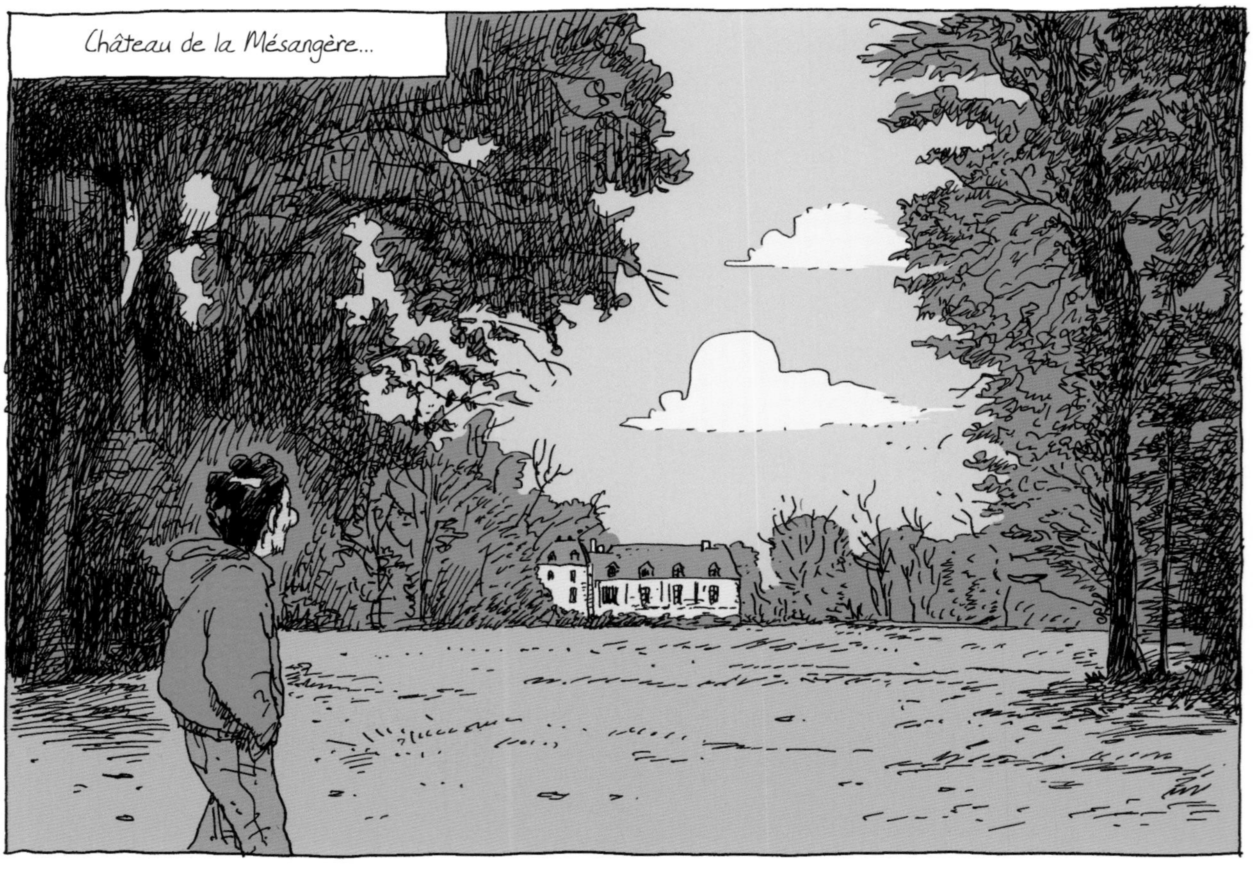
Château de la Mésangère...

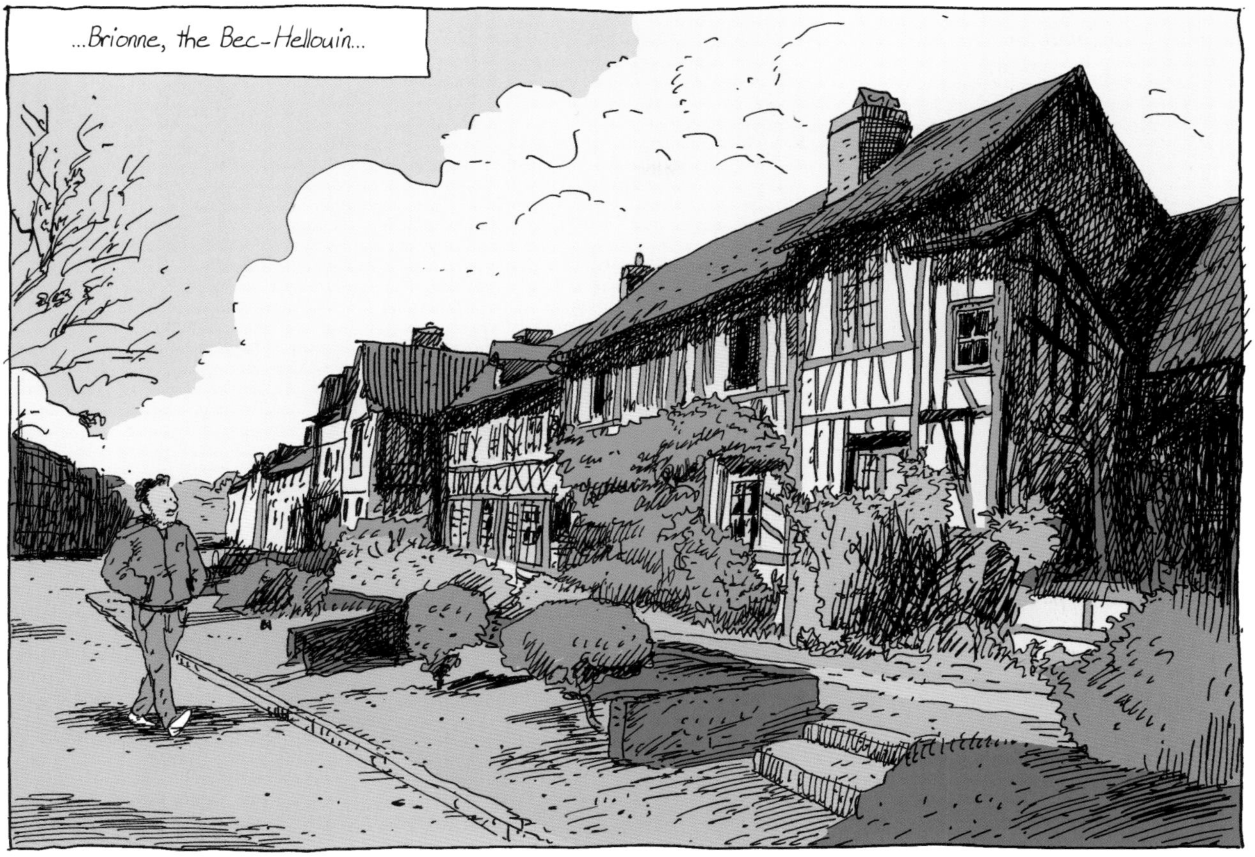
...Brionne, the Bec-Hellouin...

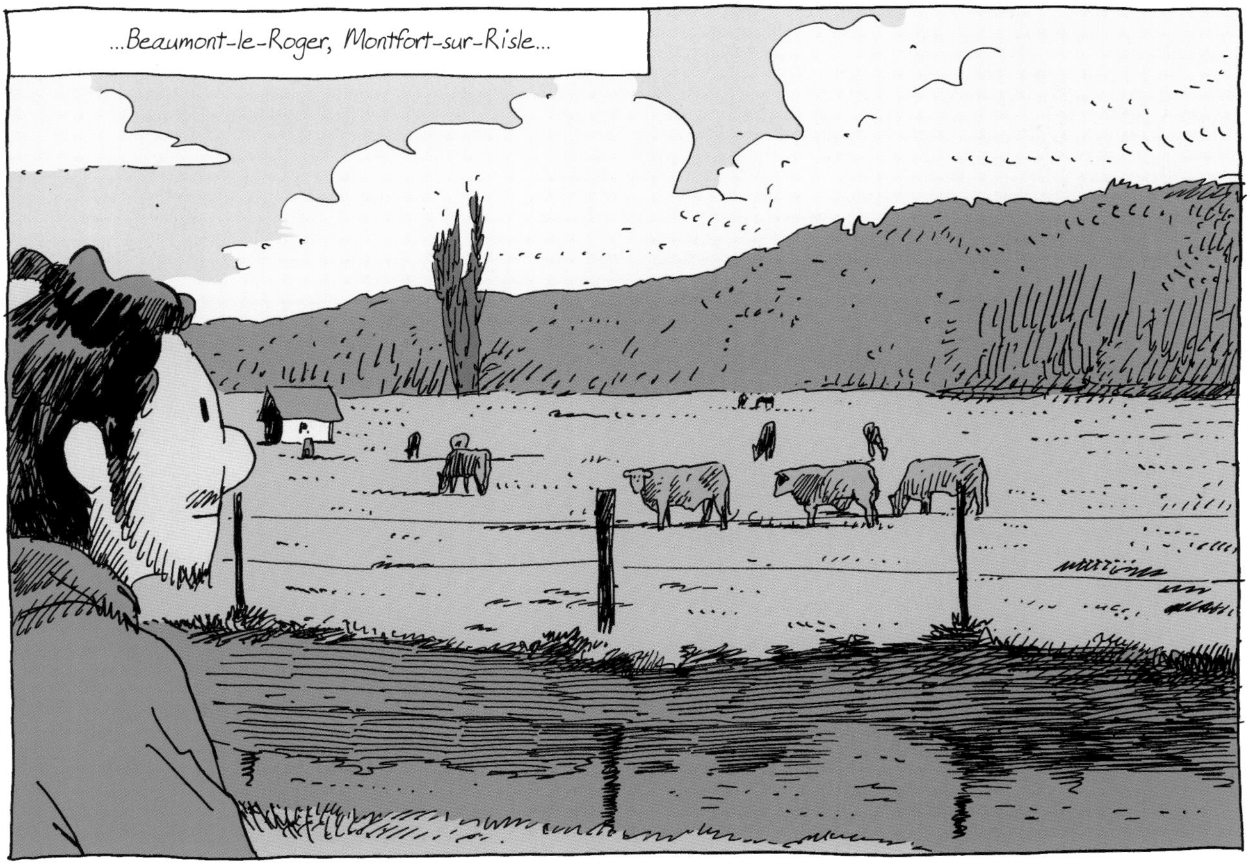
...Beaumont-le-Roger, Montfort-sur-Risle...

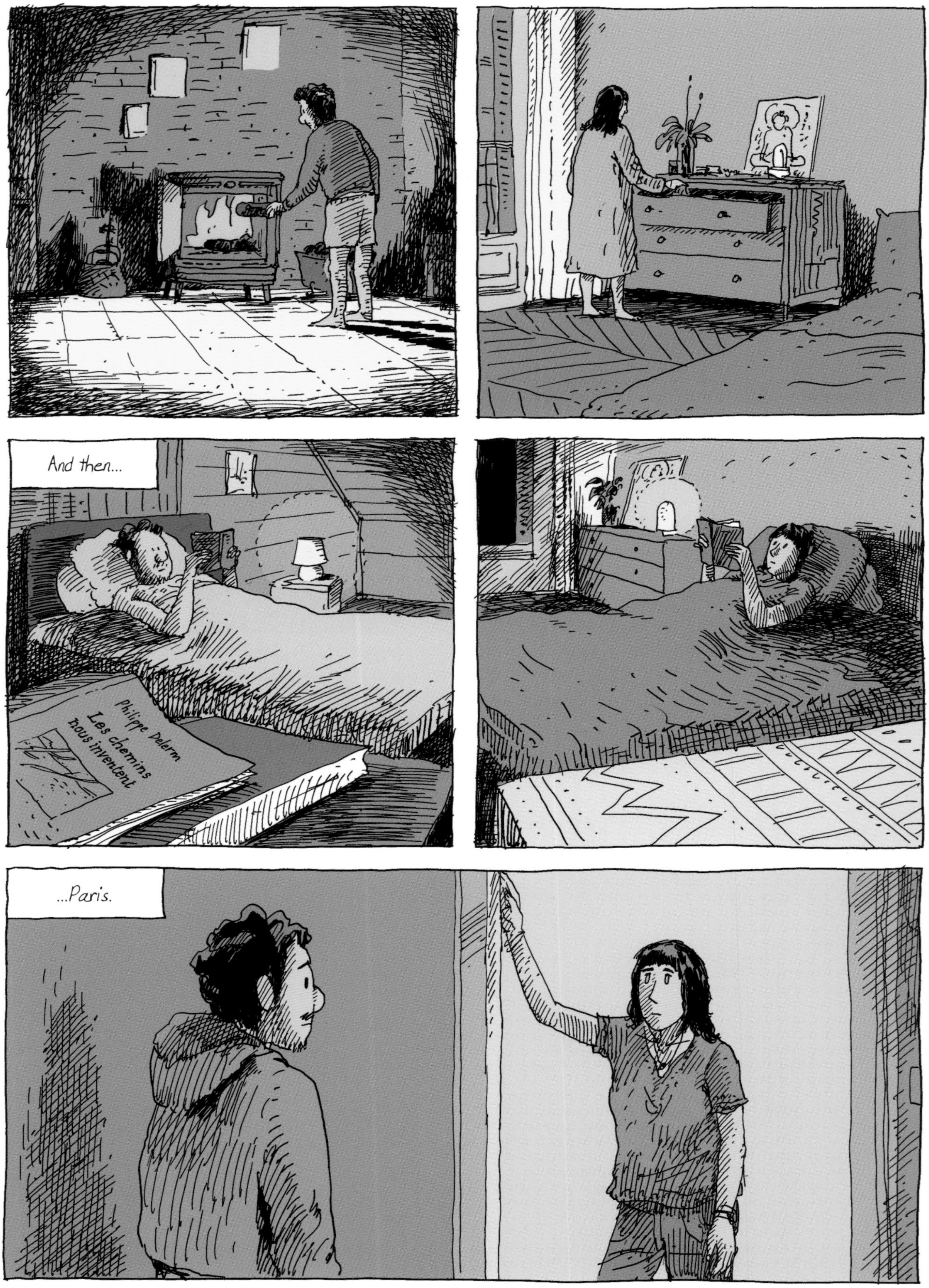
And then...
Philippe Delerm
Les chemins nous inventent
...Paris.

Chapter Seven

Reemergence

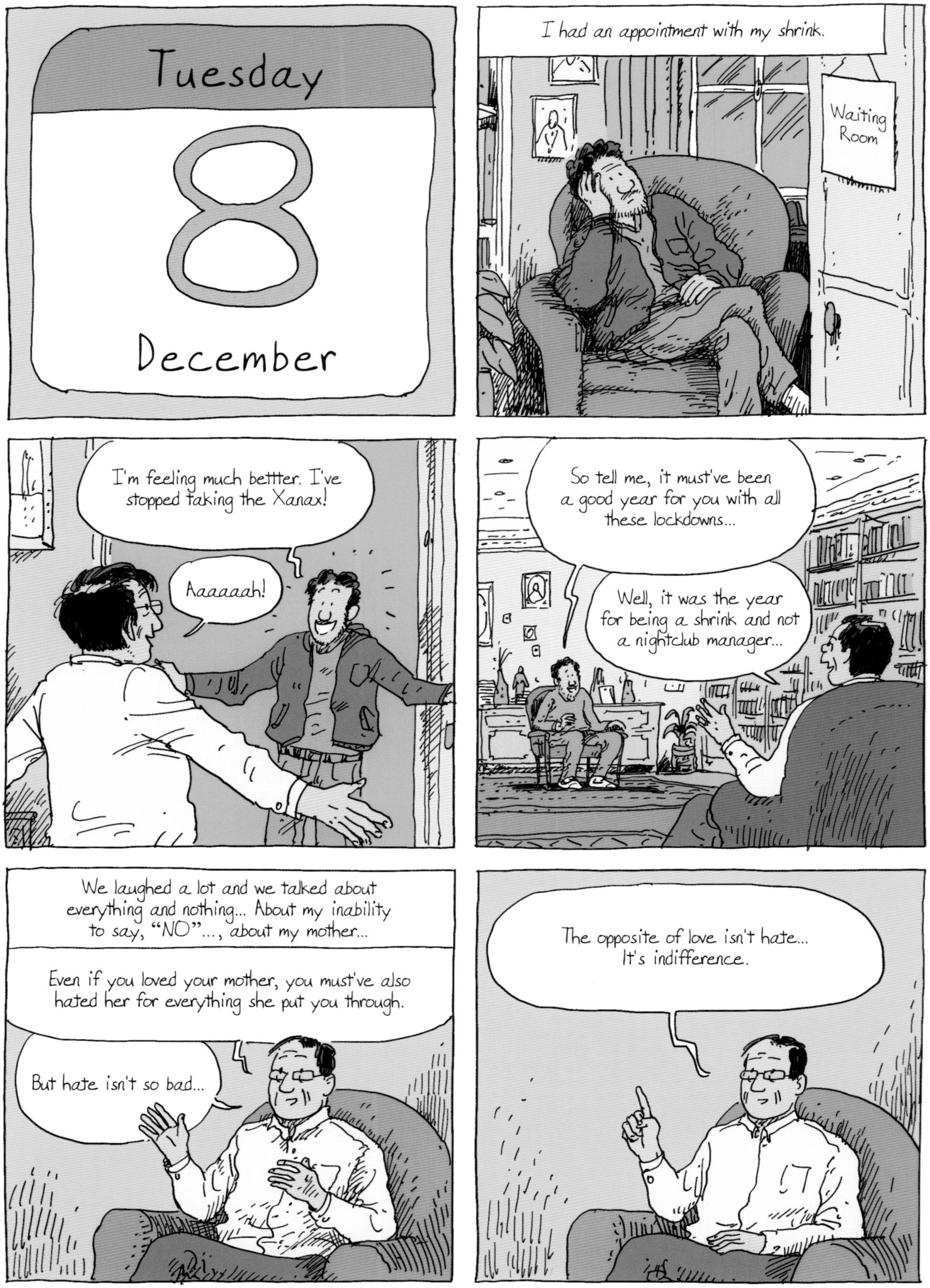
Tuesday
8
December
I had an appointment with my shrink.
Waiting Room
I'm feeling much bettter. I've stopped taking the Xanax!
Aaaaaah!
So tell me, it must've been a good year for you with all these lockdowns...
Well, it was the year for being a shrink and not a nightclub manager...
We laughed a lot and we talked about everything and nothing... About my inability to say, "NO"..., about my mother...
Even if you loved your mother, you must've also hated her for everything she put you through.
But hate isn't so bad...
The opposite of love isn't hate... It's indifference.

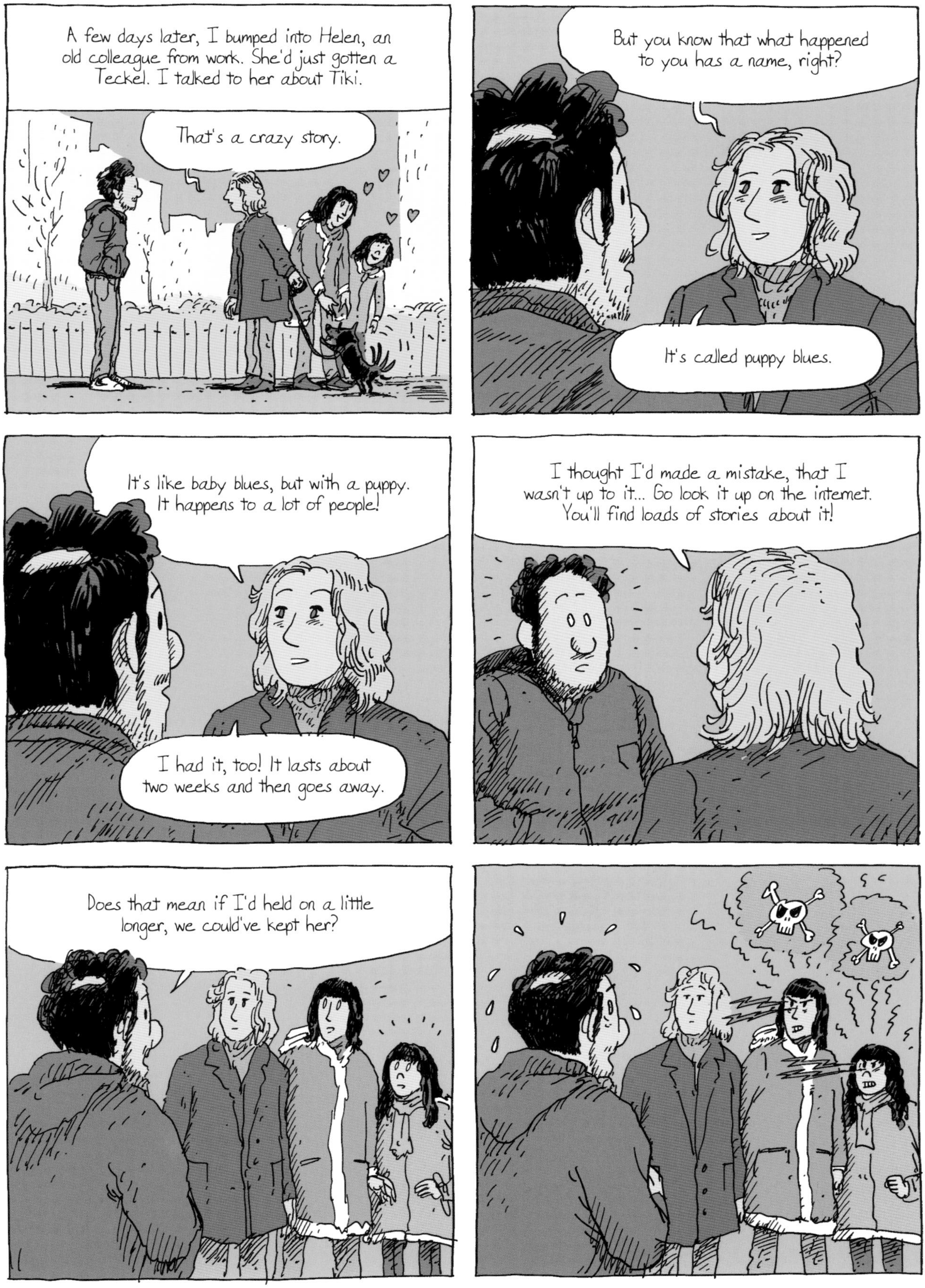
A few days later, I bumped into Helen, an old colleague from work. She'd just gotten a Teckel. I talked to her about Tiki.
That's a crazy story.
But you know that what happened to you has a name, right?
It's called puppy blues.
It's like baby blues, but with a puppy. It happens to a lot of people!
I had it, too! It lasts about two weeks and then goes away.
I thought I'd made a mistake, that I wasn't up to it... Go look it up on the internet. You'll find loads of stories about it!
Does that mean if I'd held on a little longer, we could've kept her?

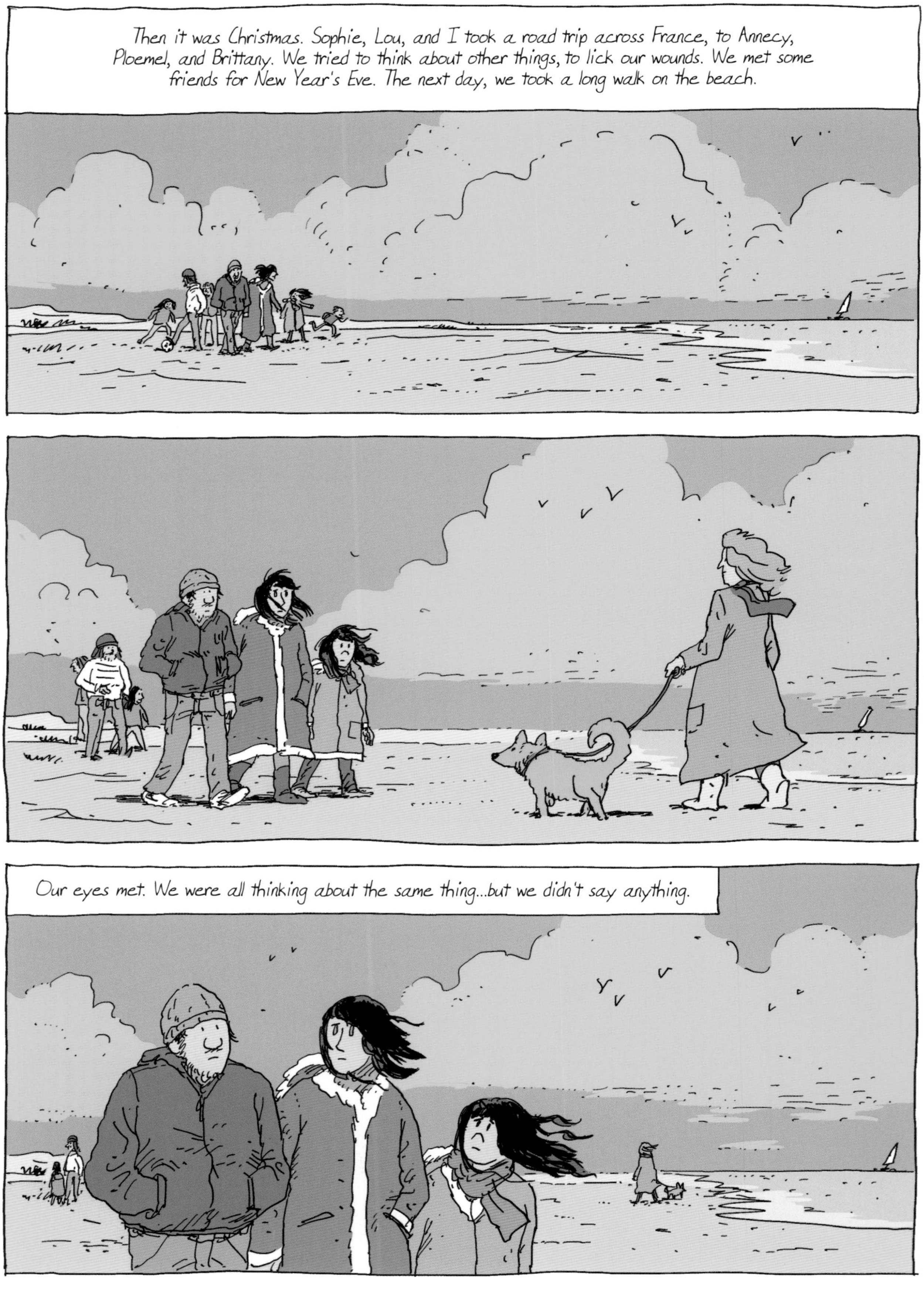
Then it was Christmas. Sophie, Lou, and I took a road trip across France, to Annecy, Ploemel, and Brittany. We tried to think about other things, to lick our wounds. We met some friends for New Year's Eve. The next day, we took a long walk on the beach.
Our eyes met. We were all thinking about the same thing...but we didn't say anything.

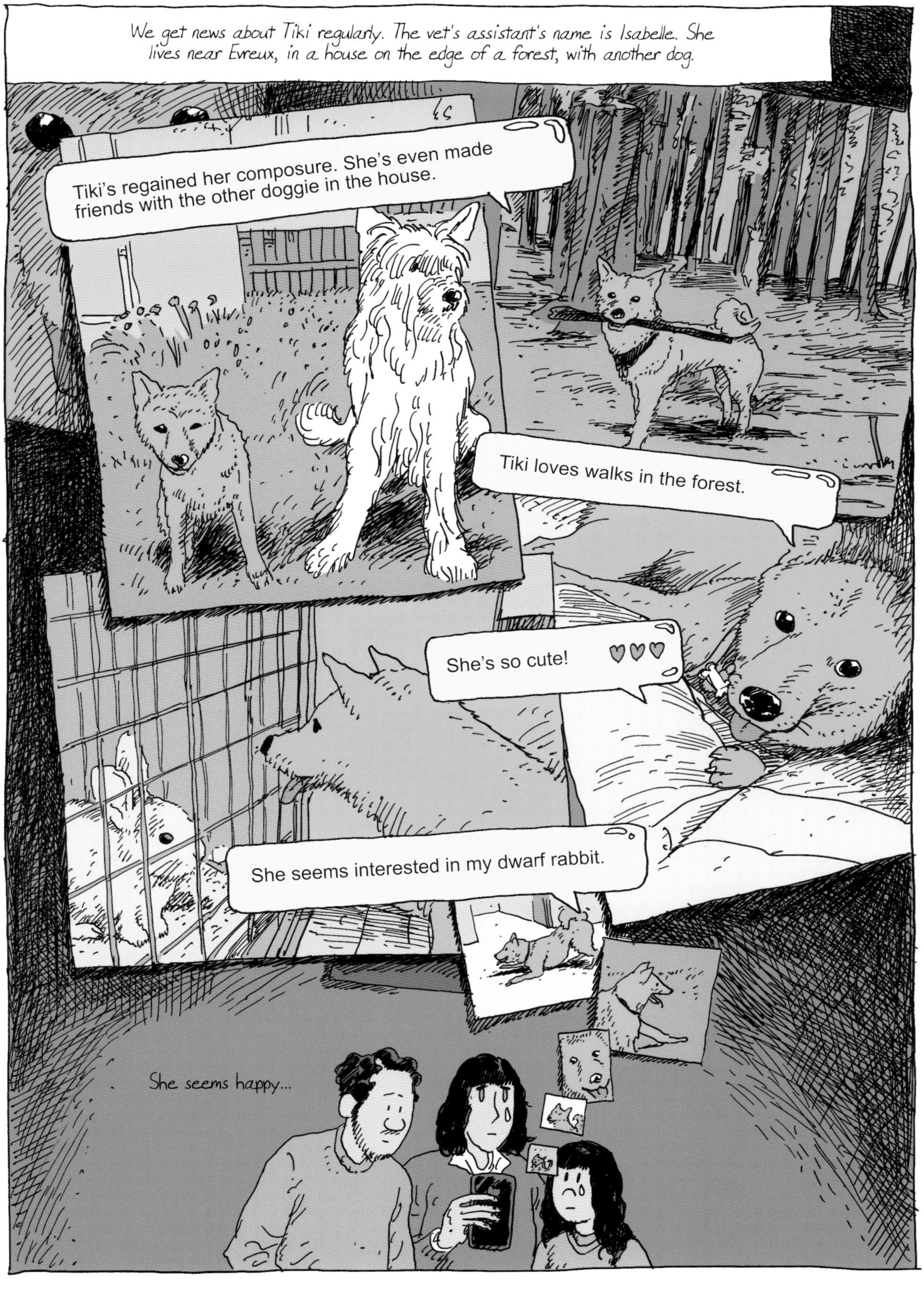
We get news about Tiki regularly. The vet's assistant's name is Isabelle. She lives near Evreux, in a house on the edge of a forest, with another dog.
Tiki's regained her composure. She's even made friends with the other doggie in the house.
Tiki loves walks in the forest.
She's so cute!
She seems interested in my dwarf rabbit.
She seems happy...

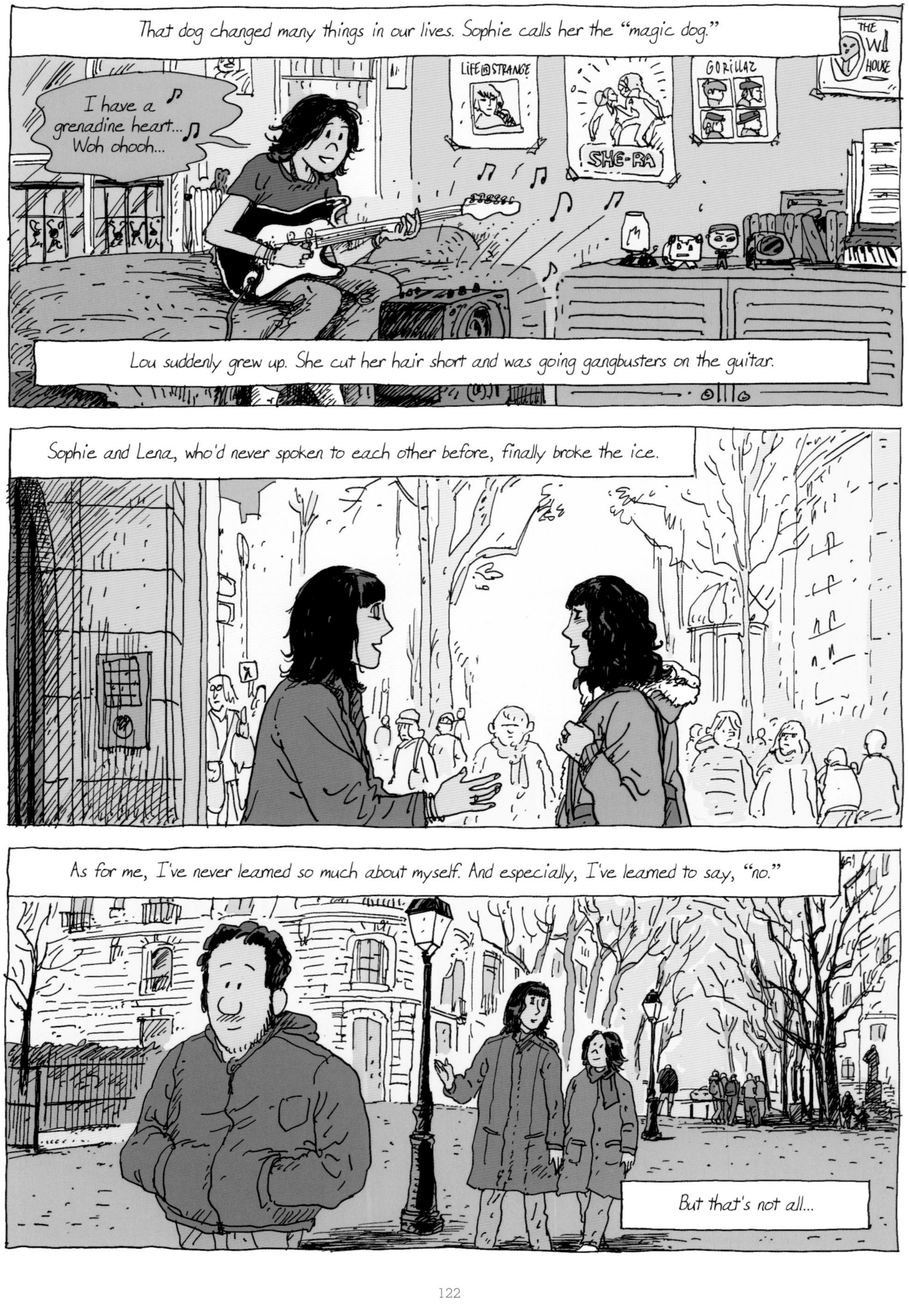
That dog changed many things in our lives. Sophie calls her the "magic dog."
I have a grenadine heart... Woh ohooh...
GORILLAZ
SHE-RA
Lou suddenly grew up. She cut her hair short and was going gangbusters on the guitar.
Sophie and Lena, who'd never spoken to each other before, finally broke the ice.
As for me, I've never learned so much about myself. And especially, I've learned to say, "no."
But that's not all...

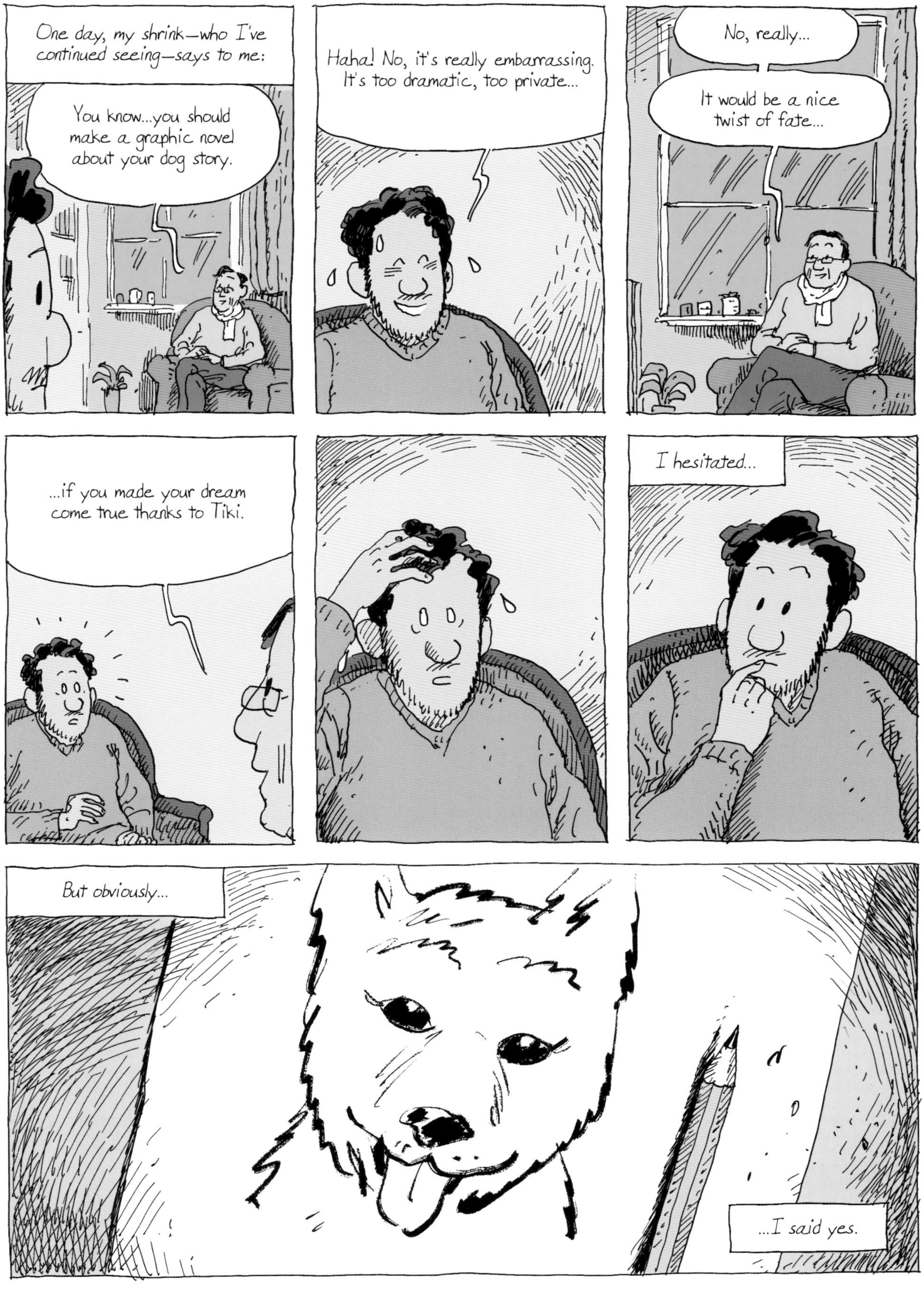
One day, my shrink—who I've continued seeing—says to me:
You know...you should make a graphic novel about your dog story.
Haha! No, it's really embarrassing. It's too dramatic, too private...
No, really...
It would be a nice twist of fate...
...if you made your dream come true thanks to Tiki.
I hesitated...
But obviously...
...I said yes.

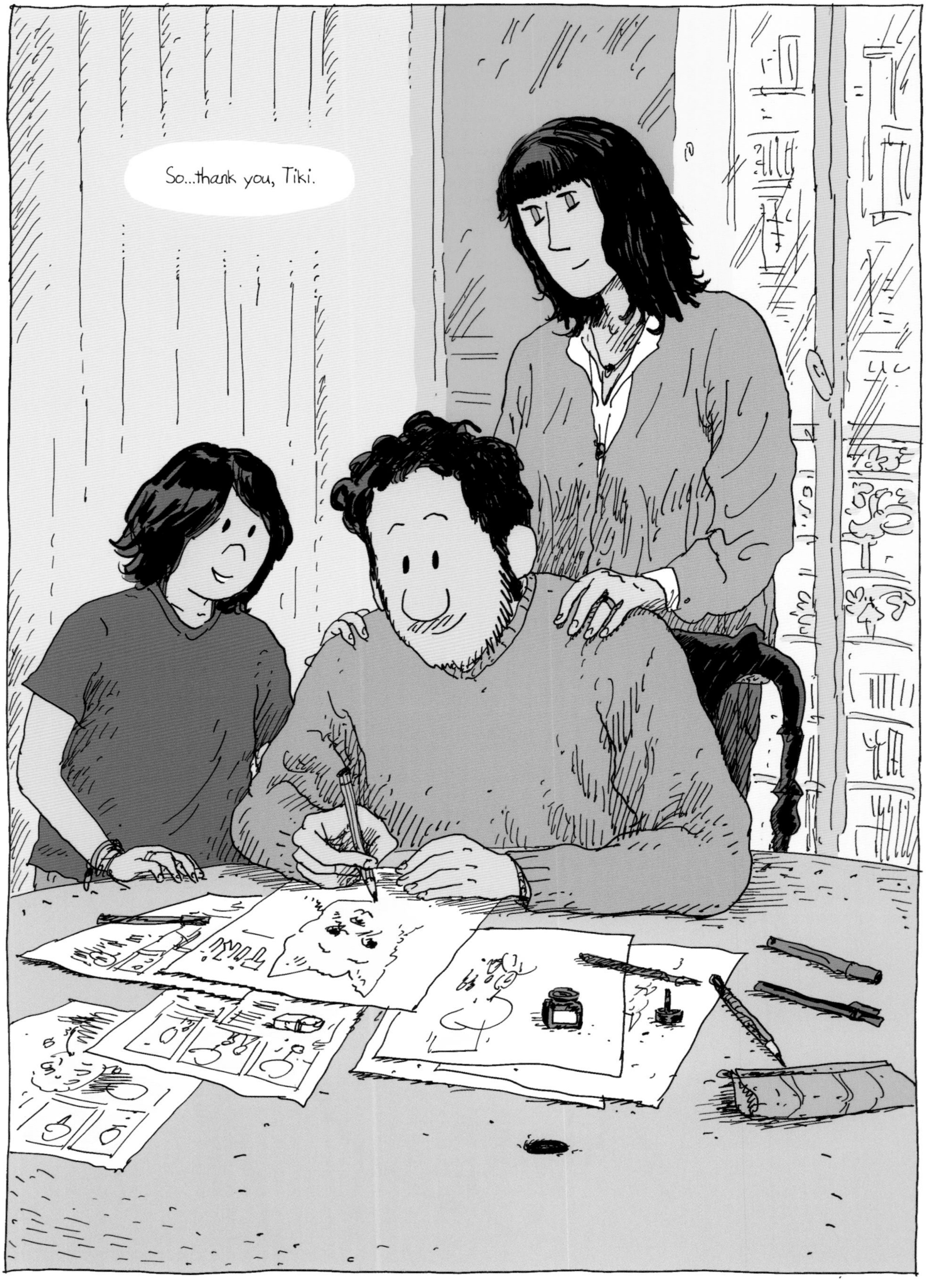
So...thank you, Tiki.

Epilogue

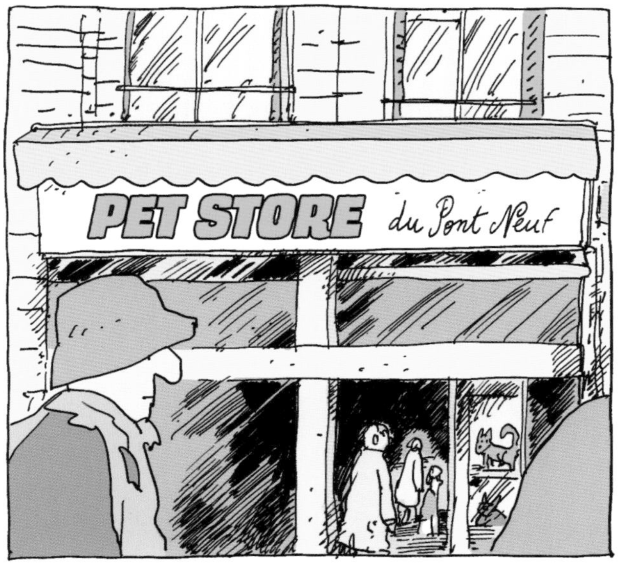
PET STORE du Pont Neuf

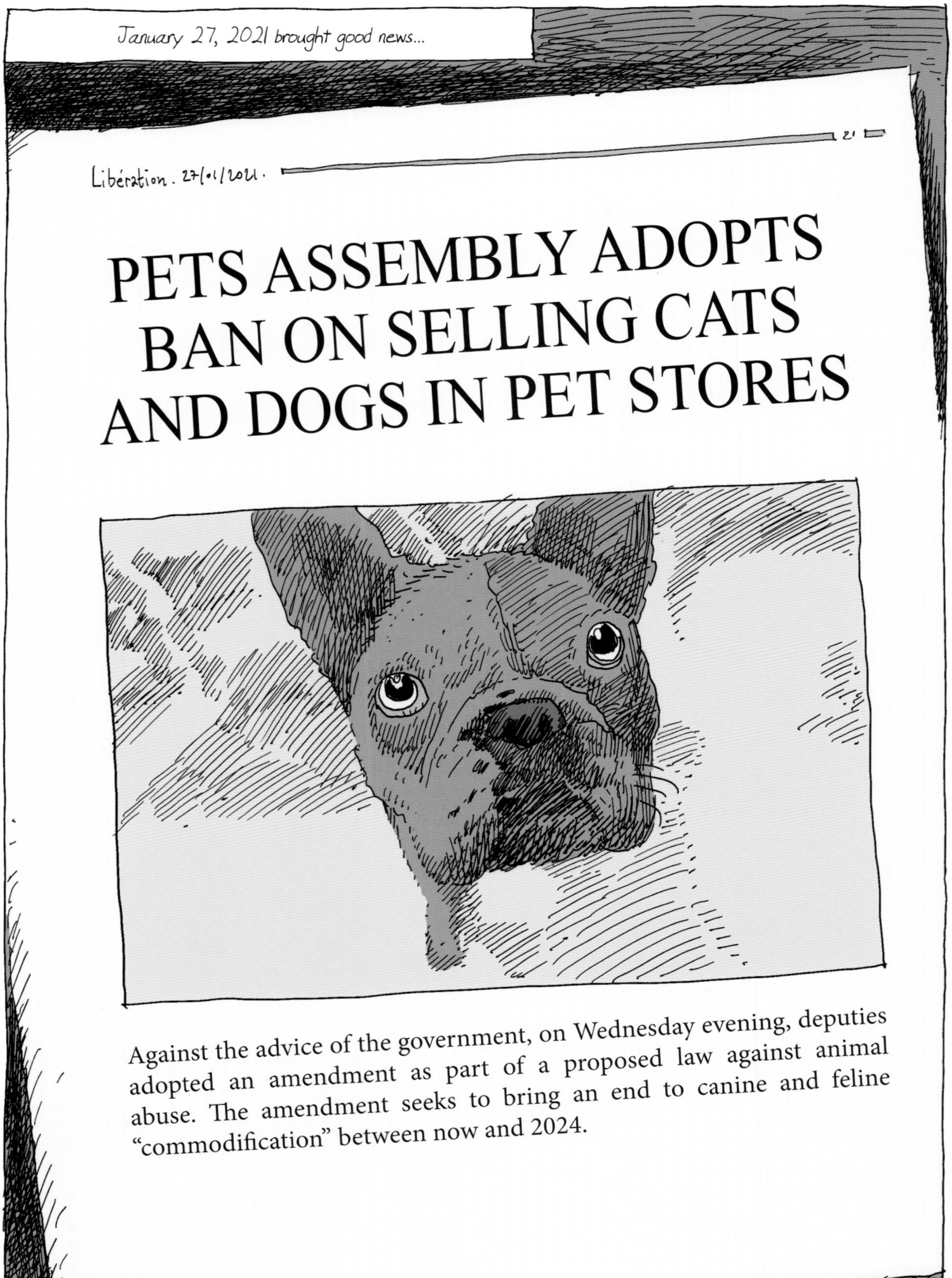
January 27, 2021 brought good news...
Libération. 27/01/2021.
21
PETS ASSEMBLY ADOPTS BAN ON SELLING CATS AND DOGS IN PET STORES
Against the advice of the government, on Wednesday evening, deputies adopted an amendment as part of a proposed law against animal abuse. The amendment seeks to bring an end to canine and feline "commodification" between now and 2024.

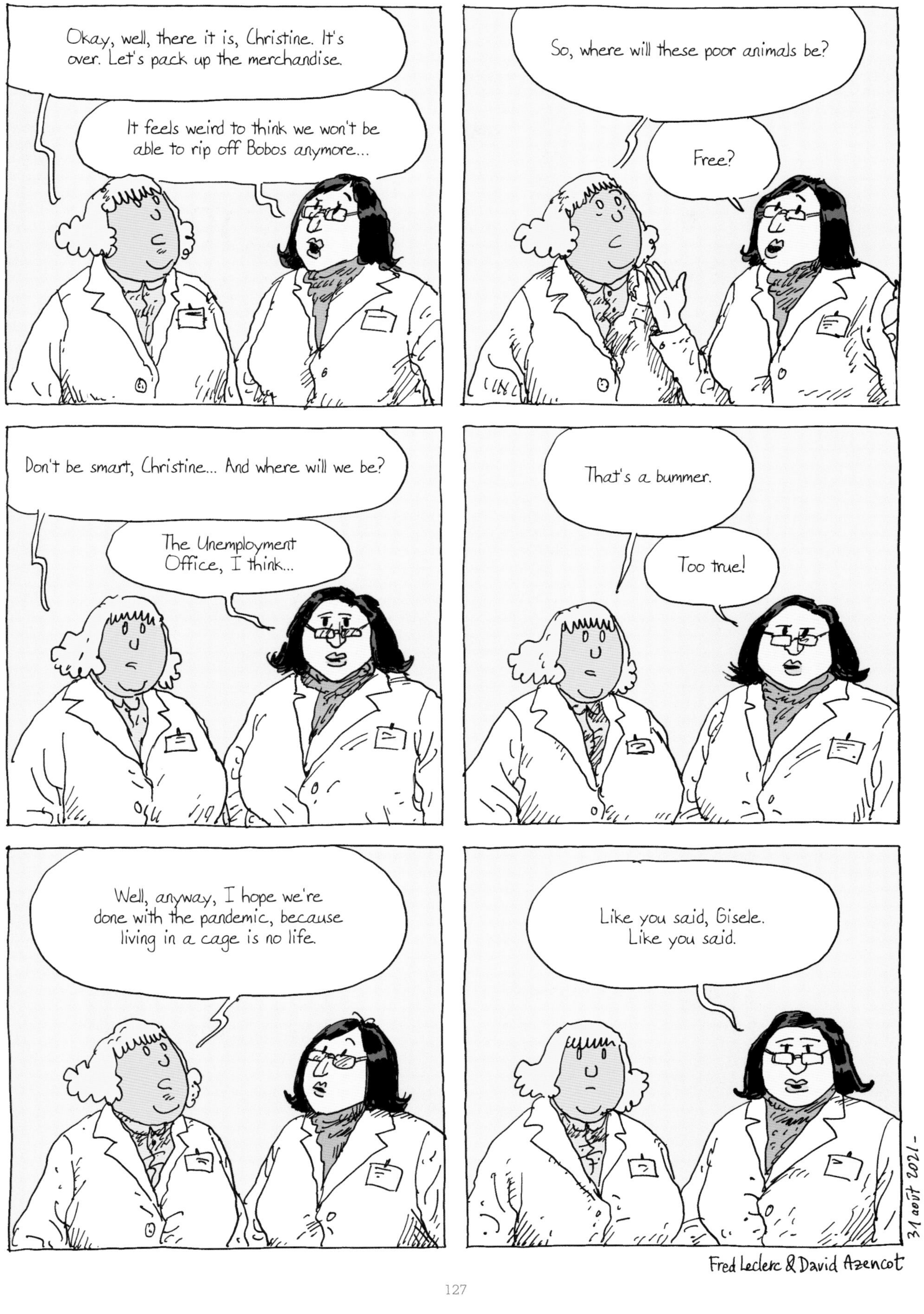
Okay, well, there it is, Christine. It's over. Let's pack up the merchandise.
It feels weird to think we won't be able to rip off Bobos anymore...
So, where will these poor animals be?
Free?
Don't be smart, Christine... And where will we be?
The Unemployment Office, I think...
That's a bummer.
Too true!
Well, anyway, I hope we're done with the pandemic, because living in a cage is no life.
Like you said, Gisele. Like you said.
31 août 2021 -

Fred Leclerc & David Azencot